T0386751

MRS
PANKHURST'S
BODYGUARD

Praise for *Mrs Pankhurst's Bodyguard*

'This highly readable book tells the story of the Bodyguard formed to protect the great suffragette leader Emmeline Pankhurst. Skilfully weaving the personal stories of women such as artist Kitty Marshall, whose unpublished autobiography is threaded throughout this account, this book vividly conveys the commitment, excitement and fear of suffragettes who dared to challenge the Liberal government of the day ... The many courageous "mice" mentioned here often evaded the "cats" of the state. Beautifully told, this book brings a fascinating and compelling story to a wider public. A "must read" for those interested in women's lives in the past.'

~ June Purvis, Professor (Emerita) of Women's and Gender History, University of Portsmouth, UK

'This important and absorbing book presents a unique history of one suffragette. This is the tale of Kitty Marshall, martial arts expert and Mrs Pankhurst's bodyguard; a tale of "cat and mouse" tactics told from the perspective of the detective who hunted her, and Kitty's own memoirs. This is first-class history and a first-rate thriller.'

~ Professor Clive Bloom, author of *A History of Britain's fight for a Republic*

'A fascinating and brilliantly written account of what Mrs Pankhurst called the "warrior spirit" of the Suffragette movement. Godfrey shows how the measured embrace of violence – including less-lethal weapons – allowed the suffragettes to make their indelible mark upon British history.'

~ Jonathan Ferguson, Keeper of Firearms and Artillery, Royal Armouries

'Drawing substantially from bodyguard Kitty Marshall's unpublished memoir *Suffragette Escapes and Adventures*, Emelyne Godfrey skilfully conveys their many escapades of evasion, deception and – when necessary – confrontation with much more powerful opponents.'

~ Tony Wolf, author of *Suffrajitsu: Mrs Pankhurst's Amazons* and co-producer/director of *No Man Shall Protect Us: The Hidden History of the Suffragette Bodyguards*

'This is a welcome book that delves into the inside story of the Suffragette movement, with fresh insights into the heroic women's lives and, indeed, some of the police officers who necessarily found themselves having to apply the law against some of their activities.'

~ Alan Moss, author of *Scotland Yard's History of Crime in 100 Objects*

MRS PANKHURST'S
BODYGUARD

ON THE TRAIL OF 'KITTY' MARSHALL AND THE MET POLICE 'CATS'

Emelyne Godfrey

Cover images: Shadow of jujitsu suffragette. (Re-enactment photo, courtesy of Jennifer Garside); Detective Ralph Kitchener. (Courtesy of Jan Janet Dennis and family)

First published 2023

The History Press
97 St George's Place, Cheltenham,
Gloucestershire, GL50 3QB
www.thehistorypress.co.uk

British Library Cataloguing in Publication Data.
A catalogue record for this book is available from the British Library.

ISBN 978 1 80399 175 7

Typesetting and origination by The History Press
Printed and bound in Great Britain by TJ Books Limited, Padstow, Cornwall.

Trees for Life

Contents

Preface   9

Some Notes on the Text   13

Prologue: No Way Out   15

1. Married Alive   21
2. Mental Equipment   35
3. Body Armour   45
4. The Winsonosaurus   55
5. Winston Churchill's Fanlight   67
6. Charge!   79
7. Toothbrushes at Dawn   89
8. Into the CID   101
9. Infernal Machines   113
10. The Month of Flowers   123
11. The Rules   131
12. Dancers in the Dark   141
13. Shadow Play   153
14. Under the Fig Tree   159
15. The Battle of Glasgow   167
16. Their Last Gasp   175
17. Broken Hearts and Hammer Toes   187

18. Twinkle, Twinkle, Little Star   199
19. Firestarter   207
20. The Final Hideout   213

Epilogue: Enid's Wrecking Ball   221
Acknowledgements and Adventures   223
Notes   229
Bibliography   233
Index   253

For Peter and Martin

I have no idea how to write a book, but there are
many interesting stories relating to the struggle for
votes for women that it seemed a pity they should not be told
by someone who was a great friend of Mrs. Pankhurst.

Kitty Marshall, *Suffragette Escapes and Adventures* (1947)

Emmeline Pankhurst by Georgina Agnes Brackenbury. Oil on canvas, 1927. (National Portrait Gallery, 2360, London)

Preface

The story ought surely to give more than just the names and dates of the various persons; it should show at least something of how they spoke and acted, and even on occasion how they thought and felt. ... If I could but make the different characters come alive the story would truly be an interesting one.

Ralph Frederick Kitchener, *The Kitcheners of Olney: A Family Saga*

There are two memoirs which form the basis to this book. When looked at together, the eyewitness accounts offered by Kitty Willoughby Marshall and Detective Inspector Ralph Kitchener give us an insight into the campaign for women's suffrage from both angles. Typed up by Rachel Barrett, who was Kitty's friend, neighbour and a veteran suffragette, Kitty's *Suffragette Escapes and Adventures* is kept in the Suffragette Fellowship Collection at the Museum of London. The collection also features Kitty's necklace in the form of three medallions inscribed with the dates of her three spates in jail and the various cell numbers on the reverse. 'Mrs Marshall' was arrested six times – once for shouting 'charge!' – which earned her a WSPU medal, which is also in the collection. During the course of her story, it becomes apparent that Kitty's role as a soldier within the elite Bodyguard accords her a unique place, not only in the story of the suffrage movement but within the history of martial arts, of women's empowerment and their emergence into male space. Kitty's close friendship with Mrs Pankhurst singles her out, too. Not all prominent campaigners could claim this privileged position.

Unlike Kitty's memoir, Kitchener's autobiography, *Memoirs of an Old Detective*, was carefully prepared and neatly presented, bound in a red Brampton Springback Binder. The text within was personally typed up by Kitchener. I first read the similarly titled *The Memoirs of an Old Detective* in Cambridge University Library, one of the few copies in Britain. This version of the autobiography was edited by Ian Adams who co-wrote, together with Ray Wilson, *Special Branch: A History 1883–2006*. For a while, the book sat boldly in duck-egg blue, side-by-side with the purple, white and green suffragette volumes on the display tables outside the Museum of London shop, beckoning a historical comparison. A chance introduction to Ray resulted in him offering to put me in touch with Kitchener's descendants, who very kindly entrusted me with his original manuscript. When comparing the two versions of the manuscript, it was obvious that much material had been cut out of the edited version. Kitchener's tone had been altered subtly by the replacement of exclamation marks with full stops. Some typos had crept in, too. Even the dedication, which hinted at his personality, was missing. Writing his memoirs was one of his passions, alongside family history. His granddaughter Janet remembered hearing him at work and she used to ask him about his detective days. And so, as the original manuscript reveals, his memoirs are dedicated thus: 'For JANET, who asked for it. Grandad 1969.'

Kitchener's autobiography casts light on the perspectives of officers themselves. So frequently in films and in history, the duality of police versus suffragettes persisted, and still does. One strong visual example of the popular boardgames of the Edwardian era was *Suffragetto!* which consisted of a suffragette team, represented by green pawns, and an opposing side of blue officers and inspectors who attempted to reach the Albert Hall while keeping the suffragettes away from the House of Commons! There was a tendency to represent the police in one of two ways, either as 'Policeman Plods', who were always a few breathless strides behind the criminals they pursued, or as a hostile faceless column of regulation moustaches, cudgels and helmets. The film *Suffragette* (2015) appears to offer a more nuanced depiction of the interaction of the two sides. We see Brendan Gleeson's Special Branch character Inspector Arthur Steed given voice. However, his reasonable perspective on the dangers of the militant campaign is crowded out by the unsympathetic comments he makes about the women he is trailing. As the police worked for Asquith's government, it is still hardly ever deemed necessary to look beyond the police reports, but although the police were under instructions from the Home Office, it did not mean that they were all enemies of women's suffrage. Even the suffragettes themselves made this point. For example, Cicely Hamilton, who wrote the lyrics to the rousing suffragette anthem 'The March of the Women', said her relations with the police were amicable; the officers' work required them to arrest suspects and they just happened to be suffragettes.

What Kitty Marshall and Kitchener have in common is their strong sense of justice and their appreciation of the light-hearted moments in what was an earnest campaign on both sides. As Edwin T. Woodhall recalled:

> I always think the Women's Suffrage Movement when it was at its height was the sharpest thorn the Special Branch has ever had in its side. I am certain that the suffragettes were more troublesome than all the other problems put together. It was so difficult to know who was or who was not in the movement. Titles conveyed nothing at all.[1]

In exploring new angles on the suffrage campaign, *Mrs Pankhurst's Bodyguard* is, on the one hand, the product of the many online resources that are available at the click of a button. On the other hand, the spirit of the book principally stems from my own 'shoe-leather' investigations, making local enquiries, speaking to descendants and visiting the places where much of the action of this book occurred, to intriguing effect. In 1982, Noel Burch's *The Year of the Bodyguard* offered a docudrama depiction of Edith Garrud's dojo. When interviewed by martial arts historian Tony Wolf, Burch discussed how his film had been received:

> I remember one reaction by a former student of mine at the RCA, at the time a promising independent director but who now does routine work for the BBC. He felt that the scene where the bobby comes down to the gym where the women have just hidden their street-clothes under the tatami (mats) should have been filmed from the point of view of the police; it would have been more suspenseful, he thought. I tried to explain that I was on the side of the women, that the film was on the side of the women, that such a view-point would have been out of the question.[2]

It seems to me that the story of the suffrage movement becomes more multidimensional when scenarios are related not only from the perspective of the pursued and light-footed suffragette 'mice' who feature in Burch's documentary but also from the perspective of the opposing force waiting outside, looking in. The action intensifies when we can glimpse events as if we were standing beside the officer in the shadows, struggling to extinguish his hot and malodorous oil lamp and negotiating the contents of his new-fangled thermos flask, before he is spotted.

Some Notes on the Text

While Kitty could call her Mrs Pankhurst 'Dearest', her friend was intensely private. When Mrs Pankhurst visited Chicago in the winter of 1909, journalists asked how many 'm's were in Emmeline and Mrs Pankhurst winced and replied that in England people did not give out their Christian names to the public; this was reserved for the home. So with that in mind, I have called her Mrs Pankhurst. Wherever possible, others have been called by the names by which they used themselves. For example, the Pethick Lawrences hyphenated their surnames and my spelling of their names reflected their omission of the hyphen during the suffragette campaign. The 'cats' in the title of this book refers to the slang name for the police who were tasked with following and capturing the militant campaigners, both men and women (the 'mice'), but the term 'cats' also includes the government, those sceptics of militant suffragism who witnessed events in the House, who saw missiles fly through their own windows.

Jujitsu or jujutsu has a variety of spellings. This book has adopted the spelling 'jujitsu', as this was the most common spelling I encountered in my research.

Unless otherwise stated, the voices of Kitty Marshall and Ralph Kitchener have been quoted from their respective memoirs: *Suffragette Escapes and Adventures* (1947) and *Memoirs of an Old Detective* (1969) by permission of the Museum of London and Janet Dennis and family.

Mrs Pankhurst at the Battle of Glebe Place, 1914.
(Museum of London, 50.82/1264)

Prologue

No Way Out

The building is haunted. She is sure of this as she lies on guard in the dark. Over the years, visitors have talked of disembodied singing echoing between the floors. Some have even stalled icily halfway down the stairs, subjected to the caress of a small, unseen hand on the banisters. The house in which the main protagonist of this story finds herself tonight was built in the seventeenth century as a clergyman's home for a neighbouring Huguenot chapel. At twilight, anyone who happens upon the panelled room tucked away at the top of the house feels that they are interrupting a private conversation. The compulsion to leave immediately and shut the door, flit back to safety and the known world is overwhelming. Near palpable, the atmosphere is said to be so historically charged that the previous owners moved out partly on account of the disturbances. But right now, there is safety in numbers; a brigade of women is grabbing history by the wrist and braving the supernatural together. The room is filled with real, living sounds, the creaking of chairs and whispers and the voices of around a dozen women plotting, directing and anticipating mayhem.

It is part of the plan that Kitty should be here before the big event, to prepare. The women are sheltering indoors from the miserable February night as well as from the armed 'cats' prowling around. There is a distant hoot from a barge as it makes its way up the Thames; tonight, this building contains its very own precious smuggled cargo. Kitty thinks back to those 'cats' that surround the building. All she has for protection is the Indian club that the famous Madame Garrud has taught her to use. Then at some point during the darkness, the first scintilla of Saturday morning edges its way across the curtains. With the coming of the dawn, Dearest's great escape mission is put into action.

Dearest. This is what Kitty calls Mrs Emmeline Pankhurst. During the suffrage campaign these two women have become close. Their Lancashire and Manchester connections, not to mention their experience of being married to eminent lawyers, have further cemented the bond they are forging in their fight for social, political and legal justice for women. For decades, campaigners have fought within the law for women's suffrage, seeking support from sympathetic MPs, presenting petitions to Parliament, raising awareness within political societies, and using the power of the pen and the typewriter. And while some concessions have been gained, the suffragettes remind the public that the parliamentary franchise is still out of reach for all women as well as 40 per cent of the adult male population. In contrast, a sizeable number of women living in, for example, New Zealand, Australia, Finland, certain states of North America and the Isle of Man, where Mrs Pankhurst's mother was born, have the parliamentary franchise.

Exasperated by the failure of carefully worded petitions to Parliament, Mrs Pankhurst's team founded the Women's Social and Political Union (WSPU) in Manchester in 1903. As Mrs Pankhurst has learnt, the just cause of votes for women must be fought verbally and physically as much as possible by women themselves. When Mrs Pankhurst's demands meet with resistance, her followers cause havoc by disturbing political meetings, ruining public performances, wrecking property and tampering with communication systems. And now, Mrs Pankhurst, who is dodging a three-year jail sentence, is further inciting them to disrupt Britain's infrastructure.

This morning's papers have announced that Mrs Pankhurst is to make a public appearance at an undisclosed address in Glebe Place, Chelsea. No doubt, there are many onlookers in the gathered crowd in the street, scanning the houses for signs of action, who believe that women would be unsexed and that the domestic order of the home would be destroyed if women could cast their votes. The usual taunts are being primed and are ready to be fired. *Go home and darn your husband's socks. Why aren't you married? Can't you get a husband? You're a disgrace. You should be boiled alive. Go home and mind the baby. Don't you wish you were a man?* But even to these sceptics, the shows the suffragettes put on are still worth watching.

Shortly before Kitty's arrival, a decoy managed sufficiently to fool the authorities into arresting the wrong woman. As this was happening, Mrs Pankhurst's friends quickly spirited their leader to this charming three-storey refuge at 63 Glebe Place, Chelsea, near the Thames embankment. Lined with artists' studios, Glebe Place might be a street of genteelly unconventional goings-on but it is also not exactly London's typical number one hotspot for a Saturday afternoon confrontation. The home in which Mrs Pankhurst is holed up belongs to the bacteriologist Dr Harry ('Peter') Schütze and his new wife, Gladys Henrietta. Gladys gives him a warm, conspiratorial smile, her dark, curling hair bobbing. She is steeling herself for a challenge. She needs a chance to prove herself.

The Schützes look out of the window and begin to wonder about the enormity of the scenario in which they have willingly placed themselves. As the inhabitants of 63 Glebe Place can see, the crowd of men and women below is continuing to grow and is quickly filling up the road. Flat caps, turned-down collars and mackintoshes jostle for space with police officers' uniforms and substantial ladies' hats, which are kept in place with fierce-looking hatpins. Without guard tips, these pins, often up to 16 inches long, are lethal, and are causing anxiety as to their use as fashion accessories. One London magistrate has declared them to be as dangerous as guns; hatpins have even been used as stealth murder weapons in fiction and in real life.

Some spectators are taking a professional interest in the events. They are the detectives – 'tecs' for short, or 'shadows' – who come disguised as loafers and their numbers continue to increase. Among the crowd stands a young man in plain clothes whose appearance is, by his own admission, wholly unremarkable. And yet, from his short stature, he does not look like the average policeman. His story has crossed Kitty's path before and now he considers the scene with the mischievous, shrewd and piercing gaze which would overawe his grandchildren. Mrs Pankhurst's organisation presents a threat to public order and he is involved in trailing the women trained by Edith Garrud. As a result of his own hazardous spy work and the extraordinary activities of fellow officers in pursuing wanted suffragettes, the Metropolitan Police know how many men to send to bohemian Chelsea. Indeed, the Schützes find themselves on tenterhooks. What if the police force can also figure out who is concealing Mrs Pankhurst, obtain a warrant for an arrest and raid the premises? In any case, the minute she sets foot outside she is a target.

And so, Mrs Pankhurst is late; her protectors are busily considering their options. The throng of people outside has been kept waiting in the street for fifteen minutes as the clip-clop of horses' hooves and the rumble of wheels on the wet cobblestones pass by. Inside, there is much shuffling about, changing of clothing and there are also debates about whether to employ a hosepipe to help keep climbing enemies at bay. In an attempt to calm her, Gladys's illustrious guest gives her a smile and a kiss. Finally, just before 5 p.m., the French doors open and the great lady steps out on to the balcony, a veil over her face. A feather points out proudly from Mrs Pankhurst's toque. Reporters surmise from her motoring attire that she has only just arrived. In reality, she came last night, preceded by a number of maids and trades people. Suspiciously new faces. The policemen wait below, their helmets almost within touching distance of Mrs Pankhurst and her friends on the balcony. And Mrs Pankhurst is so tempted to reach down for just a second with her dainty gloved hand and to make that connection.

Mrs Pankhurst considers her sizeable audience, her deep violet-blue eyes ranging across the growing crowd. She stands above them, but she is not too important as to be above the ordinary trials and sufferings that campaigners have to undergo to fight for a change in the conditions of women's lives. The authorities' inability to feed her during her absurdly frequent spates in prison have repeatedly brought about her early release; the government does not want another martyr to the cause. She wears her physical strain publicly. It is plain to see that the speaker's numerous hunger and thirst strikes behind bars as well as the cycle of escapes and captures have exhausted her. The police call her a wanted criminal with a 'sallow' complexion; her friends describe her as frail and beautiful, even ethereal, with her olive skin, high cheekbones and stately bearing. Mrs Pankhurst, the star of this open-air performance, leans forward on the whiplash-thin railings, eyes the 1,000-strong crowd again and takes a breath.

When she speaks, her weakened voice is imbued with an arresting, otherworldly quality. She wants to put a stop to 'foul outrages' and to make the streets safer for women. *Foul outrages?* At this point, an observer's gaze might be drawn to Kitty's face, searching for a note of abstraction in her admiration of her friend. Dearest will not go back to jail to complete her sentence if Kitty, whose heart is beating against her tender ribs, can help it. By the end of the speech, the sky is darkening and the crowd has not completely dispersed as it ought to have done. A number of curious people have hung on to their places in the street, waiting for further events to unfold. They are not disappointed. There are now constables at each end of Glebe Place and down the King's Road. 'The game is afoot', as Sherlock Holmes might say.

As the crowd wait, two cars pull up outside 63 Glebe Place. The front door swings open and Mrs Pankhurst dashes out, Kitty in the lead, accompanied by who whip out their clubs. These accessories are the same batons used in exercise classes to increase strength and aid posture, accoutrements to aid health and beauty. On this occasion, however, the clubs are pressed into a different service. Mrs Pankhurst slips into a car which proceeds to move away. Amid a surging crowd there is a set-to between the police and the women. One of Madame Garrud's pupils is not adept in her use of the club. She aims at an officer who has one of her comrades in his grasp, but he is too fast for her and ducks as the blow comes; it is the suffragette who is struck on the head and now requires medical attention. 'Now, now, Miss, be good!' resonate the voices of the officers in an attempt to reason with the wild women. 'If you don't 'urt me, Miss, I won't 'urt you.'

The veiled woman in the car feels distinctly uneasy as the men's faces peer in through the windows. At last, a look of disgust hardens their features. 'That's not 'er! Drive on, chauffeur!' It is as Kitty has feared; despite her best efforts to look like Mrs Pankhurst, the decoy fails to outfox the police. As Gladys watches the spectacle, it seems that the police are not sure what to do or whether they have indeed made a terrible mistake in letting the veiled woman in the taxi escape. As if to compensate for this loss, they arrest some of the fighting women. However, there is doubt as to whether Mrs Pankhurst, who has a habit of vanishing in the thick of the action, is still hiding behind the doors of this Chelsea home.

Those inside 63 Glebe Place move gingerly on the blanketed parquet floor, suppressing seasonal coughs and sneezes. Two flights of stairs must be silently negotiated. If the police realise the extent of the suffragette presence in the house, their suspicions will be aroused that Mrs Pankhurst, with all her entourage, is still stranded. There will be no chance of an escape if the house is constantly under surveillance. Gladys attempts to hear what is being said on the other side of the door as detectives exchange thoughts on Mrs Pankhurst's whereabouts. Then, the sudden opening of the front door causes the occupants to jump. It is the cook's bibulous husband, a sympathiser to the women's cause. Thankfully, he shambles in and slams the door behind him before the men outside can see anything incriminating. Nevertheless, police presence is kept up. The organiser attempts to send a rescue party but the number of detectives and constables stationed outside Glebe Place and in the surrounding area is too great; by 1 a.m. all hope of an escape is abandoned. As detectives seat themselves on the doorsteps, Mrs Pankhurst slips into bed with a hot-water bottle and her group of women bodyguards flop into their easy chairs or find spaces on the floor. Some of them sleep in the remains of the Huguenot chapel which is now a drawing room. The branches of a fig tree, which was rooted in the floor, grow around an oval glass dome set in the flat roof above the room, which reaches over their heads. In plain clothes, the sharp-eyed officer who has witnessed events of what would become known as 'The Battle of Glebe Place' thinks that the authorities have succeeded in containing Mrs Pankhurst. However, his version is only half the story.

According to the papers, there is no back entrance to 63 Glebe Place. The only way that the leader can escape is out of the front door or through the tradesman's passage from the basement, either way facing arrest. How will she get out? This is indeed a locked-room mystery of sorts. Her supporters inside the house know that it will take a tremendous effort to execute their task. Early on Sunday morning, an old maid slips out of the Schützes' house. The officers stationed outside do not notice her. She returns with news that a relief party is on its way, and that evening at home Kitty, who should be resting, receives another phone call with instructions. Her husband Arthur is not pleased. He thinks that she has done enough for the cause. They both have and in doing so have become a powerhouse couple. But she simply cannot let her friends down. And besides, it is her job to lead the rescue mission.

1.

Married Alive

It is not hard to see why Kitty became a suffragette. She was brought up in what appears to have been a loving and supportive, middle-class socially active family. Her background was not only highly respectable, her family members were esteemed local figureheads whose legacy is still very publicly commemorated in the communities in which they lived and worked. Yet, there were elements in her upbringing which betokened a rebellious streak: a need to disturb, interrupt, force a change. When later provoked by events in her own life, it was this intrepid energy that Kitty inherited that would come to her aid when she found herself backed into some tight corners.

Kitty's hero was her mother's brother, William Charles Baldwin. His father, Reverend Gardner Baldwin, Vicar of Leyland, was a descendant in a long line of Baldwin vicars who had served St Andrew's, Leyland, Lancashire all the way back to 1748. Kitty's mother, Caroline, played cricket, while William, sporting a red jacket, went riding with the squire's hounds and loved to chase salmon, much to the displeasure of his nanny who ended up chasing him. As an adult, he became a celebrity explorer. His book of 1863, *African Hunting*, a classic text, was compiled from a journal of his adventures which he penned using ink, pencil and gunpowder. The book is true to its title, and with a typical imperialist's eye, he describes escaping from an elephant, negotiating with and observing the locals, and shooting buffalo, rhino and giraffes. At the Victoria Falls, he found the island where Dr David Livingstone had carved his name on a tree and added his own as the second European to reach the Falls, and the first to reach them from the East Coast. It was 4 August 1860. William Baldwin sat down with Livingstone that evening and chatted about Livingstone's discoveries. William Baldwin died on 17 November 1903 and was buried at St Andrew's Church, Leyland. His grave is marked with the epitaph: 'A South African pioneer and "like Nimrod, a mighty hunter before the Lord".' A memorial stone, which sits above the door to the vestry, reads: 'Resolute, not reckless, he was one who never turned his back, but rode straight forward.' And below is added: 'No man shall order me, I will be my own master.' The carvings would be significant for Kitty.

Caroline was living in Lytham, Lancashire, with her other brother, Thomas Rigbye Baldwin, who had taken over the post of Vicar of Leyland after his father's death in 1852. A new assistant was needed and in answer to the invitation, Leicestershire-born Kinton Jacques, an Oxford graduate, son of a successful wool merchant, came into Leyland in December of 1860 along with the deep snowdrifts. He soon set about helping parishioners affected by the embargo on slave-grown cotton from the American South with many workers supporting Abraham Lincoln's blockade. Those mills that could not adapt were forced to shut down or cut back operations. The embargo hit Lancashire hard and money was raised around the country to pay for soup kitchens and clothing. Mrs Pankhurst (née Goulden) grew up in an abolitionist family in Manchester and one of her earliest memories was of helping her family raise money for newly freed slaves in America. Then only 5 years old, she would beam with pride as her little bag filled with coins. Kinton felt that the experience of these intense times and his work in the community helped him develop as a person. He made an instant impression on Caroline. The couple worked hard during the embargo of the early 1860s but in their spare time, they often sang together. Only a matter of months after they had first met, Kinton proposed to Caroline on 7 August 1861. She didn't hesitate to accept.

The Kintons married in the parish of Lytham on 3 March 1863 and their first children were born in Clayton-le-Woods where Kinton worked as a curate. Kitty had three older brothers and a sister. William Baldwin Jacques was born in 1864; the year of James Kinton Jacques' birth in 1865 marked the end of the American Civil War and the arrival of the first consignment of cotton in Leyland, when weavers and workers surrounded the cart and sang *Praise God, from Whom all Blessings Flow*; Francis Augustus Jacques was born in 1867; and Eleanor appeared in the autumn of 1868.

In early 1869, Kinton became the Vicar of Westhoughton where many of the parishioners were silk weavers who worked either in the four mills or on handlooms in their cottages. He presided over the laying of the corner-stone of a new parish church for St Bartholomew's whose origins could be dated back to before the Reformation. The old brick chapel had been demolished and the stone one was erected in its place. In his speech, Kinton preached equality and reminded the audience that this was a church for all. No seats would be appropriated. Everyone was welcome. The church was consecrated on St Bartholomew's Day, 24 August 1870, a handful of days after the birth of Emily Katherine, who was called Kitty from a young age. She was the first child born at the Westhoughton vicarage, on 3 August 1870. Kitty was baptised by her father on 27 August that year.

Four more children were born in the eclectically styled vicarage which had seen centuries of renovations. The home even boasted its own lake. Kitty's mother's name is a clear influence in the choice of names for the last two girls who were Florence Caroline (1872) and Cecilia Caroline Jacques (1874), who inherited a passion for cricket. Arthur Patrick Jacques followed in 1876 while George Philip Rigbye Jacques appears to have been the last child, born in October 1878. Caroline's voice does not seem to have survived and it is impossible to know what her feelings were during the fifteen or so years spent in an almost constant state of pregnancy. Large families were considered the norm, most famously depicted in paintings of Queen Victoria and her family. However, many children were not expected to live into adulthood. Over 14 per cent of infants born between 1860 and 1900 in England and Wales died before their first birthday. The Jacques family endured tragedy, too. Caroline had lost her baby brother in 1843, when she was only 9 years old. Her own daughter, Florence Caroline Jacques, born in October 1872, died on 8 January 1874. Florence's epitaph expresses the heartache of the grief-stricken parents who watched her tiny frame waste away and their daughter slip into the next world. Adapted from Kings 4:26 are the words: 'Is it well with the child? It is well.' Born on 17 March 1876, Arthur Patrick Jacques died on 10 May of 'debility from birth' and was heartbreakingly buried just over a month after his father baptised him.

Westhoughton had been one of the most impoverished areas in the Manchester diocese and Reverend Jacques, no doubt touched by personal tragedy, was committed to improving the lives and prospects of the people around him. In the wake of Joseph Bazalgette's architectural feats in London, Kinton Jacques fought, amidst much local opposition from ratepayers, to have a local board to coordinate sewerage and better water supplies, much to the gratitude of his parishioners. Kinton built new churches and missions, set up night schools and reading rooms and organised regular collections for the poor, church charity fêtes and a Church Sick Society. In his work, he was helped by Caroline, who was a much-loved figure in the community. Kinton was deeply socially conscious and it is clear that his and his wife's activities form the roots of Kitty's faith and her campaigning spirit. His career influenced his family's education, too. William Baldwin Jacques, clearly named after his famous explorer uncle, became a Lancashire curate before moving to Northampton. Kinton's second son, James, also went into the church, becoming a curate of Kirkham, Lancashire in 1888. Kitty would become skilled at fundraising, a respectable pursuit for ladies. Her mother, who was active in the church and among the communities near Manchester where the British women's suffrage campaign blossomed, was her teacher. Caroline did not live to see the formation of the WSPU but she would likely have known of the foundation that nineteenth-century suffrage campaigners had laid for the battles that were to rage in the Edwardian era; of the questioning spirit that was rising up in the theatre, coming to the boil in tearooms and prompted by experiences in workplaces, bedrooms, divorce courts, railway carriages, and on the street. Religious faith was a galvanising force and while critics railed against outmoded Christian ideals of women, faith also provided a rallying point, prompting many women to look at their role within Christianity. One of Kinton Jacques' parishioners, who was considered an eccentric for her loose hair and her supposed unconventional life, scandalised society by living with another woman. She gave Kitty pause for thought. When the lady lay dying, Kinton Jacques offered up a prayer and finished with Amen. The parishioner reflected upon his words and responded with 'Ay, that's it, Master Jacques, a' for men and nought for women.'

In 1889, Kinton Jacques moved his family to leafy Brindle in Lancashire. His two older daughters, Eleanor and Kitty, had finished their education at St Elphin's Clergy Daughters' College, near Warrington. A former pupil of St Elphin's was Agnes Smallpeice, one of the earliest students admitted to Newnham Hall, Cambridge, in 1879. In the early 1870s, Millicent Garrett Fawcett had persuaded philosopher Henry Sidgwick to provide accommodation for women who attended lectures at Cambridge. Demand grew and the hall, which later became Newnham College, opened its doors four years before Agnes's arrival. St Elphin's School was founded in 1844 as part of a charity formed in 1697, which helped the widows and orphan daughters of qualifying clergy, training pupils of impoverished clergymen to become teachers. By the time Kitty was in attendance, the school's intake had widened. St Elphin's had spiral stone steps, an impressive fireplace and an underground passage and it seemed that the expansive windows beckoned a great future to those who gazed out on to the lush countryside beyond.

Kinton and Caroline may now have been turning their minds to making suitable matches for their daughters, but the nation was wondering: were there even enough men to go round? The 1851 census had revealed that there were 100,000 more unmarried women than unmarried men and the anxieties surrounding this disproportionate number had not gone away. George Gissing captured the mood when he described the excess female population as 'odd' women, like worn old gloves which could not be matched. Although single women could lead fulfilling lives and pursue successful careers, marriage was thought to be the apex of a woman's life. But there was another reason why women had to start searching early for a husband: rumour had it that as soon as unmarried females reached middle age, their mental faculties began to disintegrate!

In 1888, the *Daily Telegraph* invited readers to consider the question: 'Is Marriage a Failure?' The volume of responses for both sides of the argument was astonishing: the newspaper's offices received 27,000 letters. Nor was the reputation of marriage enhanced by the case of R. v. Jackson (also known as the Clitheroe Abduction Case of 1891), brought about after a husband had kidnapped his wife, Emily Jackson, as she was leaving church. A Court of Appeal ruling established that a husband could not take the law into his own hands and kidnap his wife and did not have the right to detain or imprison her in order to obtain conjugal rights. Elizabeth Wolstenholme Elmy, who later appeared in numerous suffragette photographs as the smiling old lady with silvery hair in ringlets, felt that the result of the Clitheroe Abduction Case was a significant step towards women's emancipation. The court decision helped to chisel away at notions of coverture, namely that a woman's person and personal belongings were ceded to her husband on marriage. (Legislation including Married Women's Property Acts sought to claw back power by giving wives power over their own personal property and independent earnings.) Yet, there was a long way to go, not least because of the violent local public demonstrations in support of Mr Jackson.

Despite the negative press surrounding the institution of marriage, Kitty found herself heading down the aisle at St James in Brindle on 7 April 1896. She was 25 years old. But there was no panic yet, as she was not considered too old; in fact, she was of the average age at which women married. The sun shone down on her as she emerged from the vicarage, dressed in a winter-weight white mohair dress, trimmed with silk, carrying a bouquet of white blossoms. Numerous flower girls preceded her and lay petals before her feet as she headed across the path to the church whose windows were decorated with flowers and ivy. Her father led her down the aisle to the tune of the 'Wedding March' from Richard Wagner's opera *Lohengrin*, a theme which had been popular since 1858, when it was played at the wedding of Victoria the Princess Royal and Prince Frederick William of Prussia. The bridesmaids – Kitty's sisters and her fiancé's sister Ethel – were dressed in white and blue blouses and hats, typical of the era when the shirt and skirt ensemble was becoming everyday wear. Encircling their wrists were gold bracelets, gifts from Kitty's husband-to-be who stood at the altar and cut a slim figure in his wedding suit as he gave her a backward glance.

She was surrounded by well-wishers, whose expectations would have crowded in on her, too. For a start, the Jacques and Finch families were closely involved in the proceedings. Hugh's own father, Reverend Thomas Ross Finch, an Oxford graduate, presided over the ceremony, assisted by Kitty's brother James Kinton Jacques and Hugh's brother Walter, Vicar of Nuneaton. Reverend Finch, now Kitty's father-in-law, addressed the church on the duties of a husband, who should offer his spouse protection and comfort, while a wife was expected to be a helpmeet, ready to submit to her husband. He reminded them that their marriage was no accident. They had been chosen to be together by God and, with a nod to the marriage sceptics, he told the couple that marriage was not merely an earthly contract that they could just break off at will. But he unwittingly added a loophole. They would be destined to be together forever, he said, provided that their love proved to be true.

We do not know whether Kitty chose Hugh or if she had responded to gentle persuasion from her parents. After all, the marriage appears to have been professionally and socially beneficial to both families. Born in

Staffordshire in 1871 (his mother was also called Caroline), the dapper 25-year-old Hugh appeared to have been an excellent catch. As was typical in his social class, he had been sent to boarding school, which in his case was Winchester College. Not only had he been a keen gymnast and rower, cross-country runner and athlete, he played polo whilst studying at Keble College Oxford and was a member of the 1st VIII in Oxford's Eighth Week, an annual rowing event. He graduated with a BA in Natural Sciences, and would obtain an MB Bac. in Surgery at Oxford in 1898, eventually taking up work at various hospitals in London. Hugh was living in Bloomsbury by the time of his marriage. He seemed to embody the principle of *mens sana in corpora sano*. His best man, schoolmaster Archer Vassall, was also a member of the university athletics team at Keble College and in 1899 he married Kitty's younger sister Cecilia. Archer and Cecilia were witnesses at Hugh and Kitty's wedding, together with Kinton Jacques and Caroline Mary Finch. After the garden party at the rectory, Kitty put on her brown travelling dress and coat and pink silk blouse, affixed her brown chip hat, which was trimmed with roses, and set off with her new husband for a life far from home, at the other end of England.

It is tempting to speculate on the thoughts and anxieties that Kitty may have had about her new life with Hugh. The poetry of Adelaide Procter, a favourite of Charles Dickens and Queen Victoria, is touchingly revealing. In particular, *A Woman's Question* (1858), which was written not long before Procter's death, combines a sense of hope and wariness:

Before I trust my Fate to thee,
Or place my hand in thine,
Before I let thy Future give
Colour and form to mine, —
Before I peril all for thee, question thy soul to-night
for me.
...
Is there within thy heart a need
That mine cannot fulfill?
One chord that any other hand
Could better wake or still?
Speak now, lest at some future day, my whole life
wither and decay.[3]

Not much is known about Kitty during these early years of her marriage in Essex. But in 1900, there was a change of circumstances for her and the new century ushered in a feeling of sorrow and dread. Hugh was working as an assistant at the Central London Throat and Central London Ophthalmology Hospitals when the couple were recalled up to the Rectory. Caroline Augusta had been suffering from bronchitis, asthma and syncope. Kinton was by her side in her final moments. He registered her sudden death on 7 January. Her funeral took place on 11 January at Brindle St James, attended by her family and many friends from Westhoughton and Leyland. Kinton and his children organised a tribute to his wife in the form of a prominent mural and a set of three stained-glass windows, known as The Three Ladies Window. The mural tablet, which sits just below three images of women, entitled 'Wisdom', 'Charity' and 'Good Works', reads: 'Caroline Augusta younger daughter of the Rev: Gardnor [*sic*] Baldwin Vicar of Leyland. For thirty seven years the beloved wife of Kinton Jacques Rector of this Parish. At rest January 7th 1900.' Running along the bottom of all the stained-glass panels is the message: 'To the glory of God and in loving memory of Caroline Augusta Jacques.' The first panel on the viewer's left shows The Capable Wife, her wedding ring prominent. We are invited to consider Proverbs 31 of the Old Testament which describes such a wife who works hard for her family, organises her servants and helps her husband who is a prominent local figure. The panel on the right, refers to Acts 9 from the New Testament and depicts Dorcas (whose name is Tabitha in Aramaic), the Good Lady of Joppa, who cared for widows and the poor. When she died, her grief-stricken community appealed to St Peter who successfully raised her from the dead. The middle window shows the Virgin Mary, holding Christ in yellow robes, watched by two young, adoring children. The scene refers to sections of 1 Corinthians: 13 of the New Testament:

> Love is patient and kind; it is not jealous or conceited or proud … When I was a child, my speech, feelings, and thinking were all those of a child; now that I am a man, I have no more use for childish ways. What we see now is like a dim image in a mirror; then we shall see face to face. What I know now is only partial; then it will be complete – as complete as God's knowledge of me. Meanwhile these three remain: faith, hope, and love; and the greatest of these is love.

The three children represented in the glass panel are symbolic of the three qualities at the end of this passage. Perhaps too, though, given the way that the scenes from the Bible interconnect with Caroline Augusta's own good works and her love of her family, the boy and the slightly older girl who kneel at the Virgin Mary's feet may have been reminiscent of Patrick and his sister Florence, whose tiny lives had been cut so short. Here they are face-to-face with us, their memories preserved in glass above the congregation.

The Jacques' home as represented in these stained-glass memorials and in the tablet was a reflection of godliness on Earth, harmonious and safe, with Kinton's and Caroline's companionate marriage transmitting the Lord's message, even after death. As Reverend Finch had told the guests at Kitty's wedding:

> And so, my dear son and daughter, when all the outer excitement and show and glitter of your happy wedding have passed away, may there still remain sounding in your heart the solemn undertones of God's Word, reminding you of the holy duties towards each other, which you undertake to-day. … When they leave their old homes, and set up a separate home and household of their own, the master of the family should remember that he is also the priest, and the mistress, that she is the deaconess, of the Church which is in their house.[4]

But when Kitty attended her mother's funeral in the very church in which she and the man standing beside her had been wed, she knew by that point that her own marriage was failing. Something went wrong very early on in the marriage and for whatever reason, Hugh had begun to distance himself from her. It did not help matters that women were so often kept in the dark about sex. As a child, suffragette and arsonist Kitty Marion was told that sex was 'a closed book'. Mary Wollstonecraft's *A Vindication of the Rights of Woman* (1792), had decried the state of innocence in which women had been kept, their minds kept ignorant and their bodies bound by the principle of 'coverture'. Her work struck a chord with late-Victorian readers, particularly suffrage campaigners like Emmeline Pethick Lawrence. On a practical level, ignorance of what to expect could augur badly for the marriage. For Gladys Schütze, who married grain merchant Louis Mendl in 1904, it was the wedding night, that mysterious event for which Victorian women were so typically ill-prepared, which caused the first rift. The event left her shaken and she felt that the experience forced her to grow up very quickly, while her husband seemed unaffected. The two were unable to surmount their differences and eventually filed for divorce. H.G. Wells married his cousin Isabel in 1891, but it was their disastrous wedding night which put a division up between them and made Wells feel rejected and resentful. Wells would continue to find Isabel attractive but his attention also drew towards his student, Amy Catherine Robbins, and soon he and Isabel would find themselves faced with the prospect of ending their marriage.

The Matrimonial Causes Act 1857 set up divorce courts in London which made divorce easier to obtain for many, albeit with stigma attached, more so if the parties came from backgrounds as close-knit as Kitty's. Although divorce was more widely available, there was a catch. Whereas a husband seeking a divorce only needed to prove a wife's infidelity, a wife would have to prove adultery and other fault such as desertion, bigamy or cruelty. It was only under the Matrimonial Causes Act 1923 that both men and women could divorce on grounds of adultery alone. Louis Mendl obtained his divorce from Gladys by proving that Gladys had been unfaithful; he named Peter Schütze. Peter and Gladys were married a matter of days after the divorce came through. Isabel Wells was required to show that her husband had been unfaithful – the co-respondent in his case was Amy Catherine ('Jane') who would become his long-term wife and would run his household while he engaged in his many affairs. But Isabel also had to show that he had been guilty of an act of cruelty which in Wells' case was desertion; he had failed to return to the marital home.

Under the Matrimonial Causes Act 1884, Wells could no longer be imprisoned but this act of desertion meant that he could be threatened with divorce. A copy of Isabel's letter to Wells imploring him to return was duly enclosed in her affidavit, and a statement of his failure to do so contained the necessary wording that a court would have been looking for in order to prove heartbreak, desertion and that her 'conjugal rights' had been infringed when he continued to ignore her court order to return to him; grounds on which to start the divorce proceedings. She got her divorce and Wells was ordered to pay her alimony.

In April 1899, Hugh had an affair. Kitty was determined not to begin the new century married to him and she marked the New Year of 1901 with a divorce petition. It was an age of endings. Kitty's divorce proceedings were set in motion just as Queen Victoria's diminutive coffin was drawn by black-plumed horses through the streets of London to the strain of Chopin's *Funeral March*. The death of the then longest-reigning British monarch left the general public with a sense of being unmoored, left to drift into a new century, just as Kitty's decision to unhook herself from her marriage would result in a battle which would at best confer on her the insecure social status of divorcee. The case of Finch v. Finch was heard before the Right Honourable Sir Francis Henry Jeune KCB, who had worked for the plaintiff in the Tichborne v. Lushington case of the early 1870s in which corpulent Australian Arthur Orton claimed to be the slim and dashing long-lost heir to the Tichborne baronetcy. When Jeune, who had presided over the Wells v. Wells case, eyed Kitty's divorce petition, he decided in her favour. Hugh was staying in London hotels with Alice Carr, who had divorced her own husband in 1895 on grounds of cruelty and adultery. It was not uncommon for the husband, with the wife's full knowledge, to be conveniently seen with another woman in a hotel to fulfil the adultery requirement. This tactic was the subject of A.P. Herbert's 1934 novel *Holy Deadlock* in which one character announces that those who are unhappily married and cannot divorce are 'joined together in unholy matrimony' and are 'married alive!'

As far as the court was concerned, Hugh had treated Kitty with cruelty. In April 1899, Hugh had contracted a venereal disease, which he then 'wilfully and recklessly' communicated to Kitty and 'was thereby guilty of cruelty towards her'. Both adverbs were important. In fact, two previous cases gave rise to a vocabulary which framed Hugh's treatment of Kitty as an act of cruelty and ultimately helped Kitty obtain a divorce. The first of these was the 1865 case of Brown v. Brown. It was not the numerous examples of her husband's drunkenness, his repeated desertion of her, his threatening presence at home or his shabby treatment of her father, whom he threatened with a pistol duel in 1863, that convinced the judge of the husband's cruelty. Rather, the judge felt that Brown had committed an act of cruelty by 'wilfully' communicating a disease to his wife. To sufficiently establish wilfulness, Judge James Wilde argued, one must look to the circumstances around the husband's behaviour and assume that his health was 'within his own knowledge'. The Liverpool divorce case Boardman v. Boardman of 1866 importantly broadened the definition of cruelty from an intentional action to a reckless deed. Effectively, the case extended the grounds on which a woman could obtain a divorce. In 1860, 18-year-old Martha married commission agent James Boardman; after five years, Martha fell ill. Serial adulterer James Boardman knew he had had a disease prior to marriage. The doctor's conclusion was that only James could have given Martha syphilis. James gaslighted his wife and tried to darken her reputation, but a court decided that it was James and not his wife who was guilty of adultery, with James also considered guilty of cruelty. But, looking back on these cases with modern eyes, it is clear that the medical profession was also committing its own act of cruelty in withholding the truth. The doctors who had treated Margaretta and Martha told their husbands what was wrong with them but the women, their patients, were kept in the dark about the true nature of their physical complaints. They were indeed victims of a common doctor-led conspiracy of silence.

Kitty's husband may well have suspected that he was suffering from a venereal complaint. At some point, Kitty deduced the nature of her physical complaints and was appalled enough to seek medical advice. All three women bravely put themselves through the ignominy of appealing for a divorce, proceedings for which were held in a male-led court, an experience which could be devastating for a wife's reputation. One of the most famous cases of a wife contracting syphilis was Campbell v. Campbell in which playwright, journalist and artist Gertrude Elizabeth (known as Lady Colin Campbell), whose circle included Oscar Wilde and Sir Arthur Sullivan, received a judicial separation in 1884. The couple's divorce case of 1886, in which four co-respondents were featured, attracted much press attention although the divorce was denied as no evidence could be found that either of them was having an affair. Gertrude could never clear her name from scandal.

Mrs Pankhurst did not need to watch Henrik Ibsen's widely influential play *Ghosts* (1882) or read the 1890s novels *The Heavenly Twins* (1893) by Sarah Grand and *A Superfluous Woman* by Emma Frances Brooke, which see women becoming infected by their husbands and giving birth to ailing children. The founder of the WSPU already knew all about the effect of VD on young lives. When Richard Pankhurst died in 1898, Mrs Pankhurst relinquished her unpaid work as a Poor Law Guardian. Chorlton Board of Guardians offered her the position of Registrar of

Births and Deaths, a post which came with a salary. She remembered how some mothers, who had come to register the deaths of their children, were unaware that the accompanying sealed doctor's letter stated venereal disease as the cause.

While the Contagious Diseases Acts of the 1860s placed the responsibility of the nation's health on prostitutes and made women who happened to find themselves in the wrong areas of garrison towns subject to arrest, in *Ghosts*, *The Heavenly Twins* and *A Superfluous Woman* it is men's bodies and past actions which are seen as a source of anxiety, of physical and moral pollution. In her book *The Great Scourge and How to End It* (1913), Christabel had maintained that three-quarters of British men had been infected with VD and she backed up her claim with quotations from medical experts to counter allegations of exaggerations. The widespread concern over venereal disease before the advent of Salvarsan in 1910 for treating syphilis, followed by antibiotics, could not be dismissed. In 1913, Kate Parry Frye, a 35-year-old suffragist, had an awkward conversation with her fiancé over venereal disease during a Christmas shopping trip:

> Everyone is telling of Christabel Pankhurst's book and certain Diseases. … And then the remembrance of the statistics – the number of men who must use women – sent me reeling over – just as if I had had a blow in the face – why should I think John different to the rest – how should he be? … Is any man possible if the physical relations have been made so repulsive and dangerous between man and woman – and if no-one is delicate and decent about them? I never wanted to marry, though I did not know why, and now the whole idea is repulsive to me.[5]

Kate seems to have set her qualms aside, as she and John were later married.

When it came to how Kitty was affected by the disease she caught from her husband, she kept her own council. Recovering from the invidious experience of having her private life displayed before a male-dominated courtroom, Kitty went to stay in Withycombe, near the Somerset coast, with her sister Eleanor. Kitty waited out the customary six months for the decree nisi to become decree absolute, which it did on 4 November. Hugh emigrated to Australia where he married a further two times and served in the New Zealand army as a medical doctor during the First World War. He died in New South Wales in 1934.

In 1904, Kitty married Arthur Edward Willoughby Marshall, a 33-year-old solicitor and bachelor, the son of a clergyman. One of ten children, he was born just under a month before Kitty on 14 July 1870. The marriage took place in Hammersmith at St Matthew's Church, rendered distinctive with its striped yellow and red bricks and sleek bell tower. The building was designed and built in 1870–71 by Sir Arthur Blomfield, an advocate of early Gothic design, who was influenced by William Butterfield and G.E. Street. The church wedding was unusual as second marriages would normally be civil ceremonies. Notably, on her marriage certificate, Kitty was recorded as being 'single/unmarried', not divorced. Bar her surname, now appearing as Finch in contrast to her father's, who was present at the ceremony, it is as if the Hugh Finch episode in her life had almost never happened. Kitty gave her address as Brindle Rectory, her father's home, and on 16 June, Kitty dropped the name Finch and became Mrs Marshall.

Soon after their wedding, Kitty and Arthur Marshall moved into a house named 'Kenilworth' in Theydon Bois, a village situated on the outskirts of the popular market town of Epping. A cosy spot off a main road in Theydon Bois is St Mary's Church where women's education pioneer, suffragist and Kensington Society member Frances Buss, is buried. Just after her death in 1894, two stained-glass windows were put up in her memory. As Kitty sat in the church, the stained-glass window was to her right. The Marshalls imbibed the fresh air of Epping Forest, with its distinctive hornbeams, holly thickets and overshadowed Iron Age fort undulations, but they could also easily commute to London. In 1906, the Pankhursts moved the WSPU headquarters to 4 St Clement's Inn to be near Westminster; Arthur's law firm was located nearby at 48 Mark Lane in the City of London. The Marshalls' new London home was at 58 York Street and from 1913, at 15 Gayfere Street, Westminster. The distance between their Gayfere Street hideout and Caxton Hall, where the WSPU would hold Women's Parliament sessions, could be closed in a matter of minutes, even in heels.

2.

Mental Equipment

Kitty's experience with Hugh had given her a reason to fight for social change, but she had not yet learnt how to translate her questioning spirit into a physical struggle. By contrast, Ralph Kitchener, the detective who would follow her to 63 Glebe Place, had learnt how to fight from an early age. The Kitcheners were used to hardship. Ralph's grandfather, Ephraim, had spent his childhood during the Hungry Forties, living with his family in a porous, earth-floor cottage in Olney. At 7 years old, Ephraim was sent out to work long hours as a farm hand, scaring crows and picking stones from ploughed land. His father scraped together enough savings to pay for a clock by which the boy learnt to tell the time which gave him a competitive edge over other farm labourers. Kitchener admired the way that his grandfather could work the tough soil in his father's allotment. 'Ah, it's the way you do it, not the strength you do it with – you must remember that,' he advised. Such a mindset would come in handy when Ralph later came to learn martial arts.

Little Ralph gained his first experience of dramatic recitals, watching the white-bearded, straight-backed Ephraim perform *The Charge of the Light Brigade*. Ephraim supplemented his income by working as a boot and shoe finisher, as did his son Joseph, who was born in 1861. Despite learning not much more than the three Rs, Joseph impressed his son Ralph with his knowledge of politics, Richard Cobden and William Gladstone. Joseph's workshop was situated at the end of a miniscule garden at the address where Ralph was born at 6 Warwick Terrace in Olney on 17 June 1889. The small family home had a kitchen and a living room on the ground floor and two rooms above this, with water being pumped from a communal pump. Joseph toiled from six in the morning until well into the evening, the shoes he was working on arranged in a semi-circle around him, their soles upwards. Ralph Kitchener's earliest encounter with the police was when Ralph's father was visited by a policeman – a man whom Kitchener considered a 'bogey' – in connection with his father's refusal to have his sons Maurice (born in 1894) and Cyril (born in 1892) vaccinated against smallpox. The officer marked up the articles of furniture which were to be distrained to make up the cost of the fine Joseph refused to pay. Ralph's mother, Elizabeth Ann Coles, who was born in Olney in 1863, found inventive ways to keep her family fed on Joseph's weekly earnings of 25 shillings and helped make ends meet by taking in work as a shoe 'closer', working with uppers from a factory. Both parents made sacrifices for their children and Ralph Kitchener remembers his parents' marriage as a happy one. The couple were well loved by their own children and those around them.

Against a background scent of leather and polish from the workshop, the three brothers engaged their father in wrestling and tumbling matches. Joseph enjoyed outdoor exercise, rugby (his father was in the local Olney rugby team), football and wild swimming and taught a little Ralph how to fish. Elizabeth read to her boys and Ralph devoured *Aesop's Fables* from the family collection, while popular magazines like *The Strand Magazine*, with its Sherlock Holmes adventures, could be borrowed from the Congregational Church Society. Ralph attended the local elementary Board School until he was 7 and then the 'Big School' where girls and boys were separated. As was common, especially in large classes, children were caned for misdemeanours and on one occasion one unruly pupil was asked to buy a new cane only to be whipped with it on his return! Thankfully for Ralph, learning was easy and he was always at the top of the class.

When Ralph was around 12 years old, his mother could no longer take in any more shoe-finishing work so, to make ends meet, he worked half-time in a boot factory, alongside attending school. This arrangement meant that he had to learn in half a day what others learnt in a whole day of schooling. Despite the remonstrations of his uncle, whose two sons were teachers, Ralph, who was still a star pupil, had to leave school at 13 to take a job fixing eyelets in the factory. He then toiled in an ill-lit and ill-ventilated room as a clicker, a key worker in a shoe factory who cut out the uppers of shoes. This was a skilled job which required accuracy in matching the grain of the leathers and avoiding wastage. (The job title of 'clicker' was derived from the clicking noise the hand knife made when it separated from the clicking board.)

Ralph knew that if he wanted to improve his lot, he needed to continue to educate himself and so, in addition to buying as many fortnightly copies of *Cassell's Educator* as he could, he attended night classes. These classes were insufficient, but one of the teachers encouraged him to study for the Oxford and Cambridge senior local examination with a view to entering the teaching profession. He studied three hours a week on top of a full day's work, finishing at 7 p.m., trudging in total darkness to the teacher's house for tuition 2 miles away, Milton's *Paradise Lost* in his mind. One of his evening walks took him towards his first encounter with the suffragettes on 22 July 1909 at Bedford Town Hall. Kitchener tells us in his autobiography that he observed that the women were massed in full force, and loudly interrupting the speakers. They were violently ejected and a man, who was sporting a sash bearing the words 'Votes for Women', was also thrown out. Kitchener and his friends walked 12 miles back to Olney, but he was still up in time for work the next day.

Ralph taught himself shorthand and passed an examination in 'Theory of the System'. He took down notes from political meetings and, with the blessing of the local minister, recorded in shorthand the sermons in church. Just before he began work at 6 a.m., Ralph's father would read passages for him to take down, such as parliamentary speeches on Old Age Pensions and the People's Budget, which provided 'dictation material'. He timed the lad and both noticed that by the time he moved to London he had reached 100 words a minute and was able to transcribe his notes accurately. He also taught himself basic typewriting skills, borrowing a machine from a Northampton commercial school. He felt that he ought to learn a foreign language and approached Thomas Wright, a local eccentric who wore dark glasses, a 'shovel hat' and a frock coat, who ran a private boarding school and was the author of *The Life of William Cowper* (1892). Wright set him French lessons and English essays, which were corrected on a weekly basis, and introduced him to Thomas Carlyle's *The French Revolution* (1837) – one of Mrs Pankhurst's lifelong favourite works – which, at the time, Ralph was too time-pressed to appreciate. In the little spare time they had, he and his brothers practised boxing in what they called their 'gym' at the end of their father's workshop, while Joseph looked on at work, amused.

Ralph wanted to expand his horizons and language skills, and he soon aspired to join the police. Attracted by better working conditions and the opportunity to move up the ranks and improve their social status, constables were often drawn from what would have been considered to be working-class backgrounds. As the WSPU was gearing up for a monster rally in Hyde Park on 17 June, Kitchener turned 21. He had wanted for some years to join the police force. Given the scale of unemployment at the time, a career in the Metropolitan Police, which came with a pension, was attractive. So, he took an overnight train from Olney to the metropolis. His height concerned him, however. Despite his best efforts to stretch himself through exercises, he could not reach the minimum height requirement, which was 5ft 9in (for City of London police it was 6ft). However, he hoped that if he could sleep on the train, he could go straight to his interview first thing in the morning, at a time in the day at which it was believed people were at their tallest. One of his confident competitors, who was working in an iron foundry, towered over Kitchener. The medical officer remarked that Kitchener was short of the height requirement by five-eighths of an inch, but he also noted his physique, his interest in swimming, rugby and boxing. He saw too that Kitchener had learnt shorthand. Most of the candidates, despite their navy or army training, were dismissed and told they would have their results by post but Kitchener was asked to return after lunch to take a written examination. Much to his and his tall competitor's surprise, Kitchener was offered the job on the day.

Six weeks' training followed at Peel House, including parade drill, education in the law, first aid, the three Rs and physical training which included jujitsu. Jigoro Kano had founded Kodokan Judo in the storeroom of a Buddhist temple in Tokyo in the 1880s. It was the era of the Meiji Restoration, of modernisation and industrialisation, and Kano, an expert in physical education and a politics and economics graduate, sought to update and bring together the best elements of traditional jujitsu styles which were associated with the old Samurai ways. His reforms omitted some of the more dangerous, battlefield-orientated techniques so that judo could be practised at an international (and ultimately Olympic) level. Kano was inspired by Eastern and Western teachings and his new school offered students a moral and spiritual – as well as physical – education. His philosophy paid off when his judoka defeated a rival jujitsuka in a match with local police jujitsu groups. And although judo started to take off – it would be taught in schools and to police officers in Japan – Kodokan was indebted to and respected the old styles of jujitsu, recognising them as valuable aspects of Japanese cultural heritage. While some of the self-defence schools that Kitty might encounter referred to their art as jujitsu, a number of them had adopted elements of judo.

Kitchener's CID colleague, Cecil Bishop, relished a fight. He had escaped to sea at the age of 13, then became a stockbroker's clerk. Feeling stifled by deskbound work and dreaming of his earlier adventures at sea, he resigned. He admired the figure his brother had cut in his Life Guard army uniform and was inspired by his brother's police friends to join the Met in 1903. He was posted to the K Division, Limehouse, in the East End of London. On occasion, jujitsu saved his life and for him one benefit of knowing the martial art was that he could defend himself without injuring his opponent unduly.

Japanese martial arts and boxing were often taught in section houses and various forces, such as the Glasgow Police Jujitsu Team, displayed their physique in police magazines. In 1904, City of London Police Sergeant (later Inspector) George Henry Edwin Wheeldon wrote *Self-Defence: A Treatise upon the Art of Defence Against Attack, Specially Designed for Police Instruction* (1904), which offered methods of countering knife attacks, tips on how to extricate oneself from the indignity of being restrained in a 'Chancery hold' or being gripped by the waist, collar or coat. Wheeldon offered his own unique form of self-defence, combining Cumberland and Cornish wrestling and jujitsu. Sir Howard Vincent was impressed and Wheeldon's tip for conducting a miscreant to the police station and his advice on countering knife, pistol and dagger attacks were printed in *A Police Code and Manual of the Criminal Law*. By 1912, all officers were being taught ten key jujitsu holds during their probationary training.

Kitchener was dazed by the immensity and loneliness of the city. He lived in a section house with around fifty other men. Although the Police Disabilities Removal Act 1887 had enfranchised the police, he was unaffected by the legislation. The large numbers of unmarried men living in cubicles did not get the parliamentary franchise because their living spaces were not considered separate dwellings; partitions between the cubicles failed to reach the ceiling which meant that the men shared air and light, and on that basis they were ineligible to vote. On Kitchener's first night, he heard a commotion further down the dormitory. All new recruits were being tipped out of their beds. But when the men approached his cubicle, he roared at them and they meekly retreated. He hoped he would not be posted to east London's darkest streets, to alleyways so dangerous that constables dared not venture there alone. To his relief, he was sent to E Division and was later based at Bow Street where he spent two years.

Before an officer could become a detective, he had to gain experience and develop intuitive powers by working as a beat bobby. Kitchener's daytime shifts at Bow Street came in two batches of four hours and nightly beats ran to eight continuous hours from 10 p.m. to 6 a.m. He helped those who needed assistance on the increasingly busy throughfares of Oxford Street and the Embankment, which were frequented by pedestrians, and a plethora of horse-drawn vehicles, bicycles, motorbuses and motorcars, leading to traffic incidents. Checked by his superior officer, the notebook he was required to keep recounted various incidents and expenses. Sergeant Frank Bunn, who was on duty at Tattenham Corner where suffragette Emily Wilding Davison was killed at the Epsom Derby in 1913, famously listed the items found on Emily's body, however, the rest of the pages of Bunn's police notebook, which are far less well known, also reveal the kinds of everyday incidents which an officer could encounter. Writing in a large, clear looping hand, Bunn's notes intimated the ironic story of a suicidal man who has a change of heart but whose decision to hide his gun under a pillow results in the accidental shooting of a woman who enters his room. In a collision between two cyclists, the police paid the doctor's fees for the teenage cyclist as she was too poor to pay. Bunn's record of the incident illustrates the hazards the newly emancipated female cyclist could encounter and also demonstrates the ways in which police officers could go above and beyond their expected duty of care towards the public.

The formation of the Met in 1829 sparked concerns that the organisation could be an extension of the military and might pose a threat to civil liberties. To assuage fears, the colour chosen for the uniform was not army red but blue and the police officer was, in the main, minimally armed: Kitchener carried with him a truncheon and whistle. He also became familiar with *A Police Code and Manual of the Criminal Law*. Handy, too, was the more nifty *Policeman's Pocket Almanac* which contained tips on first aid, the locations of foreign embassies, London penitentiaries, women's refuges, fire brigade stations and the times of the rising and setting sun. As Kitchener learnt, a good officer was book-smart as well as street savvy and knew when to exercise discretion. The beat bobby needed to possess excellent 'mental equipment' and legal knowledge and be prepared for action at any moment.

The suffragettes soon put the ability of the police officer to react in all circumstances to the test when Kitty's friend, Mrs Pankhurst, and her eldest daughter, Christabel, changed the direction of the WSPU. An early catalyst for more militant action occurred in May 1905, when Mrs Pankhurst, together with Elizabeth Wolstenholme Elmy and around 300 others, had gathered in the Strangers' Lobby and in the environs of the House of Commons in great anticipation of a second reading of the landmark Women's Enfranchisement Bill, which aimed to give the franchise to women on the same terms as men. Earlier on the agenda, the Vehicles' Lights Bills was put forward by James Bigwood, MP for Brentwood, on the expectation that, given the increased volume and varieties of traffic on Edwardian roads, such a sensible safety measure would not even need much discussion. But, parliamentarians unsympathetic to women's suffrage also used the measure as a way of tactically eating into time, edging the Women's Enfranchisement Bill off the table. When the House finally came to the topic late in the day, the usual old chestnuts were slung around: women could not be useful citizens as they were unable to be policemen or soldiers and besides, there was not much interest in the female franchise. Then time for discussion ran out.

A few months later, at the Free Trade Hall in Manchester in October 1905, a bloody, scratched and determined Christabel Pankhurst narrowed her eyes and lifted her chin in defiance as her arms were pinned to her sides. Like her mother, she was fed up with being sidelined. When Sir Edward Grey had failed to mention women's suffrage in his speech, and the questions she and her friend, millworker Annie Kenney, asked of the speakers were repeatedly ignored, the two women unfurled a calico banner bearing the words 'Votes for Women' in black polish. That was when the fight had broken out, and Christabel's blood had found its way on to Annie's hat. It was imperative that she and Annie were noticed and the cause they supported was given publicity. The women needed to be arrested. Christabel, who had studied law but was barred from practising as a lawyer due to her gender, knew that she had to commit a technical assault. (Christabel's knowledge of the law and her skills she had acquired in her debating and logic classes would be essential tools in the WSPU's armamentarium.) With her arms bound and her movements restricted, Christabel reasoned that she could still commit a 'technical assault': she could 'spit' in the police officer's face. Of course, it was not a real spit, but a dry pursing of the lips, a mere gesture of intent, a performance. And it worked. The police officers on the scene arrested Christabel and Annie. Both women refused to pay fines for their misconduct and instead served a short jail sentence, which earned them and the cause further attention.

Chief Inspector Charles Scantlebury did not have to contend with spitting women, but he was presented with an unexpected security problem. Christabel's and Annie's actions at the Free Trade Hall inspired more acts of rebellion and Scantlebury was to encounter one of the very earliest protests. On 23 October 1906, over a hundred women gathered by the Strangers' Entrance, each of these visitors requesting an interview with a Member of Parliament. As soon as Mrs Pankhurst and Emmeline Pethick Lawrence were told that Henry Campbell-Bannerman's government would not be considering the question of women's suffrage, a group of these female visitors created what was commonly referred to as 'disturbance' in the Central Lobby of the House of Commons, climbing onto the soft, padded seats, shouting and making speeches. Mrs Pankhurst was knocked over and as her friends formed a protective barrier, they could hear the jeers from parliamentarians over their shoulders. Those who remained standing on the seats resolutely desisted from making their protest when Chief Inspector Scantlebury, his Cornish heritage apparent in his accent, asked them to do so. Scantlebury suspected that the demonstration was no sporadic display of annoyance and had been a prearranged invasion. He acted quickly to prevent the group from gaining further ground within the building, had the women arrested and was praised by his colleagues for his swift action. Among the women who were apprehended were Anne Cobden-Sanderson, the daughter of Richard Cobden of Corn Law repeal campaign fame, and claustrophobic Emmeline Pethick Lawrence who, in 1907, would become the co-editor, along with her husband Fred, of *Votes for Women*, a publication to which Kitty subscribed. The memory of terror that Emmeline Pethick Lawrence felt when presented with the inside of the police van stayed with her for decades. As the women were thrust into the daunting space, she saw that there was not a row of seats as she had expected, but an arrangement of cages, each barely big enough to accommodate an adult. Only a thin wisp of air and light trickled in through the bars in the passageway between the rows. As the cab jolted arrhythmically on its way to Holloway, she tried to still her wildly beating heart.

When Christabel Pankhurst mimed a spit in the face of a police officer, she began a performative dialogue between the suffragettes and the men who were to arrest them. Scotland Yard came to the conclusion that, at least when it came to apprehending the more famous protestors, ideally a more experienced police officer, such as inspector, would have the knowhow to play the game and react with the necessary delicacy to avoid giving the suffragettes positive press whilst maintaining the Yard's reputation. In October 1908, Inspector James Jarvis displayed his tact when he was given the task of arresting Mrs Pankhurst, Christabel, and Flora Drummond in connection with a proposed 'rush' on Parliament which Christabel had incited. A deputation had headed to the Houses of Parliament from Caxton Hall at 7.30 p.m. Kitty Marion's memoir relates how she saw plain-clothes officers breaking their ranks and diverting the women, pushing them along the road and flinging them to the ground. To keep her balance, she leaned back whilst being 'run'. But she could distinguish between the 'brutes' who seemed to enjoy acts of violence and the 'men' who were reluctant to do such an uncomfortable job. The incident involved thousands of police; traffic was diverted, crowds were rerouted and women were seized. Jarvis knew that he had to humour the Pankhursts and Flora ('The General') Drummond and saw to it that they were not to be roughly handled. So, he politely waited for Christabel's missive to say that they would meet him at the WSPU headquarters at Clement's Inn. One of the iconic images duly appeared in the press in which Inspector Jarvis read out the warrant for the arrests of the trio while Mrs Pankhurst looked on, unimpressed.

Refused a trial by jury, the women argued their case at Bow Street with Christabel acting as their lawyer. Christabel had been a gifted law student and had achieved a First Class Honours in 1906, the only woman on her course and one of only two students to be awarded the category in her year. The trial now offered her an opportunity to showcase her talents. Fortified by sustenance brought to the prison by the Savoy Hotel, Christabel cross-examined Chancellor of the Exchequer Lloyd George. Christabel claimed the 'rush' that had been planned was not intended to be an act of violence. The definitions of 'rush' which she offered, which irritated the magistrate, Curtis Bennett, included a pressing 'urgent demand' or 'rushing' at hockey. She furthermore questioned whether violence was advocated during the meeting. As she suggested, Lloyd George would not have brought his child to the meeting if he had considered it to be hazardous and violent. Christabel, who wore a plain white dress and the WSPU sash, contrasted with the stuffy courtroom officials. She threw her head back when emphasising points and her fluid arm and hand gestures coupled with quick responses were her form of self-defence. Her interrogation of Gladstone won over the audience.

The women were, nevertheless, sentenced to three months and Christabel to ten weeks in prison, in the Second Division. As the sentence was being read out at the Rush Trial, a press photographer, Arthur Barrett, watched from the press stands. He had hidden a camera in his top hat and had cut out a flap for the lens. The resulting image was taken clandestinely, the sound of the snap carefully drowned out by his strategic cough. He told the story of his photographic stunt which was passed down through the generations of his own family.

3.

Body Armour

Omnibus drivers could take enquirers there and pedestrians would stop and stare, for the scene was exceptionally hard to miss. It was the middle of May 1909 and the WSPU fundraising event at the Prince's Skating Rink was in swing. The setting was affluent Knightsbridge, situated on the lower corner of Hyde Park. Sylvia Pankhurst, Christabel's younger sister, had excelled herself. Not only was the exterior decorated in purple, white and green colours but a mural, designed by Sylvia, extended the length of the building, depicting the birth, progress and success of the movement. She also designed the programme cover, with its trumpeting angel. Every corner was considered in this brilliantly branded event; even tea tables were laid in suffragette colours.

On bazaar opening day, Mrs Pankhurst told visitors that the purpose of the event was to raise funds and to show that the women possessed of the vote would help beautify the world. This was a clever reshuffle of John Ruskin's idealistic image of womanhood in his famous essay, 'Sesame and Lilies'. Ruskin had implied that women ought to confine themselves to beautifying the home while their husbands, possessed of financial and political power, braved the excitement and danger of the world. Yet, in a clear use of Ruskin's ideas and gender stereotyping, here the WSPU was showing that the world, and not just the home, could benefit from women's 'queenly' aesthetic vision if women had the franchise.

Benefiting from corporate backing, the bazaar offered a variety of suffrage-themed items. The Women Writers' Suffrage League bookstall sold signed copies, there was an ice cream soda fountain, crafts, including needlework, art and flowers, were exhibited, while palmists and artists offered their services. Mrs Pankhurst had a millinery stall and was assisted by her 19-year-old son Harry; the Aeolian Ladies' Orchestra made an appearance too. Kitty Marshall was also flexing her muscles. At the Prince's Skating Rink, she headed the Farm Produce Stall. She was well suited to the task. In November 1907, Kitty had masterminded a poultry show in Theydon Bois, which had attracted 400 entries, with Arthur's law firm offering a significant cash prize. Dressed in an eighteenth-century mob cap (a tribute to Mary Wollstonecraft), Kitty ran the stall at the Prince's Skating Rink with her good friends, Edith and Ellen Beck, Quaker sisters born in the 1840s who commuted to weekly WSPU meetings from Sussex and gave generously to the cause. At the Prince's Skating Rink fair, prizes were offered for the best farm produce, including fowls, butter and vegetables.

Visitors were amused by a display of wax models depicting scenes from WSPU cartoons in which women were chasing cabinet ministers protected by burly police officers. The living exhibition drew attention to the plight of suffragettes in prison. A woman dressed in prison garb of the Second Division sat on a plank bed and made bags while the contrasting First-Division cell showed a wax model of a man, sitting in his more comfortable cell. When suffragettes went to jail, for the first month they lost contact with the outside world and reading matter was extremely limited. Once in jail, a female political prisoner was expected to be silent.

A 'polling booth' offered all visitors a chance to vote on current issues. While most voters agreed that women should serve on juries and that married women should not be excluded from teaching, the votes were split when it came to the idea of women being police officers, with 197 against and 196 for the motion. It was an intriguing result, as in other instances the WSPU was heavily campaigning for career equality for women. But it may be the case that the public was reminded of who the good and bad guys were supposed to be. Police officers, or at least men dressed as bobbies, were directly pitted against suffragettes in a lively demonstration by jujitsu instructor, Edith Garrud. During the filming of *Suffragette* (2015), Helena Bonham Carter had the first name of her character, a jujitsu instructor, changed to *Edith* Ellyn[6] in honour of Mrs Garrud, who herself had starred on the silver screen. Audiences may well have recognised Edith from Gaumont's production, *Ju-Jitsu* (1907), billed as a sensational comedy. Sadly, the film has been lost over time but contemporary reviews and stills offer a glimpse into the plot. After taking classes in jujitsu, two ladies go shopping in Piccadilly. When they get on the tube at Leicester Square, they are followed by some unsavoury characters all the way to Hampstead Heath. Unable to outrun them, they fight them on the Heath, with Mrs Garrud felling them to the ground using her skills in jujitsu. The film highlighted the experiences of female pedestrians being stalked, recasting these experiences as comedies, but it did at least show women taking matters into their own hands.

Edith's husband, William, was due to give the jujitsu demonstration but was taken ill at the last minute and Mrs Pankhurst encouraged the nervous Edith to take his place. A couple of weeks earlier, she had showcased her talents at the Green, White and Gold Fair at Caxton Hall, hosted by the breakaway militant organisation, the Women's Freedom League (WFL). A newspaper reporter pretended to garotte Edith Garrud, steal her bag and raise a knife to her. The image of the jujitsu-suffragette captured the imagination. In December that year, the popular physical culture magazine, *Health and Strength*, offered a cartoon depicting 'the next Raid on the House of Commons' featuring women tackling police officers to the ground using jujitsu.

Edith Garrud had dark, curling hair and a steely yet jaunty countenance which she often presented to the press. She was 4ft 10in tall and was wearing a short zubon (trousers) and an uwagi (jujitsu jacket), which was secured with a wide sash or obi (a jujitsu belt). Under her trousers, Edith sported some form of bloomer over dark stockings. A formidable 6ft-tall police officer faced her. In a fictional tale, Sherlock Holmes, using his knowledge of Japanese martial arts, had blocked Professor Moriarty's plans to hurl the great detective into a watery oblivion in Sherlock Holmes' great comeback story, *The Adventure of the Empty House* (1903). Conan Doyle had succumbed to public pressure and perhaps also a private suggestion from Herbert Asquith's son to bring this much-loved character back; now, in real life, Edith would attempt to stymie this officer's plans to trounce her.

Edith was born in Bath in 1872. Her mother, Clara Williams, a piano teacher, was in her very early twenties and unmarried when she gave birth to Edith on 7 April 1872. It was a part of the family story that was hushed up. Edith was sent to live with her aunt and uncle at 60 Thornhill Square,

Islington in the shadow of Islington's Royal Agricultural Hall, famous for Royal Military Tournaments with assault-at-arms displays and tightrope feats. In 1893, Edith married physical culturist William Garrud who was a pupil of Sadakazu Uyenishi, a jujitsu instructor who had come to Britain with Edward William Barton-Wright, an Anglo-Scottish engineer with a handlebar moustache who himself had learnt jujitsu in Japan. Barton-Wright founded the Bartitsu Club at the turn of the century to promote his new mixed martial art, Bartitsu, in harmony with the nineteenth-century zeitgeist in which violence was considered an increasingly less acceptable way of resolving issues in everyday life, whether defending one's reputation or one's property.

Bartitsu avoided the use of weapons and employed everyday items instead. A Bartitsu Club instructor, Pierre Vigny, founded *la canne* which inspired Barton-Wright's walking-stick defensive strategies. Vigny was a self-confessed *flâneur* (urbane city explorer and observer) who had tried out his system in the no-go areas of cities around Europe. His wife, Marguerite, known as 'Miss Sanderson' or 'Madame Vigny', taught umbrella and parasol self-defence at Vigny's club, which was taken up by increasing numbers of women. Umbrella self-defence was a useful skill: Adela Pankhurst dramatically used a green umbrella to ward off successive numbers of stewards and crowds swamping the WSPU's car in Abernathy where Churchill was speaking in October 1909. Barton-Wright's Japanese assistants became celebrities in their own right, opening their own dojos (schools). Uyenishi taught Emily Diana Watts who wrote the first known women's martial arts manual in English, *The Fine Art of Jujutsu* (1906), featuring various exercises and 'kata', choreographed movements. William Garrud worked at Uyenishi's Golden Square dojo and when Uyenishi went back to Japan in around 1908, Garrud took over the school, with his wife assisting in classes for women and children.

As Edith demonstrated to the audience at the Prince's Skating Rink, jujitsu was based on the principle of using the enemy's weight and strength to one's own advantage and causing the assailant to submit by applying a lock so as to render it impossible for the opponent to move the locked limb without injuring themselves. Edith would tell her heavier adversaries to beware. When Mrs Garrud caused her male opponent to lose his helmet, the audience chuckled with amusement. She slipped out of the grasp of one of the officers just like Sherlock Holmes, with his knowledge of Bartitsu (misspelled in Conan Doyle's story as 'baritsu'), eluded Moriarty's lunge as the two fought together to the death on a ledge of the Swiss Reichenbach Falls. Edith's adversary turned into the air and landed hard on his head on the mat. Dazed, he considered the dreadful possibilities for him if such an encounter had taken place on the pavement. In fact, during a suffragette event when an officer told her that she was causing an obstruction, Edith replied that he was impeding her view. She jerked her head and threw him over her shoulder and melted back into the crowd. Jujitsu was not intended to be deadly, but on unforgiving surfaces, it could be. Commandant Mary Allen, who would become involved in the creation of the women's police force, felt that 'a woman with a knowledge of ju-jitsu can, if necessary, take charge of the roughest criminal of either sex'. If she possessed martial arts' skills as well as weapons, she would have 'that further means of persuasion at her command should it be needed'.[7]

The Prince's Skating Rink event raised £5,664 for the cause and attracted 250 new members; no doubt inspired by Edith's performance which was considered by the WSPU to be one of the highlights of the fair. Christabel Pankhurst's stellar performance at the Rush Trial had showed up the cabinet ministers as an unsure and insincere bunch. Through the image of the thrown and winded bobby, Mrs Garrud used her unique skills to help the militant suffrage groups discredit the actions of the Home Office and the government that the toppled man in blue represented. Edith ended her performances with a parting message to all the charmed journalists standing around the mat: thirty suffragettes were now proficient at jujitsu and they were not afraid to trounce any man who, by his behaviour, was asking for it. While the suffragettes saw police as tools of the government, they were also, through these jujitsu tableaux, tools in the suffragettes' campaign.

During the summer of 1909, Kitty was staying with a friend in London. As she recalled to Rachel Barrett, the women were getting dressed for a night out. It was 29 June and they were off to see the prime minister. Kitty held her new undergarments up to the light to check their suitability. They really weren't much to look at, just a couple of stiff cardboard pieces to be worn at the back and the front, underneath a blouse. Newspapers could also be used to pad out the chest. Such accessories were all the rage among militant suffragettes, however, and very serviceable when it came to cushioning the women from the pummelling they might receive from the police and public. But the armour was messy and when the women took the cardboard bodices off after a campaign, dust would scatter all over the floor.

These suffragettes were, of course, right to be prepared. Just giving a speech was hazardous enough and it was not long before the stink of bad eggs, rotten fruit and even deceased cats became synonymous with the cry of 'Votes for Women!' in the minds of the British bobby. According to her memoir, on one occasion in Hereford, Kitty and her group had faced some flying garden produce:

> The next evening we hired a cart and took it to a nice square with trees round it and a wall. We got a good crowd, including a cowardly young man, who thought it good fun to throw ripe tomatoes at us. He was not a particularly good shot because he hit the mayor below the chin and the tomato burst all over his face, which did not please the Mayor. He was very annoyed with the young man hiding behind the wall and very unsympathetic with us and quite a supporter when he understood and heard what the campaign for Votes for Women was really out for.

A ripe tomato, whilst damaging to clothing, was not a particularly painful missile to receive; but to have one's motor veil – Kitty loved wearing these – plastered with rotten eggs was worse. Some suffragettes were happy to throw food themselves: a group of women lobbed a bag of flour at the car of Augustine Birrell, the Chief Secretary for Ireland. Unfortunately, the flour instead smacked into the face of a dignified Special Branch officer, causing him and his colleagues and Birrell to fall about with laughter. In Hereford, Kitty and her friends had been carrying sandwich boards in the gutter to avoid being arrested for obstruction. This took no small amount of courage. The women were approached by a policeman, who was becoming familiar to Kitty, who told them that they could not announce their meetings. He noted their names with a blunt pencil and was impressed when Kitty told him that her father was a canon. Then she told him that they would carry on every day with their sandwich boards and off they went.

One of Kitty's friends who also intended to see the prime minster was Grace Roe, whose chosen method of breast padding was cotton wool. She dressed in her hockey outfit. It was her first deputation and she was told to prepare for a scrum. Grace had taken an interest in women's suffrage when she was 6 years old. She was staying with her aunt and uncle in Ireland when Annie and Christabel were thrown out of the Free Trade Hall. Her uncle was disgusted. 'Put back the hands of the clock fifty years!' he thundered. But Grace was intrigued. She had been charmed by Christabel composedly standing on a swaying platform in a tussore dress as the crowd jeered and sang, 'Put Me On an Island but Oh, Don't Put Me On an Island with a Suffering Jet!' But it was a quietly rousing speech given by Emmeline Pethick Lawrence whilst the Rush Trial trio were in prison that inspired Grace to actively join the movement.

And now Christabel had honoured Grace with the task of mobilising, or 'working up', the Kensington, Hammersmith and Ravenscourt Park divisions in preparation for the deputation of 29 June. Preparation began around three weeks in advance and famously, the artist and sculptor Marion Wallace-Dunlop stencilled the Bill of Rights on the wall of the lobby of the House of Commons, with information about the deputation. Chief Inspector Scantlebury confiscated the stamp and let her go, but when she returned on 24 June to commit the same offence, she was arrested. The deputation in which Grace Roe and Kitty took part became known as the '108 Deputation' (108 women would be arrested along with 14 men). Mrs Pankhurst had announced that if Asquith failed to meet them, then she would escalate militancy. Asquith had repeatedly rebuffed her and her organisation, but this time Mrs Pankhurst was feeling positive. Surely Asquith would listen to her latest cunning argument? 'Shadowed!' said the caption accompanying a drawing of Mr Asquith on the front cover of the 25 June edition of *Votes for Women* which showed the premier frightened of the suffragette-shaped shadow he was casting on the pavement. It was in this striking way that the deputation was publicly announced, giving Sir Edward Henry, Commissioner of the Metropolitan Police, some time to prepare 3,000 policemen. The women were coming.

An advance small group set off for the House on the evening of 29 June in the resplendent sunset. Among the group was Mrs Pankhurst, Georgiana Solomon and Dorinda Neligan, a 70-year-old former headteacher. Born in 1844, Georgiana Solomon was the widow of Saul Solomon, a newspaper proprietor and a renowned Cape Colony politician. When the women arrived at St Stephen's gate, Chief Inspector Scantlebury handed Mrs Pankhurst a note from Asquith's private secretary stating that he would not receive the women. In late June, Marion Wallace-Dunlop stencilled an extract from the Bill of Rights of 1687 on the wall of St Stephen's Hall. Under the terms, the king's proxy, the prime minister, could be petitioned and Mrs Pankhurst, a subject of the king, was within her rights to expect an audience with Asquith. There was an outcry when she was arrested.

Knowing that trouble was in the air because she was ignored and an outcry would follow from the women accompanying her, Mrs Pankhurst was keen to secure a quick arrest for the two older ladies in her small group, so she committed a technical assault and lightly slapped Inspector Jarvis on the cheek. Under his breath, he told her to do this again so that his colleagues would see and arrest the women, which they did. Mrs Pankhurst had an apology at the ready which she always offered after causing any trouble. Kitty was keen to keep a record of this event; a photograph of Inspector Jarvis appeared in the *Daily Mirror*. Kitty's version has crosses marked on the cheek on which he was slapped and the hat he was wearing, which she knocked off.

Whilst Mrs Pankhurst was being apprehended, Arthur reached Caxton Hall. He attempted to hear as the women's drum and fife band was playing to entertain the waiting suffragettes. Where was Kitty? He was told she had already left. Kitty was part of one of the subsequent groups of women who were trying to reach the Houses of Parliament from Caxton Hall through Victoria Street to Parliament. They walked in groups of six with their petition rolls. She was in a group of women whose surnames began with the letter M. The police had cordoned off sections of the street to allow Members to go to and from the House; members of the public who attempted to enter the cordoned path faced arrest.

When Grace, who was carrying the WSPU flag, noticed that the Palace Yard gate was open, she ran towards the barrier as if she were sprinting at a game of hockey. She was not intimidated by the approaching mounted police with their whickering horses; she was used to working with horses as she had hunted in Ireland. She shouted to her group to keep moving forward. Suddenly, she found herself under the hooves of a horse. Although Grace was not scared, the mounted officer had become dreadfully pale. The police closed in and lifted her off the ground, rescuing her from the crush. All the women in her team were apprehended. At the police station, two Westminster police officers approached the breathless Grace and one asked her if he might have her purple, white and green badge. As she proudly informed the author Antonia Raeburn, who interviewed her for the BBC in 1968, she was happy to grant him his request and he admiringly tucked the badge into his helmet.

German and American tourists gaped at the spectacle of women being grabbed by officers, the crowd's cheers turning into boos. Amidst the pulsating throng of bodies, Arthur found Kitty standing on an island in the road opposite Broad Sanctuary. He instinctively wrapped his arms around her to protect her from the police, but the couple both knew that it was his gentlemanly status that was a more particularly effective weapon of self-defence. Officers were reluctant to use force against gentlemen in top hats and morning coats. Kitty pressed home her advantage and quickly grabbed a policeman's whistle. Neither he nor the reinforcements who had been sent to help him could prise her fingers from the accessory. Kitty was relieved when a voice uttered 'Take her away' and she was sent to Bow Street Police Station. It was her first arrest. As she signed the forms and waited, other dishevelled women arrived.

At Rochester Row Police Station, Grace Roe was approached by a police officer who was a sympathiser and she gave him her badge, which he put into his helmet for safekeeping. That night, the arrested men and women were charged with a selection of offences including obstruction, violence against the police and malicious damage. Among the apprehended women were also Mabel Capper, Maud Fussell, Lillian Dove-Willcox, Emily Wilding Davison and Kitty Marion. A brief biography of each woman appeared in *Votes for Women*. Kitty's was next to Kitty Marion's and it is clear that Caroline Augusta's daughter wanted it to be known that a sense of derring-do ran in her veins:

Mrs Marshall, of Theydon Bois, Essex, is the daughter of Canon Jacques, Rural Dean of Leyland, Lancs, and the niece of Captain Baldwin, the lion hunter and great African explorer, who was the first European to reach the Victoria Falls of the Zambesi from the East Coast, where he met Livingstone, who had approached them from the West Coast. Two of her brothers are in the Army, and have seen active service, one holding three medals gained in the East, and the other one medal won in South Africa. Mrs. Marshall has worked among poor women all her life in Lancashire. Her first acquaintance with the W.S.P.U. was in 1907, when she attended the early meetings at Clements Inn, and since then much of her time has been devoted to furthering the cause of women's enfranchisement.[8]

Soon after, Kitty received a new addition to the Jacques family. On 21 October 1909, Kinton Jacques, aged 72, remarried in Hove. His new wife was Norah Frances Rassam, who was in her early twenties. Norah had been seated next to Kinton Jacques at the dinner table. 'Canon Jacques, when the time is right, will you marry me?' He replied: 'But my dear, this is very sudden!' Norah corrected him: 'No! I mean I am asking if you will conduct the ceremony at my wedding, whenever that is.' The comment prompted Canon Jacques to reflection.

The cases of Mrs Pankhurst and the Hon. Evelina Haverfield were treated as test cases for the right to petition the king and his proxy (they were eventually fined and their fines were paid without their consent). Once the window breakers had been dealt with, the remaining charges against the other ninety-two women who had been arrested on 29 June (including Kitty) were heard. Arthur Marshall represented them. To the Marshalls' delight, the charges were dropped, but the 108 Deputation and subsequent events challenged Mrs Pankhurst's right to literally stand her ground when asked to leave. Sir Edward Henry was moved to send out a memo to all Met divisions, indicating that arrests should ideally be made, if necessary, by no less than an inspector as had been the case with Inspector Jarvis who had the authority to come to an understanding with Mrs Pankhurst. If anyone remained standing for a duration outside a minister's home, whether or not they carried placards, and refused to move once being cautioned, they would be taken into custody and charged with wilfully obstructing officers in their work.

4.

The Winsonosaurus

During her time behind bars, Olive Wharry thought about the impact of forcible feeding on the frail human body. How can a woman protect herself? As if in answer to the question, she produced a hallucinatory pencil sketch of a 'Winsonosaurus', a prehistoric creature with webbed feet, bulbous eyes, winding spiky tail and a long, developed neck 'so as to render the process of forcible feeding impossible'. But what events had led up to Olive's creation of a monster that had evolved for the purpose of its own defence?

When Marion Wallace-Dunlop was arrested for the second time for stencilling the Bill of Rights on the wall of the lobby of the House of Commons in June 1909, she went on hunger strike to protest against being placed in the Second Division. It had taken staff two hours to clean off the violet stamped message of 24 June but it was her ninety-one-hour hunger strike and release which actually left an indelible mark on the militant campaign: suffragettes started going on hunger strike, the women rebelled in prison, smashed their windows and refused to tidy their cells.

One arrested suffragette was Mary Allen, who was inspired to join the campaign for women's suffrage when she heard Annie Kenney speak. Mrs Pankhurst was sympathetic to Mary, looking at her with 'magnetic eyes' and told her to sacrifice more. So she became one of the first hunger strikers, despite suffering from weak health. Mary was arrested when she took part in an attempt to deliver a petition to Parliament, subject to lewd comments from the crowds. 'The police were our protectors far more than they were ever our adversaries,' she concluded from her time in prison. Yet, however helpful the male police officers were, Mary felt the Met needed women police officers:

During our detention in the police cells before our trial, we discovered at first hand the need for women police. It was degrading and revolting, despite the clumsy efforts that the policemen made to be tactful, for women to have to apply to men in the exigencies that arose during the twenty hours or so of our confinement there. That, in fact, was how I first envisaged the idea of Women Police, to arrest women offenders, attend them at police-stations, and escort them to prison and give them proper care. [9]

On 17 September 1909, Asquith, accompanied by his family, was speaking at Bingley Hall, Birmingham. The streets down which Asquith was to travel were lined with high barriers and the premier was accompanied by mounted police. Local authorities had expected missiles to be thrown – which they were – and the meeting was interrupted by calls for 'votes for women'. However, what had not been anticipated was that two suffragettes, Mary Leigh (who had led the drum and fife band at the Prince's Skating Rink bazaar) and Newcastle-born Charlotte ('Charlie') Marsh, would climb on to the roof. From there, they loosened slates and bricks and used these to hit Asquith's car, injuring a detective. The women were soaked and dislodged with a fire hose and police officers and the fire brigade climbed up to grab them, the women shouting 'no surrender' as they were arrested.

Others who had taken part in the protests at Bingley Hall included persistent offender Patricia Woodlock, who broke windows and whose release from Holloway after a three-month prison sentence was the cause of celebration that summer. Laura Ainsworth advanced through the barriers with a hatchet, Mabel Capper was arrested for striking a police officer and Hilda 'Byron' Burkitt, WSPU publicity officer for the Midlands, had thrown 'missiles' at Asquith's train. They were taken to Winson Green Prison, an imposing castellated fortress in Birmingham, where the women went on hunger strike. Laura Ainsworth was forcibly fed, as were Hilda, Mabel Capper and Mary Leigh.

Patricia Woodlock heard the feeding table rattle down the corridor. The trolley stopped at her door, the wardresses entered and she saw the forcible feeding preparations like a silver service laid out to serve a ghastly set menu. The first offering was the feeding cup, which sounded benign, but this unassuming vessel could cause injury to resisting patients who refused to drink. The second course of action (for those who resisted the cup) bore a tang of wood and oil and coiled menacingly on the metal table. It was the oesophageal catheter, which was inserted using a wooden or steel gag during which the patient was laid down and subdued by five assistants. As the tube was inserted, there was the risk of the catheter entering the windpipe. If this happened, the medical officer would notice exhalations of air through the catheter. Next to this apparatus was a jug full of liquid mixture. Broth? Custard? Egg or milk? Supposedly softened pieces of bread and meat? The third option was the nasal catheter which could cause extreme sinus pain. Persuaded by the ghoulish implements before her, quite possibly the apprehensive matron and the giddy grip of hunger, Patricia consented to eat.

Like Mary Leigh, Laura Ainsworth made a formal complaint and when she went to court, pressing assault charges, Kitty's husband, Arthur Marshall, defended her. Laura was released after serving her two-week prison sentence and was taken to a nursing home where she told Arthur what had happened to her behind bars. She related how she had not eaten for three days and was then taken to the matron's room where two doctors and six wardresses waited. She was pushed into a chair. Whilst her head was held back by the wardresses, a doctor inserted his fingers into her mouth to create an opening through which milk was poured using a feeding cup. Shortly afterwards, a nasal tube was used which caused her great pain. Due to an injury when she had been hit with a stone, her nasal passage had closed up so the doctors decided to force the tube down orally using a cork gag to wedge open her mouth. She was violently sick. Laura was fed in this manner twice a day; in addition, during the day some meat extract was pushed through her teeth by a wardress who held her mouth and nose shut. The doctors sent her to the prison hospital where she was forcibly fed by the cup. She charged Herbert Gladstone, Captain Percy Green, Governor of Winson Green and the medical officer of Winson Green Prison, Ernest Hasler Helby with assault.

Mary Leigh, whom Arthur Marshall also defended, told Helby that if he attempted to feed her by her nose, he was committing an 'outrage', a term often used in reference to crimes or scandalous behaviour; one which was also synonymous with rape. Requiring the recipient to be restrained, forcible feeding naturally created a sense of powerlessness and often mental and bodily disconnection. Mary Leigh was made to consume milk and brandy by mouth and staff later fed her using a 2-yard-long nasal tube, in alternating nostrils. She broke the windows in her hospital cell, was locked in a padded cell and was returned to a hospital cell in which she managed to barricade herself for three hours, after which she was seized and force-fed, causing her indigestion and pain.

Arthur was deeply shocked by what he heard. He did not imagine that the women could be treated in this way, but he admired their courage. Gladstone had refused to let them see their lawyer but gave way. Arthur's name and the law firm he represented – Hatchett, Jones, Bisgood and Marshall – were gratefully mentioned on the front cover of *Votes for Women* of 8 October 1909.

Mary Leigh's action against Gladstone, Captain Green and Dr Helby was heard in December. During the hearing, medical authorities were interviewed, including neurosurgeon Sir Victor Horsley who opposed forcible feeding and had been active in putting together the memorial of 116 signatures which was presented to Gladstone. Horsley spoke of rectal feeding adopted in hospitals, and while he would try this method on an unresisting male prisoner, he clearly considered it indelicate to anally forcibly feed a female prisoner. The Attorney General, appearing for Gladstone et al., invited the jury to consider a militant suffragette on a moral par with the fictional Dickensian murderer, Bill Sikes. Without even leaving the room, the jury swiftly ruled in Gladstone's favour.

When Emily Wilding Davison was forcibly fed, her tooth was broken. After this incident, she barricaded herself in her cell with the prison plank bed in a desperate attempt to keep at bay the medical officer and his ghoulish forcible feeding apparatus. A hosepipe of freezing water rained down on her for fifteen minutes. The door was prised open and she was forcibly fed but then released after serving eight days of her sentence. Emily was impressed by Arthur, whom she thought to be very clever and friendly. In January, she won her case against Strangeways Prison for the mistreatment she had undergone, but only received 40 shillings of the £100 in damages that she had claimed.

The vision of a delicate Laura Ainsworth at the nursing home prompted Lady Constance Lytton to become a militant suffragette. Fed up with the preferential treatment sometimes accorded to suffragette prisoners due to their looks or higher social status, she disguised herself as working-class woman, 'Jane Warton', and was arrested on 14 January 1910, along with Elsie Howey, when she took part in a protest outside Walton Gaol, Liverpool. When she refused food, she was slapped on the face. She was not tested for a heart condition before the forcible feeding began. When Adela Pankhurst was assessed, it was recommended that she be released as her pulse was wild and she was mentally 'peculiar, morbid and twisted' and 'of a degenerate type', which reads as a chilling depiction of the hunger strikers being unhinged and criminal.

In a report organised by Dr Flora Murray, which was signed by 116 doctors and submitted to Asquith, individual doctors came forward to protest against the measure – even medical professionals who were not supporters of the suffragettes. During a House of Commons debate, Gladstone acknowledged to Keir Hardie that he had received the memorial but dismissed the concerns expressed as less informed than those of prison medical officers, arguing that feeding by cup did not cause pain and was carried out competently and 'humanely'.

Despite the public outcry and opposition in the House of Commons, forcible feeding was generally set to continue throughout the WSPU's campaign as the only perceived solution to keeping alive offenders who would either die in prison or, if released early, simply go on to commit greater crimes in the most unexpected of locations.

On Sunday, 5 September 1909, Asquith, whilst on a visit to Lympne on the Kent Downs, was attending a church service. The churchyard backed on to Lympne Castle, built on a hill overlooking the English Channel. Disguised, Elsie Howey, Vera Wentworth and rising WSPU star Jessie Kenney hired a rowing boat which they left just below the castle and waited for him in the grounds of St Stephen's. The prime minister had made his solitary way through the sparsely spaced gravestones when he suddenly found himself wedged in the doorframe, hemmed in by angry women. He was dragged by the arm and pulled back into the churchyard. In a wordless encounter, the premier's felt hat was knocked off. Hats were an indicator of respectability and the unseating of headgear was an act of power, conveying to onlookers the victim's loss of dignity. The seizure and destruction of headgear became symbolic of the tussle for female suffrage.

Detectives would hide in bunkers while Asquith played golf but when the trio next sighted him descending the stairs of Littlestone Golf Club, his bodyguards were nowhere to be seen. Elsie swooped towards him, followed closely by the other two women. A once muscular but now portly Herbert Gladstone, who had been a promoter of Bartitsu, came to Asquith's rescue, striking out in all directions, aided by Asquith's son, Herbert Dixon Asquith.

The most surprising stunt of that day, as vividly recounted in Herbert Dixon Asquith's *Moments of Memory*, written in the 1930s, was the trio's scaling of the walls of Lympne Castle. Amid the purple glow of the darkening sky, they reached the window of the room in which the prime minister's family was dining with Gladstone and other guests. From outside, the sounds of cutlery were audible. Those who were inside were enjoying the quiet of the surrounding garden and the usual sound of grazing sheep. Gladstone was still in holiday mode despite the day's events which he was now recounting. Abruptly, the lull was broken when a hunk of granite passed by Asquith, splintering some glass panes and smashing a dinner plate. Asquith's son had the impression the missile was intended for his father; it had missed him by a few feet. One of the ladies was splattered with soup while the missile gyrated across the table and landed across the room. Then Elsie shouted through the broken window to warn him that the women would not stop taunting him until they got the vote. Asquith regarded the scene with equanimity and faint amusement while others rushed to the window. The premier's stiff upper lip had been previously commented on by Ralph Kitchener who had seen Asquith, following a division in the House of Commons, stroll unconcernedly back to No. 10, the defeat not showing on his countenance.

With alacrity, the trio escaped by boat which they had moored by the bank of the canal. Sighing with relief and joy, they watched the police erroneously train their lanterns on the castle grounds.

Later that same month, there was a commotion by the sands near the coastal resort of Littlestone-on-Sea on the Kentish Romney Marshes. Hurried tones and the chug of machinery were intermittently accompanied by a glow of light. Three uninvited newcomers to 'The Fifth Continent' were finding themselves temporarily yet intensively disorientated in this weird landscape. H.G. Wells used it as the location for the crash-landing of the sole survivor of a lunar expedition in his novel *The First Men on the Moon* (1901). Now, it seemed that something weird was stuttering its way towards the residents who, it was hoped, were obliviously asleep.

Kitty's band of women were not about to attempt a feat on the same magnitude as those performed by Elsie, Vera and Jessie, but their actions were nonetheless designed as a wake-up call, literally. The group had been told about the water tower which was conveniently near Gladstone's house; that was to be the focal point. Equipped with a large bag of stones, the women had left London at night and been driven to the Romney Marshes by male sympathisers. These men could not risk imprisonment and the loss of their jobs and so, on arrival, the women were left to their own devices. But whose car were they driving? There were a number of automobiles at the WSPU's disposal. When her husband Fred bought a car in 1903, Emmeline Pethick Lawrence enthusiastically learned to drive and devised a method of temporarily fixing a loose pipe, which conveyed petrol to the engine and dangled beside one of the wheels, using a piece of black elastic. On her release from Holloway, Emmeline Pethick Lawrence was given a car by the WSPU. It was purple with white and green lines. She dedicated it to the organisation and the car, named 'La Suffragette', was also used by Mrs Pankhurst on her tours. However, the Romney Marsh group would have needed a less readily identifiable vehicle. Colonel Blathwayt and his family, who lived near Bath, offered their home to suffragettes including Mrs Pankhurst and Marion Wallace-Dunlop, a sanctuary to recover after jail spells, where they spent time planting trees in the family arboretum. They also lent their first car, nicknamed Bodo, to the WSPU. But Kitty's husband, who was a rising legal star and could afford a set of wheels, might have helped out too.

The distinctive buildings of the seafront at Littlestone seemed to protrude abruptly at intervals from the flat landscape, like jutting teeth. Sir Robert Perks, an industrialist and an MP, was responsible for what seemed to H.G. Wells' lunar explorer Bedford to be weirdly juxtaposed structures. Sighting the undulating terrain of the Romney marshland with its arable pastures and dry, desert-like terrain, Perks had sensed a business opportunity and transformed Littlestone-on-Sea into a golf getaway; a restful resort for the gentry. Promotional postcards depicted the Grand Hotel, Littlestone Golf Clubhouse and a disused red-brick water tower, one of the town's most distinctive architectural features, which rose to just over 36 metres. Nearby were the dark single-storey coastguard cottages and the coastguard station. There were also the houses of more illustrious private residences: one postcard showed visitors how to find the house which the ardent golfer Home Secretary Herbert Gladstone, the youngest son of William Ewart Gladstone, had built close to Littlestone golf course.

Making use of these postcards, the WSPU could see that Gladstone's home stood out, isolated and proud against the sky. Kitty and two friends had been tasked with locating the house and smashing its windows, a protest against forcible feeding. Their actions were to be an expression of the WSPU's vote of no confidence towards Gladstone as a representative of the people. Kitty Marshall was a keen golfer – her local club was at Theydon Bois – and this sporting connection may also have induced her to accept the mission. Notably, the club, which was a favourite with metropolitan commuters such as the Marshalls, had a Ladies' Section and women-only facilities.

Meanwhile, in the reality of the situation ...

The women out on the Romney Marshes knew full well that petrol stations were a rarity, cambers were formidable at times and hills could be particularly unnerving as engines became hot and tyres might burst. Would they have to resolve a fuel blockage with a hat pin as Karl Benz's wife Bertha had done when she became the first motorist in the 1880s? The petrol tank sat low, close to the ground, which created an additional fire hazard. Then there were startled horses to contend with and the odd walker, frightened by this new panting, spluttering vehicle. To some, the vision of three women behind the wheel that late September night would have seemed a most unearthly sight indeed.

Kitty and her friends were soon hopelessly lost on the misty terrain, the lights of their car sure to attract attention. For a couple of hours, they groped about for their bearings, stopping frequently to look at signs with their torch light. When they finally happened upon the water tower, their raucous engine attracted attention and they were discombobulated by a pack of baying dogs. With moments to spare, they caught sight of what they hoped was Gladstone's house and took aim at his windows. But before a single stone hit glass, they heard rallying men's voices coming from nearby bushes. The men jumped out. In a scramble to get away, Kitty slipped through some railings, fell down a bank and lost her railway ticket as well as the bottle of brandy she always carried to steady her nerves. Her friends were seized and taken to the water tower. When the men learnt that the women were not burglars but suffragettes, they listened with curiosity and did not press charges as unfortunately for the women, no damage had been caused. Very little was gained from the event and disappointingly little in the way of publicity. It was challenging, Kitty felt, to convert disgruntled locals, called from their beds on that dreary night, to the cause of women's suffrage.

As far as Kitty was concerned, the WSPU's plan of retaliation was a shambles; it was the only bit of bad planning that Kitty had come across. A key problem was that the spectacular series of suffragette stunts which had occurred a couple of weeks earlier had put the residents of Littlestone-on-Sea on their guard.

The 'Lympne gang', as Gladstone would call them, of Elsie Howey, Vera Wentworth and Jessie Kenney were members of the mysteriously titled 'YHB'. The Young Hot Bloods was a wing of the WSPU formed in 1907 which consisted of younger, single women under the age of 30 who were prepared to undertake 'danger duty'. Members signed a pledge never to reveal the meaning of the acronym. Only Mrs Pankhurst was allowed to attend their meetings, which took place in a Strand teashop. During the later conspiracy trial of 1913, at which Ralph Kitchener was present, some mirth was caused when the acronym was explained for a court which included Sir Arthur and Lady Conan Doyle, present in the press seats. The audience learnt that just as the term 'suffragette' was reappropriated by the WSPU from an insult into a badge of honour, the name 'Young Hot Bloods' was derived from a newspaper which had derided the ardency of Mrs Pankhurst's junior followers. Jessie Kenney was on the committee of the YHB, along with other members, including Mrs Pankhurst's youngest daughter, Adela.

Attacks on Asquith and his cabinet were justifiably causing concern. How did Asquith himself retaliate when attacked by members of the supposed weaker sex? He could hardly have hit a young woman with his applewood putter when he was attacked at the golf club. Such a course of action was against gentlemanly notions of fair play and, besides, he would have risked seriously injuring her. On that occasion, before the detectives could get to the scene, he was defended by his daughter, Violet Asquith, paternal grandmother of Helena Bonham Carter who starred not only in *Suffragette* but also played the role of martial arts instructor and mother to the eponymous heroine in the Sherlock Holmes-inspired jujitsu action thriller, *Enola Holmes* (2020) and *Enola Holmes 2* (2022). Violet frequently single-handedly fought to protect her father and his reputation during confrontations (Lloyd George's daughter also defended her father). The suffragettes' tactics, which included jumping out of hedges, aiming at him with their dog whips, sprinkling pepper on the statesman and tearing at his clothing while he determinedly gripped on to the lapels of his coat, further alienated Violet from the militants' cause.

The Lympne trio's stunts were the unnerving result of dogged persistence, meticulous planning and ad hoc frenzy and were so deeply disconcerting as to make the Home Secretary think of images of criminal insanity and murder. As a result, the Met was forced to consider the allocation of special resources and explore new techniques in crime fighting. Gladstone was so concerned that he sent a missive, scribbled in tight, scratchy and almost inscrutable handwriting, to Sir Charles Edward Troup, Permanent Under Secretary at the Home Office. The letter, which was marked 'pressing', was also intended for the eyes of Sir Edward Henry, Commissioner of the Metropolitan Police. 'I think it sh[oul]d be considered whether the time has not come for special police organisation for containing Suffragette violence,' he began. Gladstone expressed a disconcerted admiration for the WSPU's organisational skills, their willingness to 'supplement disorderly women in localities lacking the article', to 'prospect' target areas and to use their gathered intelligence to 'outwit the local forces'. Local police ought to be forewarned and Special Branch officers should be sent to places where cabinet ministers are due to speak. He warmed to his theme:

> There are some women who from nervous excitability or otherwise are specially dangerous. Where did the Lympne gang come from? Who housed and cooperated with them at Hythe? It is not enough to deal with these people if and when they come. We ought to know what they are up to locally, and all the more dangerous should be known to N.S.Y. [New Scotland Yard].[10]

The recollections of Special Branch officer Edwin T. Woodhall chime with Gladstone's concerns:

> What worried the Branch more than anything else, was the fear that some demented creature would commit an act for which no possible excuse (except that of madness) could be made. As with all pioneer movements, it was not the really sincere and clever workers who caused trouble but the fanatics.[11]

Moreover, Gladstone feared 'savage reprisals' from angry crowds in the event of the prime minister being injured, a comment which pointed to the conundrum facing the police forces who had not only to protect the public and property from potential militant violence but also to protect militants from an enraged public. In his letter to Troup, Gladstone warned that a possibility of a 'female Dhingra' could not be 'completely provided against'. Madan Lal Dhingra was a London student and political extremist who had only recently assassinated Lieutenant Colonel Sir William Hutt Curzon Wyllie, aide-de-camp for the Secretary of State for India, on 1 July 1909 before attempting to kill himself. Dhingra was hanged at Pentonville Prison that year.

Gladstone's choice of wording in his letter to Troup had an impact. Sir Edward Henry selected a division of highly experienced detectives for the task who would make sure to avoid any actions which could reflect badly on the police. Sir Patrick Quinn took charge, aided by Chief Inspector McCarthy and the athletic, trilingual Inspector Francis Powell who had foiled 'white slave' traders, stymied a plot to blow up the Royal Exchange and had arrested an anarchist. He had been the first on the scene when a bomb was thrown at King Alfonso XIII and Queen Victoria in Madrid in 1906. It was felt that the suffragettes would escalate disorderly behaviour into physical attacks and Gladstone had a letter sent to cabinet ministers requesting them to inform the police when and where they were due to speak at public meetings and the times of their trains. This information was to be sent three days in advance.

The death of the Liberal MP for Bermondsey, George Cooper, resulted in a by-election at the end of October (during which the voting paraphernalia was destroyed by two Women's Freedom League members). Lloyd George and Winston Churchill were heavily promoting the People's Budget, which proposed a land and income tax on the wealthy to pay for new social welfare schemes. It was part of the Liberals' plan to extend democracy to a broader base, to liberate the people. As part of the 'Keep the Liberal Out' campaign, suffragettes held prominently advertised meetings and booked out the best halls in the constituency for themselves, where they gave speeches which drew attention to the failings and hypocritical attitudes of the Liberals in power. How could the Liberals glibly talk of extending democratic rights when women, essential taxpayers, were excluded, the suffragettes asked. Kitty presided at a meeting at Bermondsey Town Hall where Christabel and Lady Constance Lytton gave speeches. The anti-Liberal propaganda paid off; the seat was a Conservative gain for John Dumphreys. Kitty also chaired a meeting at a school in St Pancras and designed a placard, 'Keep the Liberal Out', which was accompanied by WSPU posters, held in place with purple ribbon. The construction was suspended on green poles carried on the backs of campaigners who boasted flowers in the WSPU colours. It was a victory for the WSPU; again, the Conservative candidate won.

As part of his own campaign for women's suffrage, Arthur was busy attracting signatures from the Epping Forest locals, while Edith Garrud's next contribution to the cause was articulated in the form of an empowering piece entitled 'Self Defence', which appeared in *Votes for Women* in March 1910:

> Whatever the future may have for us, there is no doubt that the average woman is weaker, in muscular strength, than the average man. Yet in modern life it is not actual muscle that tells. Agility, alertness, dexterity, and endurance are usually of more importance, as the lessons of the Russo-Japanese war have taught ... Science, quickness, vitality, and brains are surely equal to brute strength in politics as well as in fights.[12]

For Edith, changes in physical development gradually helped women to become stronger in the far future but the skill she was offering to teach could help those women who signed up to her course to leapfrog over years of 'evolution'. It was brainpower and not brute force that would win the fight.

5.

Winston Churchill's Fanlight

Ralph Kitchener watched the diminutive American Dr Hawley Harvey Crippen and his mistress, Ethel le Neve, being ushered into a police van. 'What an insignificant little blighter. Who would have thought it?' remarked his colleague in response to the sight of one of the most notorious men in the world. When Cora Crippen disappeared, her friends had alerted the police and Chief Inspector Walter Dew was sent to their home where he discovered a female torso in the coal cellar. The captain of the *Montrose*, a cargo ship destined for Canada, noticed a supposed father and son behaving in an oddly intimate manner towards each other and Marconi's wireless system was used to contact Scotland Yard. On a faster vessel, Dew caught up with the fugitives at the end of July.

Ready with his secret camera hidden inside his top hat, Arthur Barrett captured another enduring courtroom image of the couple. In the photograph, Crippen's gaze is fixed straight ahead while le Neve's face is downcast beneath her substantial hat. Bent forward slightly, their hands are together on the bar in front of them as if in supplication. Crippen was hanged in November but le Neve was acquitted. Whether he was the killer would remain debatable, but at the time the case offered an example of the most hideous dangers of marriage, especially to a woman as bold as Cora who tried to make a name for herself, daring to outshine her husband. Walter Dew retired after the case, leaving with a certificate of exemplary character.

Towards the summer of the same year, momentum was gathering for a Private Members' Conciliation Bill which aimed to benefit female householders in complete control of the property they owned or rented (however small the rent and however tiny the property – even if it was just a single room) and occupiers of shops or farms worth £10 a year. Drafted by fifty MPs, this exciting step forward was set to become the Representation of the People Act 1910. A monster march took place on the Embankment on 18 June 1910 to influence Parliament to consider the Bill favourably. Over 10,000 suffragettes and suffragists took part in the 'Prison to Citizenship' procession which was 6 miles long. Kept in step by Mary Leigh's band, walkers wore their organisations' colours and academics donned their robes, while suffragette prisoners carried arrows on sticks. In the wake of the march, Asquith received delegations of suffragists and anti-suffragists; he underhandedly told the latter that they had his ear.

The Bill passed its second reading in July but it would not become law in 1910. The WSPU contested the result and planned for a giant demonstration to mark the anniversary of the tearing down of the Hyde Park railings in 1866. Just as Walter Dew was pursuing Crippen across the ocean, there was a Great Demonstration of Suffragists at Hyde Park with two processions making their way through Pall Mall, Piccadilly, the heart of clubland. Mounted police accompanied the women as they made their way to Hyde Park where forty platforms with 150 speakers awaited. Nancy Lightman, a Cambridge-educated teacher who had interviewed a number of cabinet ministers at political meetings, spoke at Platform 24. Her speaking partner was Kitty, who was introduced to the audience as a veteran of the 108 Deputation, the daughter of Canon Jacques and the niece of Captain Baldwin, the famous lion hunter. As she told the crowd, her philanthropic work among the poor had convinced her that votes for women was a pressing need that could no longer be ignored. The session at Platform 24 was chaired by Marie Brackenbury, who, like Kitty was also a landscape artist. Marie's sister Georgina, who chaired Platform 23, was a celebrated portrait painter as well as a high-profile speaker for the WSPU. She would later play a key part in Kitty's plans to memorialise Mrs Pankhurst.

The estimated turnout was half a million. Hunger strikers marched in single file and the Gymnastic Teachers impressed onlookers with their sporty posture. Banners were held aloft to the 'Women's Marseillaise'. Despite passing its second reading, the Bill's progress was blocked. It seemed ironic that Asquith, who had railed against the powers of the House of Lords to veto Bills at will, was now exercising an arbitrary control over the fate of an enfranchising and democratising measure which had tremendous public and parliamentary support. Asquith refused to grant facilities for the Bill that session, postponing matters until the opening of Parliament on Friday, 18 November and when, on that date, the Bill was kicked into the long grass, Mrs Pankhurst was furious.

Heading straight out from Caxton Hall, Kitty's friend 'Dearest' led a deputation of over 300 women, which included Kitty in its ranks, to the House of Commons. Tactically, the women marched in groups of twelve, not large enough to tempt officers to arrest them. The group who walked with Mrs Pankhurst included Anne Cobden-Sanderson; trend-setting Princess Sophia Duleep Singh; Evelina Haverfield, gripping her riding crop; Dorinda Neligan; Georgiana Solomon; and the physicist Hertha Ayrton, who cut a striking figure with her frizzy hair and arresting, close-set green eyes. Mrs Pankhurst was also accompanied by Elizabeth Garrett Anderson. Anderson's daughter Louisa, who had a pale and calm face, protectively followed close behind.

The crowds let the ladies pass through and they reached the Strangers' Entrance at 1.30 p.m. A cordon of police surrounded them and all they could do was look on at the scene which unfolded when the other women of the deputation, including Mrs Pankhurst's sister Mary, attempted to follow them but were met with a wall of police officers. As the crowd came to blows, the banners bearing the inscriptions 'Down with the Premier's Veto' and 'There is Time If They've the Will' were ripped and felled to the ground. In a piece titled 'Suffragette Raiders', *The Times* depicted the 300 or so women as 'extremists' who rushed heedlessly forward, prevented by diligent officers who kept their cool under exceptionally trying circumstances. One woman climbed on to the wall at Palace Yard and the paper tickled readers into an anti-suffragette response with a description of the undignified scene: 'She was apparently unused to mountaineering, or her dress caught on a buttress, and she was saved from a dangerous fall by two policemen, who caught her before she quite reached the ground.' A number of officers had helmets 'knocked off', a policy often adopted by campaigners to distract policemen in the assumption that they were always required to pay for lost helmets.

The Times recorded one officer being kicked in the ankle and 'disabled', an ominously vague term. The women were shown as maniacal attackers 'some of whom came up smiling every time to the attack, while a few scolded like viragoes and most were simply stolid'. The paper made light of the scene: 'As a rule they kept their tempers very well, but their method of shoving back the raiders lacked nothing in vigour. They were at any rate kept warm by the exercise, and so were the ladies who flung themselves against the defending lines.' Within this tongue-in-cheek observation lurked an admission, through descriptions of 'shoving' and 'vigour', of the women being 'pushed' and 'seized', that not all was well with the police's treatment of the women. *The Times* averted its eyes to the true horror of the confrontation as did Chief Inspector Scantlebury in his report when he mentioned that men and women associated with the WSPU had caused the disturbance which was dealt with quickly by the police.

Frightened participants felt as if they were being thrown from one officer to another, some of whom did not realise their own strength. Other officers knew exactly what they were doing. They separated individual women from their friends and backed them into corners or pushed them down alleyways where they inflicted injuries, accompanied by bad language, just to add that extra level of intimidation and degradation. Against the grunts of profanities, women's screams rang out as their backs were hit, breasts were pulled, thumbs twisted, clothing pulled up around them and knees thrust between their legs. Within the Houses of Parliament, Keir Hardie led a chorus of MPs who pleaded with Asquith and his cabinet to speak to the women's deputation who were now waiting for him in the premier's room.

While Mrs Pankhurst's group were traumatised by what they saw, they were nevertheless treated better than those outside. Complaints of police misconduct were fired off to Home Secretary Winston Churchill who was seen as the figurehead of the violence. Kitty and many others believed that Churchill had drafted in hardened officers, in sharp contrast to Inspector Jarvis with his respectful treatment of Mrs Pankhurst. The bobbies present on Black Friday were accustomed to taking a tougher stance on violent East End criminals and were prepared to do so with the WSPU deputation. However, the arrangements for 18 November 1910 were not unique in this regard. The Police Orders, a set of instructions sent out before various planned events, show that often men from all divisions were required to supplement existing manpower. These directions gave an indication of the Met's plans, but the real number of officers drafted in may indeed have been larger than stated in the Police Orders. What they do indicate is that the presence of officers from H Division, that is, Whitechapel, was by no means unusual.

More compellingly, a report compiled by Henry Brailsford and Dr Jessie Murray quoted sections of the *Police Code* to underline their argument that a number of officers present, regardless of the divisions to which they belonged, had conducted themselves in a wholly unfit manner, using unnecessary violence accompanied by 'improper language' which, the *Police Code* emphasised, could damage one's chances of promotion. It seemed that officers could be taken to task for their conduct in dealing with the suffragettes, if the authorities cared enough to pursue the matter – as Cecil Bishop learnt from his reaction to a bite to the hand from a suffragette in 1913 which left a permanent scar:

> I managed to get one of the ringleaders outside, but she was exceedingly violent, and it was on this occasion that I got the bite. I regret to say that I was so hurt that I promptly dropped my burden into a barrel of rainwater, which cooled her down a good deal. I had to answer for my action before the authorities, but they rightly said that I had not used more violence than was necessary in the circumstances![13]

Unfortunately for the victims of Black Friday, they did not get justice. Princess Sophia Duleep Singh had spotted a uniformed officer continually beating a suffragette. After scaring him off, she managed to memorise his collar number. To her great disappointment, the case against him was dropped. Churchill disregarded the findings of the Brailsford-Murray report and did not order an enquiry in the matter. Several months later, Churchill claimed that none of the 200 women arrested on Black Friday complained of their injuries or mistreatment. This was hardly surprising, given that they had been dismissed from court without the chance of airing their grievances. The year 1910 was a dark year for Mrs Pankhurst. She had lost her only surviving son, Harry, at the time of the January 1910 general election, and her mother in the spring. Her sister, Mary Clarke, with whom Mrs Pankhurst and her children shared a close bond, died on Christmas Day. Mary was considered the movement's first martyr; it was widely understood that the injuries she had sustained on Black Friday had hastened her decline.

Kitty and Mrs Pankhurst formed part of the twelve-woman deputation to Asquith on Monday, 21 November. After waiting again that next day, the women received a meaningless response from Asquith. If his response was lacklustre, their riposte was swift and forceful. The next day, Downing Street was plunged into chaos when more than a hundred women, led by Mrs Pankhurst, made their way back to the Houses of Parliament. Maud Fussell gave Kitty Marion a one-pound weight which she tried to throw at 10 Downing Street but its uneven edge caused the projectile to swerve and hit the wall instead. The mark the impact created remained for quite some time. Kitty Marshall was one of the women who were arrested after damaging windows in a number of cabinet ministers' houses. Another consequence of 22 November was that the battle cemented the friendship between Kitty Marion and Maud Fussell and they became lifelong friends.

But when considered from the recipient's perspective, the stone-throwing campaign was not always a tale of empowerment and solidarity but of isolation and perpetual anxiety. The militants targeted darkened windows of what they thought to be uninhabited rooms, yet within some of these rooms were sleeping children. Margot Asquith, who had at one point acted as her husband's bodyguard by boxing the ears of one suffragette, was at home when an iron pound weight was sent crashing through one of her windows. She immediately asked the police what reinforcements they had and was told that there were 200 officers in the vicinity. This was becoming a frequent ordeal for her; suffragettes throwing stones at her window when her young son was asleep were making her life a misery. She had received hate mail and her children were given their own bodyguards. Margot would hear these men coughing outside her house on night duty. Her opposition to women's suffrage attracted anger. As she told a friend, she felt that the few redeeming features women had, like a sense of loyalty, were no more than animal instincts.[14] And when she saw this sense of group allegiance directed towards her in the shape of missiles bearing messages, her ire towards the cause was no doubt further roused. As Margot's experience shows, in campaigning for a better world for women and their children, militants had not given as much thought as they ought to have done to the safety of the inhabitants, young or old, of the buildings they targeted, a theme that would crop up as the campaign gained heat.

The spates of mass window smashing and obstructions continued that week. On 23 November, Kitty was one of the eighteen women who tried to enter the Houses of Parliament. She grappled in the rain with a police officer, clinging on to his cape while he cursed her. Her tenacity left him with no option but to arrest her in self-defence. As soon as she was discharged, Kitty appeared in support of Emmeline Pethick Lawrence's sister Dorothy at her trial at Bow Street Magistrates Court, for her part in the Battle of Downing Street. That morning Crippen had been hanged, the report appearing alongside columns on the Battle of Downing Street.

Bow Street was now inundated with a backlog of scores of suffragettes' cases which were due to appear before the tortoise-eyed gaze of Sir Albert de Rutzen. Kitty and Arthur spent most of that week in the courts, and in Kitty's case, this was on both sides of the dock. Dorothy Pethick Lawrence was charged with obstruction and ultimately for assault, for kicking and then smacking Inspector Perkins in the face and knocking off his cap during the Battle of Downing Street in retaliation for grabbing a woman by the throat. Kitty and Mrs Pankhurst were in her car at 3.30 p.m. by St Stephen's entrance when they saw groups of women being pushed about by police officers. Mrs Pankhurst had not seen Dorothy. 'I did,' said Kitty dramatically, her voice projecting strongly and clearly through the court.

Kitty was called to the stand. She had taken the number of the officer who had been manhandling Dorothy. Herbert Muskett, the prosecutor for the police, questioned Kitty's validity as a witness by pointing out that she herself had recently appeared in the dock. Arthur shook his head. It was shameful. The report kept at the National Archives reveals that, privately, Muskett did not like Dorothy. He thought she was obstructive and he was not impressed by Mrs Pankhurst and Kitty as witnesses, whose contributions he deemed to be irrelevant. Unfortunately for Kitty, he had a point. Neither Mrs Pankhurst nor Kitty saw Dorothy kick or dislodge the officer's helmet and he extracted from them the admission that they did not see her arrest either. Dorothy was sentenced to two weeks in prison but her fine was paid without her consent.

On 14 November 1909, Theresa Garnett had accosted Churchill at Bristol railway station. The two grappled close to the edge of the platform. She allegedly grabbed him by the coat and brought a dog-whip down on his hat and across his face. He took the whip from her and pocketed it and was praised for his calm demeanour. It was not the first time Churchill had faced a dog-whip wielded by a suffragette. Flora Drummond, known as the 'Precocious Piglet', had relentlessly pursued him with a whip, banter and a megaphone! Now, in the depths of November 1910, Churchill's house would also find itself in Kitty's own crosshairs. Mrs Marshall and Kitty Marion's new friend, Maud Fussell, crept up to Ecclestone Square where the Home Secretary lived with Clemmie and baby Diana. The idea was to create a 'useful smash'. Arthur advised Kitty to avoid carrying stones and instead take a potato. Somewhat softer than a stone, the missile would cause less injury to anyone who happened to be in its flightpath. Despite her efforts, Kitty's missile ingloriously landed in the 'area', the space outside the kitchen and servants' downstairs quarters where a perambulator might be kept. Maud's weapon was riskier and superior – half a brick – and more expertly aimed. Her projectile created a loud smash and instantly attracted the attention of the police whose duty it was to guard cabinet ministers' homes.

The mission was accomplished and both women were taken to a police station in the B Division. Kitty was favourably impressed by the officers' kindness. It seemed to Kitty that the policemen understood why the women had made this protest and while they requested her to fill in her charge sheets, both women could do so before a roaring fire. Maud pleaded guilty and was imprisoned for two months. Kitty was lucky as she had Arthur to represent her. He emphasised that the missile had only struck the woodwork of the door and not the fanlight itself so Kitty was only fined 40 shillings or had to spend fourteen days in jail. She chose prison. It was her first time in Holloway.

Her admittance to Holloway did not go as she had expected. She had imagined that all suffragette prisoners would enter together, the halls echoing with their strident singing. Instead, when she arrived at the entrance to Holloway, she was met by wardresses. Her heart sank when she saw that there was no other suffragette in sight. Kitty inspected her home for the fortnight – a 12ft by 8ft cell. Then she resigned herself to inspecting the utensils, wondering what the 4-inch strip of tin was. At around the time that she was staring at the arrow markings on her linen, young Cambridge graduate Hugh Franklin, a Black Friday veteran, decided to give Churchill a piece of his mind. Like Arthur Marshall, Franklin was a 'suffragent', or a 'suffragette in trousers', a member of Victor Duval's militant Men's Political Union for Women's Enfranchisement, the male counterpart to the WSPU. Churchill had been speaking at a meeting in Bradford on 26 November about the powers of the House of Lords. 'And what you say applies equally to Woman Suffrage!' responded Franklin's friend, clicker Alfred Hawkins, who had been in the same trade as Ralph Kitchener. The stewards threw Hawkins down the stairs and out on to the street and his injuries rendered him unfit for work for several months. When the Men's Political Union for Women's Enfranchisement took action against the League of Young Liberals, Arthur Marshall's firm was involved in the case. The judge concluded that if a heckler had not been asked to leave, the stewards had in fact no legal right to evict Hawkins and that in doing so, they were committing an act of assault. He also added that to shout out an objection was not an offence. Hawkins was awarded £100 in damages.

On the train back to London that evening, Franklin, who was travelling with Laura Ainsworth in third class, accosted the Home Secretary as he was making his way through their carriage to the dining car. Franklin jumped out and brandished a dog-whip, shouting words to the effect: 'Take that, you dirty cur.' Churchill's personal bodyguard, Detective Inspector ('Cocky') Sandercock was in the compartment with Churchill. He seized Franklin before he could attack the Home Secretary, and Inspector Edward John Parker took hold of the dog-whip that Franklin intended to wield. 'That will do, Sandy,' Churchill responded, 'let him go, he's had enough.' The officers were helped by members of the public and Franklin was taken into custody.

The whip, and consequently the dog-whip, was of great symbolic importance. 'I'll horsewhip you!' was a common insult between gentlemen in Victorian novels, a stinging slur on the victim's manliness. This everyday item could be used to keep an attacker at bay and therefore avoid a closer range hand-to-hand defensive scenario. Unless an attacker came within range of the strike, the item was a relatively minimally aggressive form of defence. A dog-whip lies next to the suffragette who flexes her muscles to intimidate the police in Arthur Wallis Mills' cartoon 'The Suffragette that Knew Jiu-Jitsu: The Arrest' which had appeared in *Punch* in the summer of 1910. Edith proudly pasted the sketch into her scrapbook of suffrage exploits. University graduate Helen Ogston used a dog-whip to protect herself from the stewards at the Royal Albert Hall when she interrupted Lloyd George's speech. In fact, Lloyd George was the target of a dog-whip, wielded by a suffragent. Although Edwin T. Woodhall does not reveal the identity of the attacker he does tell us that he managed to forestall the attempted whipping at Gatti's restaurant on the Strand.[15] When Maud Arncliffe Sennett, who ran a party acces-sories business, was arrested for smashing the *Daily Mail*'s windows in 1911, she kept the receipt for the dog-whip, hammer and chain and pasted these into her own scrapbook. Moreover, for Teresa Billington-Greig, a co-founder of the Women's Freedom League, the dog-whip was a symbolic strike back at all the 'curs' who had passed discriminatory laws over the course of many centuries. For her, the woman with the whip would wield social change for all.

Arthur Marshall's law firm prepared Franklin's papers for his trial in which Patrick Quinn represented the CID. Franklin questioned Sandercock's statement that he had used the word 'dirty'; Sandercock stuck to his view. A spectator was caught clandestinely taking photo-graphs, which irritated de Rutzen, and the case was adjourned. After being remanded for a week, Franklin was sentenced to six weeks in Pentonville where he went on hunger strike. When he was released on 9 January, he was treated to a celebratory breakfast at Eustace Miles Restaurant, a vegetarian eatery. Despite the confrontation that had taken place between Franklin and Churchill's bodyguards on the train to London that night, Churchill had not let the incident come between him and his dinner.

Having unsuccessfully employed the potato to attack Churchill's fan-light, Kitty was now faced with the prospect of eating Holloway's own finest spuds. These root vegetables were boiled in their skins and when she broke them open, they had blue insides. A fellow prisoner-to-be, Jane Terrero, thought they tasted like bullets. At the bottom of Kitty's tin in which her food was served, there also lurked a mysterious piece of meat, sometimes bacon (Mary Allen suspected this was horse meat), tiredly accompanied by some carrot. But the suet pudding proved to be particu-larly spiteful. When Kitty ate a lump, the gristle stubbornly clung on in her throat for three days. She thought it was probably a piece of rubber and thereafter avoided the dish. Her mornings started at 6 a.m. with an undrinkable cup of tea with a distinct taste of potato, a loaf of bread and margarine, without jam. The bread and margarine made a later appearance in the day, accompanied by greasy cocoa. With such uninspiring food to contend with, Kitty was starting to realise why it was so easy to hunger strike. (She received a hunger strike medal which is kept at the Museum of London's Fellowship Collection.)

Kitty's life was governed by prison routine and as prisoners were not allowed a means of checking the time, Kitty gave herself the illusion that she knew what hour it was by making a clock. She used twigs for the hands and stuck the item together with Virol, which the prison doctor had prescribed because Kitty was getting thinner. Virol was a food supplement of bone marrow extract, sold in jars and was particularly marketed towards parents, with advertisements supplemented with photographic before and after testimonies. Kitty became good at guessing the time and asking matrons, doctors, the governor and the chaplain, updating her clock hands accordingly. Like Marion Wallace-Dunlop with her stencilling machines and Olive Wharry with her Winsonosaurus, Kitty demonstrated artistic ingenuity. Her witty clock gave the illusion of dividing time into neat, manageable, knowable pieces and offered a way of gaining order over her day and with it, a sense of sanity.

Kitty covered her cell peephole with a thin membrane of toilet paper soaked in milk. She was making playing cards with which she could play patience. Using the small pair of scissors in her possession, she crafted these from four postcards found in a library book. She upcycled a Thermogene medical box to make the kings and craftily obtained the writing ink by writing to Winston Churchill. A book on hygiene from the prison library lent the cards their red colour. Using a stick from the prison yard, she shaped the diamonds and hearts. Her tactic was to lean on a slate which she had tucked inside a nightdress case. Then the wardress's eye appeared in the peephole. By the time the wardress had suspected that there was something amiss with the view, Kitty would fling the lid of the case over her work or, failing that, hide the cards under a prayer book. During her fortnight-long stay in jail, she created forty-eight of these cards.

Grateful that it was not an iron bed which would have been rooted to the ground, Kitty kept herself warm by moving her plank bed across her cell next to the hot-water pipe. To soften the bed and to supplement her covers, she took in sewing work. The windows would not open and the rooms were stuffy – a common problem. When the wardresses learnt that they could trust her and the other women not to run amok, they let them open their doors on a Sunday for ventilation. The women received one hour for exercise, a walk in single file, but later, when numbers were too large for this arrangement, the women would play rounders with make-shift materials. To communicate during church service, they would pass notes to suffragettes in other wings inside hymn books. No visitors were allowed in the first month but as Arthur was Kitty's lawyer, she could see her husband.

In March 1911, the same fanlight that Kitty had attacked at Ecclestone Square once more became a target. Hugh Franklin wrote a letter to Churchill. He wrapped his missive around a stone and fastened the bundle together with the same tubing used to forcibly feed prisoners. Then, he aimed the package at the fanlight. Like Kitty, he also missed. He was promptly arrested and sent to Pentonville for a month. He campaigned to be treated as a political prisoner and went on hunger strike. In response, he was forcibly fed.

6.

Charge!

'Let me die, let me die!' The drunk was maudlin and inconsolable but the old inspector maintained his usual unruffled composure and drolly offered a response. 'All right, but give us your name first.' In early 1911, the WSPU called a truce, hoping for a mention of women's suffrage in the King's Speech. In the meantime, Met recruit Ralph Kitchener was gaining some experience as a night duty reserve, listening in on many curious conversations, observing the nocturnal oddities who might stride or stumble into Westminster's police stations. As well as offenders of more serious crimes, prostitutes and drunks who were charged had to be taken to cells. There was a man who escaped from an asylum, and later, the case of an individual who surfaced in Trafalgar Square, claiming he had swum to Britain from the *Titanic*. 'Another nutter,' muttered the inspector.

It is clear from Kitchener's memoir that out on his night duty beats, he was taken aback by the numbers of homeless men slumped in doorways, huddled on unforgiving seats on the Embankment, with sheets of newspapers for blankets. It was bitterly cold; on one occasion he and his colleagues were caught in a blizzard and returned to meet with their sergeant at a point in Kingsway, plastered in snowflakes. An old constable sympathised with Kitchener's feeling of pity towards the homeless who were growing in number with the high unemployment levels. 'It is best to give them a little rousing, boy,' he consoled, 'you don't want to come along presently and find you've got a dead 'un on your hands!' The government was planning a National Insurance measure.

After parade and instructions, Kitchener's night duty ran from 10 p.m. to 6 a.m. He would check fastenings of doors and windows and, possibly due to his vigilance or luck, he never encountered a burglary the whole time he was a constable. It could be a challenge to keep awake though and one colleague resorted to doing the Highland Fling in the road to keep himself alert. The bullseye lamp the officers carried was a constant and noisome companion. Even when it was turned off, it would emit heat and gas and was uncomfortable when fastened to a belt. The device became particularly unpleasant when Kitchener had to wear oil-skin protection on a wet night. His can of tea would grow colder during the night but he impressed a colleague with his solution to the problem: a state-of-the-art vacuum flask, frequently advertised in the *Police Review and Parade Gossip*. After their night shift finished, the officers were so exhausted that they could sleep through the rumble and clatter of the metropolitan traffic.

Before joining, Kitchener would have been aware of the dangers of police work. On 16 December 1910, Sergeants Charles Tucker and Robert Bentley and PC Walter Choat were killed and two colleagues seriously injured when they interrupted a group of Latvian immigrants attempting to break into a jewellery shop in Houndsditch. It was the deaths of these three officers, whose funerals were held at St Paul's Cathedral, which further prompted Churchill's bodyguard Walter Thompson to join the police. But everyday duties could be highly dangerous, too. Police officers were also required to direct traffic on main crossings – 'point duty' – and had to know when to stop the flow of cross currents, causing as few tailbacks as they could. As pedestrians ran the gauntlet of motorised and horse-drawn vehicles, strangers might offer their services to ladies, a seeming act of goodwill which had its drawbacks. The well-known writer and women's suffrage supporter, Elizabeth Robins, found herself accosted by a couple of 'disgusting old men' at a street crossing, whose words frightened her:

> If a young woman ... met with a certain order of disagreeables, she knew better than to discuss them. The theory was she had brought them on herself – if only by leaving home. ... It was, I think, partly the sheer ugliness of these manifestations that unnerved me, and largely the illusion that they ought not to happen to me. That they did happen was a disgrace. No one must know.[16]

The police sometimes assisted drivers whose horses had slipped, regulated traffic whilst accident scenes were attended to and took down information about accidents. Kitchener had gained some first-aid training at the St John Ambulance before joining the Met; Kitty had also trained as a nurse. First-aid skills were particularly important at a time when taking oneself or injured individuals off to a hospital could be a time-consuming and tricky process. When Kitchener had to deal with a lady who was knocked down, he hailed a four-wheel horse-drawn cab for her, but in most cases he had to obtain a stretcher (nicknamed a 'barrow') and find a policeman manning the nearest traffic 'point' to help him convey the invalid to hospital. On one occasion, he borrowed a stretcher from a floating police station at Waterloo Bridge. When he returned, the tide had fallen. He and his colleague manoeuvred the contraption carefully at first, then lost their footing, and the stretcher careered down the ramp, much to the alarm of the pontoon station inspector!

As the King's Speech at the opening of Parliament had been a disappointment, bearing no reference to plans for women's suffrage, the Women's Freedom League ingeniously spearheaded the campaign of civil resistance, inspired by Mahatma Gandhi's disavowal of stone-throwing and fighting with the police. For suffrage campaigners who were still reeling from the events of Black Friday, resisting the census offered an opportunity for the mass display of thought-provoking political action, spiced with humour and levity, risking minimal physical danger to campaigners.

Votes for Women readers were about to hear a lot more about the fiery orator and 'human gramophone', John Burns, the man who headed up the census, the results of which would be crucial in structuring Asquith's welfare reforms. Burns had served six weeks in prison for his involvement in the 1887 Trafalgar Square protests and he was the first working man to become a cabinet minister. As president for the Local Government Board (LGB), he would be chiefly responsible for the smooth running of the operations. To assist the government in collecting data around child mortality, participants were now required to give information concerning the numbers of children they had, both living and deceased. The forms were to be filled in by the occupants themselves, requesting compliance from male and female participants. In a front-page cartoon, *Votes for Women* depicted John Burns MP for Battersea as a cabinet minister haughtily dismissing a woman who approaches him demanding the vote while his pictorial LGB doppelgänger appeals to her on bended knee, appealing to her to offer up her personal details to the enumerator. If women were to be treated with contempt by the government, they would not heed Burns' two-faced supplication.

Across Britain, women and men boycotted the census, a campaign which involved a number of pro-suffrage groups. Evaders dodged the census enumerator and, like Kitty's friends Ellen and Edith Beck, did not want to be found. Resisters wrote on their forms but often added misleading information and penned statements across the form's tables. Some campaigners were both resisters and evaders, refusing to be at home on census night. There were mass evasions, too, all-night ice-skating parties and performances of Ibsen's *Ghosts*. Among the noteworthy census feats was Emily Wilding Davison's infiltration of the House of Commons when she hid in a corner of the broom cupboard in the Crypt. Not all women who were members of women's suffrage organisations rebelled. Edith Garrud's husband William dutifully filled in the census form, listing himself and his wife and daughter Isobel as being at home on the night of 2 April at 61 Hatham Road, Holloway. He described himself with a flourish: 'Teacher of JUJUTSU. The Japanese Art of Self-Defence.' It is unclear why Edith chose to cooperate. Perhaps her compliance was motivated by her concern for her business. Whether or not she intended to confound the census, that night she was neither an evader nor a resister.

Kitty organised a well-reported stunt and even found herself on the front page of a leading London pictorial, the *Daily Sketch*. While Emily Wilding Davison was finding a nook for herself in the Crypt, Kitty went on a reconnaissance mission to Putney Heath in West London. She could not see any notices which forbade wagons and even spotted ruts on the ground from previous vehicles so she began organising the fleet with which she would mount her assault on the census. Kitty chose caravans or 'land yachts' as her mode of transport. The Women's Freedom League was the first women's suffrage organisation to seize on the opportunity caravanning offered of spontaneously attracting smaller audiences in locations not connected up to the rail network, and Australian elocutionist Muriel Matters and Lilian Hicks had been chosen to spread the word.

When Kitty's own three intrepid caravans set off on the night of the census, they attracted quite a lot of attention. Kitty and Arthur engaged three sympathetic van drivers to take the Marshalls, a group of friends and a dog, on an evasion and resistance adventure. The Marshall convoy started at Paddington then proceeded down to Oxford Street, Regent Street, Trafalgar Square, down Whitehall, via Victoria and Chelsea and Fulham Road, finally coming to rest on Putney Heath. It had been raining earlier and now the air was crisp. The group savoured the peace then prepared some food, tea and coffee. The 'Pullman' caravans were luxuriously equipped with luxury long folding tables, beds with sprung mattresses, hidden cupboards for storing crockery and a stove. This was indeed Edwardian-style glamping.

The Marshalls filled in the census schedule cover as 'Mrs Marshall and Suffragist Party'. 'Kitty Marshall' is mentioned as the 'wife' of Mr Marshall 'of Theydon Bois Essex'. The report was summarised as '1 male, 10 females' although as so many women visited them and ate with the party, Kitty couldn't say how many 'females' there were. Inside, under the Occupation column, the Marshalls described themselves as 'Suffragists'. The census enumerator still caught them out though and they were recorded as the inhabitants of 'Kenilworth', Theydon Bois. The group settled down for the night. All were attempting to rest, apart from an unfortunate suffragette who was covered in honey from a jar which had toppled over. They soon heard voices outside. There were two policemen, demanding to know who was in charge of the caravans. When there was no answer, the men left. But, at 3 a.m. there was a loud bang on the door and this time Kitty was obliged to deal with the angry enquirers. These were forest keepers and officials, accompanied by police. She told them she was in charge and that they could evict her party but that the horses would not be returning until noon so they would have to wait. A journalist was taking pictures and kept rocking the caravans and the police kept a vigil, so what sleep they did have was disturbed.

Four hours later, they stepped out of caravans to discover an unexpectedly cool breeze which roused them. The intrepid group could see beyond the gorse, birch and heath to the church spires of Roehampton. But they did not have long to admire the views. A group of park keepers, some pedestrians, two bloodhounds, a police inspector and a detective in plain clothes were eyeing the party. Arthur, with his pleasant, authoritative voice, employed his charms and the Marshalls and their friends extricated themselves in a diplomatic manner from a potentially unpleasant encounter. The caravans and horses (there being two to pull each caravan) were swiftly prepared, but not before noon, when the census ended. Kitty and her friends affixed suffragette colours and banners to their vans: 'If women do not count, neither shall they be counted' and 'When Asquith passes the Women's Bill, then women the census forms will fill.' The slogans flapped in the breeze which was getting up.

Escorted by police, the caravans made their way back to central London. The Marshall party dropped off a copy of *Votes for Women* at Asquith's house. Kitty always made a point of doing this deed every week, steeling herself to pass the six policemen guarding Number 10. Downing Street was publicly accessible at the time, resulting in, as polyglot and former jeweller's assistant, Detective Inspector Harold Brust, who was in the Special Branch for eighteen years, put it, many 'doorstep dramas'. Officers would laugh at each other as their colleagues were set upon by suffragettes. When Brust's colleague seized a disguised suffragette, her friends came to her rescue and proceeded to embarrass him by removing his hat, coat and vest, making him blush when they tried to undo his trousers. His dignity was only just preserved by two buttons. Brust tells us that a tickled Andrew Bonar Law, Leader of the Opposition, suggested laughingly that the police should arm indeed themselves with steel armour. Kitty's regular visits to 10 Downing Street were generally not as rowdy. She would bang loudly four times on the door knocker, calling 'Votes for Wom-en' [*sic*] and give the paper to the staff member who told her that he would place the publication in Asquith's line of vision.

As it turned out, the caravan group had landed themselves in a bit of bother with the local authorities. The Conservators of Wimbledon Common took out a summons against the drivers of three vehicles who had committed an offence by driving over the turf. The case was heard by Hon. John de Grey on 13 April at South-Western Police court. A lawyer, instructed by Arthur's firm, appeared for the defendants. When the magistrate expressed his view that the ladies were responsible, Morley told him that the ladies were happy to take the blame. The bemused Hon. John de Grey dismissed the summonses and, with a sense of humour, instead only fined Mrs Marshall costs amounting to a couple of shillings.

The months after the census boycott were marked by relative peace. In June, the public was treated to the Great Procession of Women, a response to the Coronation of King George V and Queen Mary on 22 June, in which women had been underrepresented. Headed by Flora Drummond, rows of marchers five deep strode to the beat of Ethel Smyth's 'The March of the Women'. Mrs Garrud offered her dojo, close to Liberty's department store, as changing room for suffragettes to don the historical costumes which represented powerful women in history. Her generosity ensured that an impressive pageant swept through the capital, a visually striking international effort and a collaboration between the suffragists and suffragettes. If the government was not going to play ball and grant women the vote, then they would play their own game of evading being counted, as with the census, or turning out in public and demand to be counted as citizens of the British Empire.

However, in November 1911, the situation deteriorated and the WSPU was once more compelled to resume its militant campaign. Depressingly, Asquith's government scuppered the progress of the second Conciliation Bill and then announced that the government would introduce a Manhood Suffrage Bill. This manoeuvre was executed despite considerable displays of a nationwide demand for women's suffrage, coupled with strong support from well-wishers around the globe for the women's cause. Women who already had the franchise had marched in the Great Procession in June. More countries and states were enfranchising women; California had just granted full suffrage to women in October. Times were changing but under Asquith's new Bill, women of Britain would continue to be shut out of social progress. Elizabeth Wolstenholme Elmy, who had watched women in saris and prison garb alike march under her window during the Great Procession, had been campaigning for women's suffrage since the 1860s. Throughout her lifetime, she had witnessed the male electorate grow from the hundreds of thousands to the millions. For her, the Manhood Suffrage Bill was an offensive piece of legislation, an insult to the women of Britain.

Superintendent Patrick Quinn suspected that increased suffragette militant activity was in the air. The WSPU intended to send a deputation to Asquith and Lloyd George on 21 November. As Kitty writes:

It was arranged that as Mr. Asquith would not allow us to come on a deputation to see him, we should go ourselves to Downing Street to demand an interview. Never had the Prime Minister received a deputation though thirteen times he was asked to hear the women's point of view. Mrs. Pankhurst said if he would only receive one woman with forty policemen to take care of him, she would be satisfied. He was terrified of women and used to run like a hare when he was in Downing Street if he saw any Suffragette coming.[17]

On the night, detectives hung around Parliament Square and the WSPU offices, attempting not to look suspicious. Christabel gave a speech at Caxton Hall before the deputation set off at 8 p.m. Unlike on Black Friday, the women went armed with stones and hammers to express their displeasure and they smashed government windows. Kitchener eyed the intense throng in Parliament Square. When he and his colleagues asked the deputation to move, they refused, which meant that the officers had to arrest 220 women and three men, including Victor Duval. Chief Inspector Francis Henry Rolfe witnessed Duval standing on the green in Parliament Square, near the statue of Sir Robert Peel. Together with another inspector, he lifted Duval out of the square and arrested him. Emmeline Pethick Lawrence, who had led the deputation, was imprisoned for a month for assault without the option of a fine. Arthur Marshall had been granted permission, as her lawyer, to see her in prison, accompanied by Fred Pethick Lawrence, but after an appeal her conviction was not quashed. Scottish Janie Allan undid the bridles of the horses of mounted police while Evelina Haverfield was arrested and jailed for two weeks for leading police horses out of their ranks. Others arrested in connection with the events on the 21 November included Kitty Marion, Lady Constance Lytton, Maud Fussell and Leeds WSPU branch member and future Bodyguard teammate, Leonora Cohen. On recommendation of her hostess, Leonora donned cardboard armour, affixed with elastic bands and string. 'We are fools travelling where angels fear to tread,' added her hostess. Leonora was indeed roughly handled, and trampled by a horse, her clothing torn and covered in froth from the horse's mouth. She protested by breaking a window of the Local Government Board office. By the time Leonora Cohen was bailed out, the police had run out of charge sheets. Her husband, who had anticipated her swift return from London, was astonished to hear that his wife was given seven days in prison. Leonora was concerned that the stress of jail had robbed her of years of her life; she lived to 105.

Kitty remembered the events of that evening very well. She had held a Beck sister on each arm for they were older than her and she felt protective of them. The women were determined to reach 10 Downing Street. Then the little group saw Rosa May Billinghurst's struggle:

> Miss Billinghurst, who was always in the forefront of any battle, had a long self-propelled invalid chair, which she handled very cleverly, and she managed to get it across Downing Street and then lock the machine so that it would not wheel. It was a fearful nuisance to the police, who could do nothing but carry off the invalid Suffragette – chair and all. It always took four policemen to get her off the scene. However, we still held our ground.

Rosa was fined 5 shillings for obstructing the police. One of the Beck sisters was thrown against the steps of 10 Downing Street. Despite undergoing the ordeal, her friend felt relieved that she was at least able to make some sort of protest as it seemed to be the only way to make an impact. As she witnessed her friends being mistreated, Kitty's anger only grew. Also running through her mind was the thought that she did not have the same political rights as the gardeners and handymen whom she employed to help with household work. Despite paying their wages and paying hefty taxes, she was considered no better than a lunatic or a criminal when it came to voting rights. With this in mind, she shouted 'Charge!' This exclamation secured her third arrest.

Arthur instructed Mr Henlé, who defended some of the prisoners in court, although most conducted their own defence. Kitty's case was adjourned. She sent a note to *Votes for Women* informing readers of her arrest and requesting that Grace Roe and her team correspond with contributors to the Farm Produce Stall that she was running at the WSPU Christmas Fair in December. She appeared in court on 24 November, charged with breaking a window at the War Office. Kitty told the court that she was protesting against the Insurance Bill, the Pit-brow Bill and the Suffrage Bill. Her lawyer, Mr Henlé, argued that she had been inspired to break the law through a worthy cause. She was fined 40 shillings and 5 shillings-worth in damages or offered a ten-day prison sentence. She chose jail. This was her second imprisonment. Unfortunately, her memoirs do not reveal any details about this time behind bars.

Kitty was released on 2 December, which gave her an opportunity to run the Farm Produce Stall at the Christmas Fair held at the Portman

Rooms in Baker Street from early December. As the WSPU aimed to give the event a village market feel, stall holders were requested to dress in eighteenth-century or early nineteenth-century peasant costume, marking the epoch of Mary Wollstonecraft. The festive fête gave ladies an opportunity to engage in a rural fantasy. Kitty would have been familiar with her mobcap, having already worn a dairymaid's costume at the Prince's Skating Bazaar in 1909. On offer to visitors were stalls featuring lace, embroidery, lucky dips, antiques, undergarments, gifts for men and the thrillingly titled 'many inventions' stall, which featured toys, jewellery, and some more exotic items such as Florentine vellum. Kitty's stall boasted cheeses, chutneys and ketchups, which were labelled with the maker's name, an innovative feature she thought would make the foods interesting for customers. The fair attracted over 7,000 visitors, raising £3,500 for the WSPU. Shortly afterwards, Kitty set to work gathering together Christmas hampers for the women, who for their part in the events of 21 November, would spend the festive season behind bars. She was still collecting for hampers well into January 1912, inviting donations of fruits, jams, cakes, books, mince pies and plum pudding.

In February, Arthur Marshall accompanied a distraught Jennie Ball to Colney Hatch Asylum in Barnet. Her husband, William, was a member of the Men's Political Union for Women's Enfranchisement and he had been arrested in December for protesting against the Manhood Suffrage Bill by breaking window panes at the Home Office. He had been forcibly fed twice daily for over five weeks. Mrs Ball's letters to the Home Secretary and the governor of Pentonville Prison were ignored. Shortly before his release, she received a letter stating, coldly, that he had been declared insane and would be sent to Colney Hatch Asylum. But thanks to Arthur, Jennie was permitted to take William to a nursing home funded by suffragette sympathisers. 'It has been only owing to the superhuman efforts of Mrs. Ball and her solicitor, Mr. Marshall, backed up by the unsparing work of the W.S.P.U. and the men's societies, that Mr. Ball's release has been secured,' concluded *Votes for Women*.

7.

Toothbrushes at Dawn

Three women were seen getting out of a taxi. The vehicle stopped right outside 10 Downing Street at 5.30 p.m. on 1 March 1912. One of the ladies was Mrs Pankhurst. She had been practising her stone-throwing skills on haystacks and trees, watched by a sceptical Ethel Smyth. It seemed to Ethel that Mrs Pankhurst had never played ball games as a child as she had no natural skill. The first stone she attempted to lob at a fir tree even fell backwards out of her grasp and almost hit Ethel's dog. As Ethel's memoir relates, when Mrs Pankhurst did at last hit a target, her expression of unalloyed joy had Ethel in stitches and the celebrated composer fell into a bush of heather with laughter. Her friend, who had been concentrating ferociously, stood by, put out and perplexed, failing to see what had caused Ethel such amusement.

Another 'doorstep drama' unfolded when Mrs Pankhurst, now tutored in the art of stone-throwing, and her two friends, Kitty Marshall and Mabel Tuke (who was known as 'Pansy' for her dark eyes), took their places, standing about 2 feet apart. They threw more than one stone each. Kitty called for the commissionaire, to get him out of harm's way while she broke two windows. Mrs Pankhurst's missile only clattered into the basement, but the other women managed to break four panes of glass at the front of the premier's house. When Mabel was apprehended, she told the officer that she was glad that she had made the protest, while Mrs Pankhurst was wordlessly taken to Cannon Row Police Station.

PC Walter Merton grabbed Kitty and while the constable was holding her, she took her last stone and threw it at the Colonial Office. Kitty's missiles, together with the messages attached, reached their target, although PC Merton spotted that another stone had fallen out of her muff. 'Why did you do it?' asked the policeman nervously, who had taken Kitty into his charge. She then told him that she had no more stones left. PC Merton noticed that the stones were pebbles, smaller than his fist. Mabel Tuke and Mrs Pankhurst handed in their flint stones. This event was just the start and over the course of the evening, more destruction was to follow.

Hit low and stand well back. Use a toffee hammer. It has an eyelet so you can secretly suspend it within your clothing or hide it in your winter muff. And it fits so well into the palm of your gloved hand. Failing that, use lead, or even a pebble; stones are surprisingly hard to come by in London. As the glass cracks, there will be showers. Just remember to aim low and get out of the way. But Charlie Marsh has her own method of going about the business. She darts down the Strand as if she is playing in a hockey game. The girl takes aim where she pleases and waits just a moment to enjoy the satisfying tinkle and smash. And then she is off again with her bag of stones towards the next target, performing a sporty protest against the patriarchy.

Ralph Kitchener and his fellow constables were in Bow Street, awaiting orders for their traffic point duty posts when the station inspector rushed in. 'Every man jack of you rush down to the Strand straight away; the suffragettes are there breaking windows wholesale,' he announced. The officers ran out of the station to the Strand, encountering their colleagues emerging from Wellington Street. Kitchener noticed what seemed to be dozens of suffragettes who had been arrested in the Strand, but some of them had come from other locations. When Charlie Marsh (normally fair-haired unless wearing a black wig) had been stopped in the middle of her game, she had gone quietly with her policeman and had surreptitiously dumped her stones in the chimney at Bow Street. Kitchener made his way through this ordered throng to the Strand, the presumed scene of destruction, back into the chaos from which she had emerged. It seemed that an early dusk had set with the extinguishing of bright shop windows. His colleagues darted this way and that while groups of people announced in thrilled voices when and where a window smasher was arrested. Amid the halt of traffic vehicles grinding to a standstill, Kitchener could hear the rattles of iron curtains and the hammer of nails, as frightened shop owners sought to protect themselves and their wares from the onslaught.

A finger could be pointed at Charles Hobhouse in particular for inciting this destruction. Rather foolishly, the cabinet minister had announced that women were incapable of assertive, even violent, political protest. Emmeline Pethick Lawrence responded and said that women were wiser than the historical examples offered by men's conduct:

> Women to-day are less emotional, less hysterical and more politically minded than were the men of the country in 1832. They are prepared to go just as far in their demonstrations of public uprising as is necessary in order to convey the fact that they are determined to win their freedom – and no further.[18]

And Mrs Pethick Lawrence's view that there should be a cap on the level of violence to property exerted by the militant suffrage movement was placing her at odds with Mrs Pankhurst.

On Black Friday 1910, women's bodies had borne the brunt of the wrath of public and police. In 'The Argument of the Broken Pane', Mrs Pankhurst told prisoners who had been released since their incarceration in November that flying stones would serve as the front line in the next campaign, and attract more attention. Volunteers were requested for the mass act of militancy, proposed for early March, coinciding with the redecoration of Holloway Prison. This event imposed a logistical problem on the authorities as small groups of suffragettes – there were over 100 women arrested on that day – had to be transported to and accommodated in other prisons.

Regent Street's shops, with their roomy plate-glass panes proudly displaying sartorial finery, jewellery, toys and other expensive luxury items, offered themselves up as easy targets. Intriguingly, in reference to the women who took part in the campaign, Kitty mentions that: 'Not a single one of them was a police spy, so the public had a fearful shock when, at the appointed hour, windows were broken at most of the shops.' This suggests that there were indeed concerns about double agents operating within the WSPU rank and file. The damage was estimated at around £5,000 and for Kitty, the destruction made the public sit up and take note. To Mrs Marshall, it was bitterly ironic that Mr Asquith had been asked over a dozen times to accept a deputation of suffrage campaigners. Peaceful campaigning was becoming a source of mirth:

The Bill for women's enfranchisement of women had been before the House twenty eight times. The petition, signed by thousands of women all over the country, was so large that it had to be wheeled into the House of Commons, and the Members laughed and thought it was a great joke.[19]

Property destruction, by contrast, was no matter for ridicule and the night of the great window-smashing campaign gave the public a reminder of social injustice, and of women's political inability to change lives for the better as their voices were shut out of parliamentary discourse, a point that could no longer be ignored or downplayed.

Christabel Pankhurst remarked that Kitty, who was responsible for attracting advertising in the pages of *Votes for Women*, saw to it that the owners of the well-insured businesses whose windows had not been damaged were made to feel disgruntled due to the lack of publicity. It was therefore in the interests of the public and the business world to become involved in the vicissitudes of the campaign for women's suffrage. For her own involvement, Mrs Pankhurst received two months, Mrs Tuke was sentenced to twenty-one days in jail while Kitty faced the prospect of spending two months and twenty-one days behind bars. Ethel, who had assisted in training Mrs Pankhurst for the event, had pretended to ask an officer guarding Mr Lewis Harcourt's house for directions. As he was replying, she threw a stone and smashed some glass. She declined bail. This was to be Kitty's third time in jail. Kitty speedily fired off a message to the WSPU: 'Our sentence only makes us more determined than ever to continue to fight, which can only end in victory. The harder the fight, the sooner the victory.' No. 4 Clement's Inn was under surveillance and suffragettes were wise to the fact that they were being followed.

Then, on 5 March there followed a raid on the premises, headed by Detective Inspector John McCarthy. A couple of cab-loads of documents were seized as were Jessie Kenney and Miss Vaughan. There was also a warrant for the arrest of Christabel. At 11 p.m., she turned up at a suffragette nursing home at 9 Pembridge Gardens, run by Nurse Catherine 'Piney' Pine, a significant lady who, some had said rather unkindly, resembled a bulldog, and Gertrude Townend. By the time the police came knocking at the door, Christabel, revived with some hot milk and disguised as a nurse, had flitted to a sympathiser's house while officers nearby paced the streets. Escaping across the Channel, a dark coat and cloche hat obscured her face and figure.

Kitty's husband examined the warrant for the arrest of the Pethick Lawrences. He could not argue with the wording and the couple were duly taken away. Superintendent Patrick Quinn of the Special Branch oversaw the arrests, McCarthy and Powell being his right-hand men in this task. Annie Kenney took over the editorship of *Votes for Women* and each weekend, Annie would brave the giddy waters of the Channel to retrieve Christabel's text from Paris. Now Christabel's successor, Annie took direction from her, steering the movement away from the constitutionally run organisation envisaged by the Pethick Lawrences. She was assisted by Rachel Barrett. Mrs Pankhurst was already in jail, as was Mabel Tuke who, whilst behind bars, was also charged with conspiracy to cause damage alongside Mrs Pankhurst and the Pethick Lawrences.

The trials hit the news. At her own hearing, Kitty requested that the stones be shown to the court. They contained messages such as 'Justice for Women' and 'We demand the Vote'. She made an impassioned speech from the dock expressing her pride in taking part in a movement which sought to promote the importance of listening to women's views as part of a campaign to arrest British national decline:

I am very proud to have made another protest. This is the sixth time I have been in this court, and I am prepared to come sixty times. We have tried every means – processions and meetings – which were of no avail. We have tried demonstrations, and now at last we have to break windows. I wish I had broken more. I am not the least repentant. Our women are working in far worse conditions than the miners. I have seen widows struggling to bring up their children. Only two out of every five are fit to be soldiers. What is the good of a country like ours? England is absolutely on the wane. You only have one point of view, and that is the men's, and while the men have done the best they could, they cannot go far without women and without the women's views. We believe the whole is in a muddle too horrible to think of. We are going as far in militancy as we may be driven to go, and no further. That is all I have to say; but I am very proud to have made the protest, and I am willing to go on.[20]

Kitty went to jail for the third and last time. While all the leaders were in prison and Christabel was now directing the movement from the safety of Paris, Annie Kenney took over the running of the WSPU, too. Soon Annie would be forced to take sides: the Pankhursts or the Pethick Lawrences. It was an agonising decision but as a faithful friend of Christabel's, she became allied to the former camp.

Mrs Pankhurst and the Pethick Lawrences were sentenced to nine months in prison in the First Division. They did not see out their sentences. Mrs Pankhurst heard Emmeline Pethick Lawrence's screams as her body was violently made to accept food. She would not be subjected to the indignity and refused to be medically examined. The suffragette leader protected herself from the prison staff with an earthenware jug. Fred Pethick Lawrence was forcibly fed five times. By July, all three were too hot to hold and had been released. The Pethick Lawrences decided that they needed a vacation.

Gasping women across Holloway prison smashed windows to let in air. Kitty broke a small pane of glass for every passing hour in which no attendant came to her cell. Jane Terrero was grateful for Kitty's act of defiance. It was due to her and other 'splendid brave women' that the prison introduced sliding panes of glass. Kitty was taken to some visiting magistrates who sentenced her to five days in solitary confinement. As she left the magistrates' court, she clung to a chair on which was seated a rather corpulent man. The matrons pulled and pushed and could not release her grip and so she had to be taken out whilst holding on to the article of furniture.

She was punitively relocated. The cell was underground and there was no hot pipe. Outside it was snowing. Kitty kicked the bedstead and sang 'The March of the Women'. Both a hymn and a battle cry, the song gave a sense of momentum, of society on the move. It reassured Kitty at any rate. Things would get better, she told herself. Then suddenly, a mattress was flung into her cell which she wrapped around her shivering frame. As she told Rachel Barrett, the prison governor looked in on her too. 'Puss in a corner,' he remarked. Kitty was faintly amused, thinking that the man clearly did not know what her name was. Without a slate and prayer book, Kitty had nothing to occupy her mind and found the solitude maddening with the loneliness and state of hunger cutting into her nerves. Not even the wardresses were permitted to speak to her if she asked questions. She took to knitting wool from her stockings using her hairpins. It was all she could do to prevent herself from ruminating over the injustice done to the women who were campaigning to improve the lives of others. By the time she was admitted to the prison hospital, she was depressed.

For a week, Kitty slept in one of the sixteen hospital ward beds. There were no dividing curtains and all inmates were overlooked by an unshaded electric light at the room's centre. Beneath the unforgiving illumination sat a wardress, flicking through newspapers. Whilst painful to her eyes, hospital offered comfort. The experience gave Kitty an opportunity to meet Third Division prisoners with whom she might not have normally had the chance to speak and offered a reminder to her and her friends as to why they were risking their health and reputation: they were defending impoverished women who did not have a voice. In one of the ward beds near Kitty was a young woman who was serving a heavy sentence for stealing a brooch when she had lost her job after becoming pregnant, classed as a 'fallen woman'. Kitty never had children of her own, at least none who appear to have survived. She sympathised with the mother in distress and wanted to help the girl and her baby and enlisted the help of her fellow suffragettes Kate and Louise Lilley from Clacton-on-Sea, daughters of a boot and shoe manufacturer who co-owned a business that fashioned suffragette-themed footwear. The Lilley sisters were serving two months' hard labour for breaking a window at the War Office. They went on hunger strike and were forcibly fed. Kitty and the Lilleys were working within the limits of society's attitudes at that time and did for their fellow prisoner what they could. On their release, the Lilley sisters found kind adoptive parents and paid for the baby boy's upkeep while his mother found work and made a new life without anyone having known about her past. Kitty and the Lilleys were frequently sent photographs of him. Sleep-deprived after a week under the matron's blazing lamp, Kitty successfully requested to be sent back to a cell.

Katie Edith Gliddon also wrote an account of her experiences in prison, in March 1929. Like Kitty Marshall, Katie was an artist and a clergyman's daughter. An active member of the Men's Political Union for Women's Enfranchisement, Katie's brother Paul protected his family from scandal by using the pseudonym Charles Gray and Katie went under the name Catherine/Katherine Susan Gray. Katie was imprisoned for smashing a Post Office window in Wimpole Street on 4 March using a kitchen knife concealed inside her old black muff. The officer was 'kind and courteous' when he arrested her and took her gently to the station. He was concerned that he might have stepped on her skirt whilst he arrested her. The station staff were keen to put the women at their ease as far as possible under the circumstances. The friendly station matron at Marylebone Police station searched her, which merely involved Katie showing her the contents of her pocket and the matron running her hand down the outside of Katie's coat. She thought that the officers at the station treated her and her friend with kindness. Katie was sentenced to two months with hard labour; she thought she would only get five days. As her documents in the Women's Library reveal, Arthur Marshall told her that she and the other women had an unsympathetic magistrate, but he advised her not to worry about the hard labour part. 'It is just piffle. You just don't do it that's all,' he said to her. Arthur later managed to get her sentence reduced by ten days.

Katie was also not permitted novels for the first month. Women with hard labour sentences spent twenty-three out of twenty-four hours in prison; others were let out twice a day. She was hungry and like Kitty she disliked the sludgy tea. Kitty filled her wooden salt bowl with water for pigeons and gave them her unappetising prison bread, wondering if they were cooing 'look at the food' or 'look at the fool'. Katie created an evocative pencil sketch of her prison cell, a view of both the window and the cell door. She stood on her stool to look out of the window, observing the colour of the clouds and the position of the stars. Katie imagined Holloway as a ship with its iron stairs leading to upper decks and its windows twinkling in their sockets.

Her view was of the hospital entrance and a gravel path down which numerous suffragettes would tread. Like Kitty, she was given knitting to attempt. Kitty managed to earn eight pence for her striped red wool sock which took her two months to complete. For company, Katie had a secret copy of Shelley's poetry. In the wide margins of the anthology, Katie revealed that on 12 March, she saw Kitty, Mrs Pankhurst and Mrs Saul Solomon pass under her window on several occasions. Women saluted the group, and they were rewarded with kisses from their adored leader. Inwardly, Mrs Pankhurst was attempting to keep herself together, bodily and mentally. During their circumambulations of Holloway's grounds, Kitty tried to reassure Mrs Pankhurst, who was unsteady on her feet from hunger and exhaustion. One day, Kitty emphasised, there would be a statue to her memory in London.

At times, Katie saw Mrs Pankhurst sitting outside, wrapped up and weak, or leaning against her strangely unmarked cell door, wearing a kimono and Japanese slippers. Mrs Pankhurst's fragility angered Katie Gliddon. To her, Mrs Pankhurst was 'natural' and 'childlike' and she hated her leader being a victim of the government. Elizabeth Garrett Anderson, who had been kept in a stuffy cell on a lower floor, also looked decidedly unwell.

Among the other celebrities she saw were Mabel Tuke and Ethel Smyth, the latter who threw a ball at rounders and conducted 'The March of the Women' with her toothbrush. All the while, Jane Terrero was checking her watch, which she had managed to smuggle into Holloway. Born in Braintree, Essex, Jane was just over ten years older than Kitty. Jane became a suffragist at the age of 18. Her husband, Manuel, was a suffragent and the couple hosted many WSPU garden parties. Jane was arrested on 1 March and was sentenced to four months in jail for her part in the window-smashing campaign. For her, the determined hunger strike was the suffragette's greatest weapon.

Katie was training herself to see beyond its ugliness of the prison dress. Hospital had given Kitty an opportunity to speak to ordinary prisoners, but Katie and those in her division were kept remote from others. In church, Katie sat behind a row of exhausted and pallid ordinary prisoners wearing white caps and buff or blue bodices over their ungainly skirts, topped with blueish checked aprons. As she watched one woman, who had severely brushed hair beneath a white cap, she could almost convince herself that she was looking at a painting by German-born fifteenth-century artist Hans Memling. Kitty did not have such an aesthetically inspired response to chapel. It was so stuffy that the women arranged a mass fainting fit which resulted in one wardress taking a turn and Kitty using her Red Cross skills to revive her. Home Secretary Reginald McKenna took away many of the privileges which Churchill had granted in 1910 under Rule 243A, which allowed suffrage prisoners to have their own clothes, needlework, books and food in jail, to chat to other prisoners during exercise, to have visitors once a month and occasional letters sent out and to receive them. Jane Terrero thought that McKenna was a fool; his rules were designed to break imprisoned suffragettes but instead, they would destroy his regulations.

McKenna only permitted suffragette prisoners, unlike those serving ordinary hard-labour sentences, to fraternise when they exercised and to wear their own clothes. Yet, looking presentable in chapel, where the women would communicate with each other by passing notes inside Bibles, was a challenge. Suffragettes were not permitted hatpins in chapel. These essential modes of affixing enormous headgear – hatpins were veritable stilettos and could reach lengths of 16 inches – had become so commonplace that customers could simply pluck one out of a 'peacock' hatpin stand at a shop counter like prising a lollipop from a selection of fanned-out sweets at a newsagent.

Holloway staff went to great lengths to prevent women from injuring themselves or others, or causing damage. There were no mirrors in cells and the mysterious 4-inch-long slip of tin was a margarine 'knife', stamped with the arrow motif. Prisoners were watched by wardresses while they had baths, and toilet chains were hung outside a cubicle to be pulled by the wardresses. Journalists and novelists had ample material for horror stories from some real-life incidents with hatpins, including punctured eyes, injuries in crowded lifts and fights between rival children. As the matrons knew, hatpins could be weapons of stealth, easily obtained and wielded by all. In *That Affair Next Door* (1897) by Anna Katherine Green, a man thrusts a hatpin into the brain of a woman who, in the dark, he believes to be his wife. In 1902, a bricklayer's labourer, William Rosser, was murdered by a gang who punctured his lung with a hatpin. At their trial at the Old Bailey, the medical consultant warned that the hatpin had been so hard to detect, that it had been unnoticed for a month, leading to the development of the blood poisoning which killed Rosser. One Marylebone magistrate declared with some relish how thoroughly fed up he was with the new woman and the sex war she seemed to be conducting with the hatpin. The hatpin was, stated Alfred Chicele Plowden, 'one of the most dangerous weapons of modern civilisation'. At the end of July 1913, when Mrs Pankhurst was arrested at the Pavilion, the *Manchester Courier* grabbed its audience by cramming in a mélange of unsettling images in its title: 'Suffragists' Fury. Re-Arrest of Mrs Pankhurst. Fight with Police. Hatpins Used; Officer Nearly Strangled.'

But by 1909, the image of the hatpin-wielding suffragette had already been sufficiently embedded in the public mind that Grace Roe wore a cap because suffragettes were accused of injuring police officers with their hatpins. Lack of a hatpin meant that Kitty's headgear kept dislodging itself so she used her toothbrush to affix her feather toque as she bent her head in prayer. She made a hole on either side of the hat through which to thread the toothbrush. Her little, humorous act of rebellion caused heads to turn. When their collars and waistbands were sent out to be washed, suffragettes smuggled notes inside to tell others of the suffrage campaign's progress. There were no adequate places to store clothes away from the dusty floor along which cockroaches scuttled. Kitty expressed her dissatisfaction by using the strings of her undergarments to hang up her combinations near the door, eliciting a blush from the chaplain. The women were deemed too wicked to attend Holy Communion for the first month and the governor weepily told Arthur that the women's antics were 'driving him mad'.

Over sixty women who took part in the great window-smashing campaigns of early March contributed sewn signatures and initials to a handkerchief, a crafted memorial which is believed to have been organised by a nurse, Mary Ann Hilliard, who donated the handkerchief to the British College of Nurses. Near the bottom of the handkerchief and next to Louise Lilley's name is Kitty's signature in orange stitching: 'E. K. Marshall'. This was not the only time that Kitty's name was embroidered on a cloth memento – the Women's Library has in its collection a cloth which bears an even greater number of suffragettes' names – but Mary Hilliard's handkerchief best represents the appearance of Kitty's signature with its distinctive capitals.

Just after Kitty had been released from prison in mid-April, *Votes for Women* printed a tribute in the 26 April edition to W.T. Stead, the editor of the *Pall Mall Gazette*, in the wake of his death in the *Titanic* disaster. Stead's paper printed Kitty's piece entitled 'No Vote, No Insurance Act'. Just as she was penning her missive, it was announced that the Manhood Suffrage Bill would not contain a women's suffrage amendment. This news likely firmed up her resolution to counter the government:

Sir, — Will you allow me to appeal to my fellow Suffragists to join in resisting the Insurance Act? So long as women remain unrepresented in Parliament the constant cry of our opponents is 'Women's place is the home.' When legislation penetrates into the home like this Act does, and we are not only taxed, but constituted tax-gatherers, without asking our consent or wishes, it is high time that self-respecting women should rise up and say 'this thing we will not have'. Respect for the law is all very well in a perfectly-constituted State, and should command our attention, but in our present voteless condition we regard the Insurance Act as an additional stigma on our womanhood.

Full particulars as to how the Act adversely affects women, and pledge cards and leaflets, also tickets for the Albert Hall meeting on Thursday, June 27, at 8 p.m, may be obtained from the Servants' Tax Resistance Defence Association, 61, South Molton-street, London, W.—
Yours faithfully, Mrs E.K. Marshall
Theydon Bois, Essex, June 18.[21]

In late June, Emily Wilding Davison was nearing the end of a six-month sentence when she attempted on several occasions to throw herself down the staircase of Holloway Prison, causing her severe back pain. She was forcibly fed nonetheless, but released on 28 June. In the House of Commons, Keir Hardie had asked how Emily Wilding Davison's accident had occurred and enquired whether or not she was being forcibly fed. Asquith refused to comment on her situation but responded that she and other women could leave jail if they wished. George Lansbury turned puce with anger as he regarded Asquith. The prime minister's own normally stoic countenance too was reddening as he crossed his arms against the verbal onslaught. Cries of 'Order!' grew louder, matching Lansbury's rising invective and the Speaker was then prompted to request Lansbury leave the House. 'You ought to go down to history as the men who tortured innocent women!' Lansbury thundered, before he made his exit.

William Charles Baldwin.
(Image courtesy of Chris Jacques)

Kinton Jacques.
(Image courtesy of Chris Jacques)

Westhoughton Vicarage. (Image reproduced with kind permission from Manchester Libraries, Information and Archives, L122/1/24/2)

'1st Torpid 1893.' Hugh Finch is in the middle row with the dog. (Keble College Archives, KC/JCR 1 C1/1/3)

'Athletics 1893.' Hugh Finch is fourth from the right, bottom row; Archer Vassall is third from the right, top row. (Keble College Archives, KC/JCR 1 C1/1/3)

Gravestone of Frances Mary Buss FCP, St Mary's Theydon Bois. Inscription reads: 'Founder of the North London Collegiate and Camden Schools for Girls, born August 16th 1827, died Christmas Eve 1894. Blessed are the Dead which die in the Lord: They rest from their labours and their works do follow them.' (Photographer Hugh Meteyard)

Ralph Kitchener as a boy. (Image reproduced with kind permission from Janet Dennis)

PC Ralph Kitchener. (Image reproduced with kind permission from Janet Dennis)

Inspector Jarvis watching Clement's Inn, 1908. (Women's Library, LSE, 7JCC/O/02/049)

The arrest of Flora Drummond, Mrs Pankhurst and Christabel Pankhurst at the WSPU offices at Clement's Inn, 1908. (Women's Library, LSE, 7JCC/O/02/064)

The Farm Produce Stall at the Women's Exhibition, 1909. Kitty is third from the right. (Photographer Christina Broom. Museum of London, IN1307)

'If You Want to Earn Some Time Throw a Policeman!' Jujitsu suffragette Edith Garrud shows how to tackle a policeman, *The Sketch*, July 1910. (© Illustrated London News Ltd/ Mary Evans, 10493265)

Pencil drawing of 'Winsonosaurus', 1912. (Museum of London, Z6084c)

Photograph of Arthur Marshall (right) taken during his work for the WSPU. Undated. (Women's Library, LSE, TWL 2002 583)

MR GLADSTONE'S HOUSE, LITTLESTONE-ON-SEA   55653

Postcard of Gladstone's House, Littlestone-on-Sea, dated October 1908. (Image courtesy of John Henley and Colin and Margaret Walker of the Dymchurch & District Heritage Group)

The Census image of Kitty and her friends. (Museum of London, 2012.1/20)

Kitty's necklace. (Museum of London, 50.82/1149)

News cutting depicting scenes outside Buckingham Palace on 21 May 1914. The arrest of Mrs Pankhurst by Chief Inspector Francis Henry Rolfe was captured at various angles. (Museum of London, 2003.46/187)

'Votes for Women, Holloway Prison March 1912.' Handkerchief. Kitty's signature is near the bottom right-hand corner. (The Priest House, West Hoathly, West Sussex. Reproduced with kind permission from Sussex Archaeological Society)

Mrs Pankhurst leaving Epsom Police Court, 25 February 1913. Arthur Marshall can be seen standing just in front of her, briefcase in hand. (Museum of London, NN22852)

The Fig Tree Room, from Henrietta Leslie (Gladys Schütze)'s *More Ha'pence than Kicks: Being Some Things Remembered*. (London: MacDonald & Co., 1943)

Arrest of Mrs Pankhurst by Chief Inspector Francis Henry Rolfe. (Museum of London, 2003.46/187)

Ralph Kitchener with his wife Nellie and son Joseph Alfred (Janet's father). (Reproduced with kind permission from Janet Dennis and family)

Kitty (far right) at Mrs Pankhurst's funeral procession. (Museum of London, NN29124)

Mrs Pankhurst's funeral, with the coffin in the background. (Museum of London, NN29131)

Unveiling of the statue of Emmeline Pankhurst, 1930. Manuscript inscription on reverse reads: 'With great care. EK Marshall, 15 Gayfere St', printed 'Copyright Keystone View Company, 12 Wine Office Court, Fleet Street, London EC4'. (Women's Library, LSE)

Right: Emmeline Pankhurst's gravestone, Brompton Cemetery. (© The March of the Women Collection/Mary Evans Picture Library/10825211)

Below: Unveiling of the statue of Emmeline Pankhurst in Victoria Tower Gardens, Westminster, in 1930, two years after her death. (Mary Evans/SZ Photo/Scherl/10570256)

Detective Inspector Ralph Kitchener. Image captured at around the time of the Bees Bomb case; his firearms are visible under his coat. (Reproduced with kind permission from Janet Dennis and family)

Detective Inspector Ralph Kitchener. Photograph taken to mark the award of his prize-winning essay in 1934. (Reproduced with kind permission from Janet Dennis and family)

8.

Into the CID

Superintendent Patrick Quinn regarded Kitchener with his piercing blue eyes. The slim-built head of the Special Branch, who was known to staff as 'P.Q', had a pointy imperial-style beard with a turned-up moustache and spoke with an Irish accent. He made it clear to his men that the Special Branch was a prestigious institution and that it was up to every detective to uphold the Branch's reputation. And above him hung a curious and arresting photograph to which eyes were often drawn. The candidate before him had applied to join the Special Branch shortly before completing his second year in the Met. He was clearly keen and as he told Quinn, he had joined the Met, hoping to enter the Special Branch. Kitchener had satisfied the required standard for entry into the Branch by passing the examination. He could now write 120 words per minute in shorthand. The man was clearly self-motivated and was studying hard in his own time. He had brains and pluck and besides, the Branch needed bright, quick-witted and tactful men like Kitchener, given that suffragette activity was growing in severity and intensity and required careful handling from a public relations perspective. As Kitchener's colleague Walter Thompson realised, the promotion to the Special Branch came with a warning:

> It takes a great deal more time and care to turn out the 'Special' than his confrère, the criminal detective. ... Whereas the ordinary detective can always feel that the Law stands squarely behind him, the 'Special' more often than not lacks this advantage. ... The slightest indiscretion on his part may not only put himself and his chief, but possibly

the Government itself, into a quandary. The situations he has to face demand the greatest possible tact in the face of problems kaleidoscopic in variety.[22]

Quinn and Kitchener talked about the work of the Special Branch. Kitchener, who took pride in research and preparation, would already have been familiar with its history. When the Metropolitan Police was first formed, the force was given the task of preventing crime; Parliament had declared that it was illegal for officers to conduct investigations over concerns that Met police were acting as government spies. Following a series of murders and attempts on Queen Victoria's life, the Met's Detective Department was finally in official operation in 1842, publicly endorsed by Charles Dickens who famously admired the department's quiet and reliable efficiency. In the 1850s, John Hitchens Sanders, who spied on French refugees, was given the job of heading a proto-political branch which included Constable Adolphus ('Dolly') Frederick Williamson. But this experimental branch ended in 1859 with Sanders' death.

In the 1860s, the Fenians waged a terrorist campaign for Home Rule. After a failed assault on Chester Castle, two arrested Fenians were being transported to prison in Manchester when their comrades attacked the police van. Sergeant Charles Brett, the officer in charge of the vehicle, was shot dead. Emmeline Pankhurst's older brother told her of the incident whilst taking her home for dinner from a friend's house. As the dusk drew in, she imagined the pistol shot and the dying policeman, surrounded by a concerned crowd. Mrs Pankhurst was appalled by the subsequent public execution in 1867 of the Manchester Martyrs who had taken part in the raid:

> I saw that a part of the prison wall had been torn away, and in the great gap that remained were evidences of a gallows recently removed. I was transfixed with horror, and over me there swept the sudden conviction that that hanging was a mistake – worse, a crime. It was my awakening to one of the most terrible facts of life – that justice and judgment lie often a world apart. ... I tell [this story] also to show that my development into an advocate of militancy was largely a sympathetic process. I have not personally suffered from the deprivations, the bitterness and sorrow which bring so many men and women to a realisation of social injustice.[23]

The memorial to Sergeant Brett in St Anne's Church read: 'Dare not I must do my duty'. The Fenians later blew up a section of the wall of Clerkenwell House of Detention in December of that year to free one of their members. The rescue attempt was unsuccessful and the bomb killed a dozen and injured many more. The incident was dubbed the Clerkenwell Outrage.

A lull in Fenian activities coincided with the Trial of the Detectives of 1877 in which four high-ranking police officers appeared in court, charged with accepting bribes from confidence tricksters involved in placing false bets on horses. Reeling from the scandal which had shown up corruption in the heart of the establishment, Scotland Yard adopted Sir Howard Vincent's reform suggestions and with 'Dolly' Williamson as superintendent, Assistant Commissioner Vincent headed the new Criminal Investigation Department (CID), founded in 1878, four times bigger than its old counterpart. Now the collection and centralisation of criminal records would begin in earnest.

A resurgence of Fenian terrorism across Britain in the early 1880s left the public shaking. No one knew where and when the next explosion would happen. In London, a wave of attacks culminated in 'Dynamite Saturday', 24 January 1885, when a bomb exploded at the Tower of London, resulting in sixteen people being injured. A letter was sent to Scotland Yard which threatened to 'blow Superintendent Williamson off his stool'. The image which was proudly displayed in Quinn's office depicted what happened next: a bomb was planted in a public urinal in the floor below Williamson's office. Part of the building was blown up and customers at the Rising Sun public house were injured as glass windows shattered. No Met staff were injured, but one narrowly missed death by quarter of an hour. It was a warning to keep vigilant. However, the image was also a testament to Scotland Yard's indomitable spirit in the face of deadly threats.

Kitchener had access to the defused explosive 'infernal machines' used by the Fenians. Under the Prisoners' Property Act 1869, officers were given the power to confiscate objects used in crimes and consequently, in the following decade, the 'Black Museum' (the Crime Museum) was established in 1875 as a training resource. The bombs were rendered inert by Colonel Sir Vivian Majendie, one of the earliest security and bomb disposal experts, who was also Chief Inspector of Explosives. The sheer volume of attacks carried out against the public by the Irish Republican terrorists made it clear that the threat finally needed a directed response from a department dedicated to the gathering of intelligence specific to these politically motivated crimes. In the early 1880s, the Political Branch of the CID was set up at Scotland Yard to counter the terrorist threat, its name being changed to the Special Irish Branch. This team was led by Chief Inspector John Littlechild who had been a junior officer during the Trial of the Detectives. Among the detectives from Irish backgrounds selected for this Branch was Patrick Quinn, then a sergeant, who later became the first police officer from the ranks to be knighted. In 1887, the Special Irish Branch became the Special Branch and its duties widened. Detectives in the Special Branch not only tracked suspected Irish terrorists but also followed suspicious revolutionaries and groups associated with practising values, such as free love, considered to be counter to notions of British decency. A firm grasp of foreign languages was highly desirable in tracking foreign anarchists. A multilinguist, Detective Constable Herbert Fitch, who joined the Special Branch in 1905, found himself hiding, cramped in an airless cupboard in an Islington public house, hearing fists banging on tables and words uttered by Lenin himself. To stop himself from fainting, he pricked his skin with a knife.

The Branch dealt with treason, sedition, the protection of British and foreign royals and foremost cabinet ministers, counter-espionage, particularly rooting out German spy networks in Britain. Under the Official Secrets Act 1911 (which included amendments to an earlier Act of 1889), if Kitchener (or his colleagues) divulged any information, or kept or passed on any sketches, plans, models, photographs or documents entrusted to him or others which might also help the enemy, he could face a prison sentence. Quinn asked Kitchener whether, despite all the risks and potential penalties, he still wanted to work in the Special Branch. Kitchener again emphasised that this work was his great ambition. Quinn, who had been devoted to the Special Branch ever since he was recruited into the Special Irish Branch in 1883, was pleased and flattered. He gave Kitchener a warm smile as he welcomed the young man from Olney into the fold.

Kitchener's team was an all-male department of detectives. A master of disguise, Maud West was running her private detective business from the same building as the infamous Dr Crippen. However, there were no women police detectives actually employed in Britain at the time; Lilian

Wyles was the first woman in the CID in 1922 and was attested with a woman's warrant in 1923. Female detectives had appeared much earlier in America – Chicago's first police detective department employed 23-year-old Kate Warne in 1856, while Lola Baldwin was the first official American female police officer, working in Portland, Oregon, around a decade before women's police patrols were established in Britain. But women connected with the police force could, nonetheless, assist in cases, to search and keep an eye on and help arrested women and crime victims. Early in his career, Kitchener came to the aid of a little girl who was able to identify her attacker. Not long after, Lambeth social worker Eilidh MacDougall was appointed in a civilian capacity as the Lady Assistant to the Metropolitan Police in 1912, helping the police with taking statements from women and girls who had been sexually abused. She had convinced Metropolitan Police Commissioner Sir Edward Henry that she thought these types of interviews ought to be handled by a woman. MacDougall started the Mary Leaf Fund to help sexual abuse victims and she would later be awarded an MBE.

Protection duties were a key feature of Special Branch work and could entail much discomfort. Kitchener, a third-class constable in the CID, knew what it felt like to be hungry for hours at a time whilst on duty. Hunger was a common feature of everyday life across all classes; even in wealthier homes and in public schools, access to food could be denied as a way of teaching children self-discipline. On the job for sometimes ninety hours a week, Kitchener had to grab food on the go or go without. As he stood at his post on the route between Buckingham Palace and Westminster Abbey during the coronation, the only sustenance offered to Kitchener and his colleagues to both slake their hunger and quench their thirst was confectionary: chocolate and sherbets. They fared better than the police officers on the scene at the Siege of Sidney Street, the sequel to the Houndsditch Murders. The men's superior officer refused offers of food for his staff much to the distress of members of the public willing to help.

The task of guarding important personages also offered some unexpected challenges. Royals and cabinet ministers did not always appreciate being watched over by the Special Branch and some reasserted their freedom. Reginald McKenna took pleasure in giving his bodyguards the slip, while King Albert I of Belgium disliked protection – at home he wheeled out a bicycle in the early hours of the morning when he could have the Ostend streets to himself. The Belgian monarch tolerated protection on special occasions and Kitchener was advised to be discreet, which entailed following him down Trafalgar Square and Fleet Street where the monarch caught a bus back to the Carlton Hotel whereupon he asked Kitchener's recommendation for a good cinema! The king liked to play the unobtrusive *flâneur* but did thank the detective for shadowing him and looking after him during his stay in London. On one occasion, Sir Edward Grey informed Kitchener's colleague, Detective Sergeant Walter Hay, that he would walk home from the House of Commons but when he reached Birdcage Walk, the Foreign Secretary broke into a sprint, losing the detective. When Ramsay MacDonald was prime minister, he attempted to lose Kitchener and Detective Sergeant Renshaw on the way back to Downing Street. Renshaw, who was known to his colleagues as 'Lumpy', was outpaced as the prime minister amusedly increased his speed. However, he met his match in Kitchener who relates in his memoir that he was training in speed walking and reached him as the man got to 10 Downing Street. MacDonald smiled. 'Where's your colleague? Have we lost him?'

Protecting government ministers led to irregular hours which Kitchener learnt when standing in for Lloyd George's two protection officers. Lloyd George, for example, returned home at 3 a.m. and was back at work at 9 a.m. Walter Thompson realised that protecting Winston Churchill had an impact on his personal life as he was sometimes called away urgently. Churchill, who had braved a stray bullet at the Siege of Sidney Street, was not to be intimidated by the suffragettes and caused a nuisance for his protectors. To the chagrin of the Special Branch, he would order a taxi and walk alongside the vehicle while his bodyguards, including Inspector Sandercock and Harold Brust, were forced to follow, on the lookout for suffragettes.

Kitchener's short stature was helpful; a taller detective would soon have attracted suspicion and so the man from Olney was often called up for observation duty. He felt that the ideal man for shadowing was the man who could spend a considerable amount of time in one street without drawing attention to himself, a great skill that was hard to master. One way Kitchener could avoid suspicion was to unlearn the constable's manner of walking and not to talk with an officer in uniform or wear police boots with plain clothes. Saluting officers in public was a dead giveaway. Despite these efforts at disguise, suffragettes became adept at spotting familiar faces. At one meeting, Flora Drummond recognised Kitchener but 'sportingly' said nothing and merely smiled and nodded at him as he began to take notes. Knowing her words were being recorded, she governed her tongue. Afterwards she bounded up to him. 'Well, you hav'na got much tonight, have ye!'

Kitchener's ability to write shorthand was invaluable and he was enthusiastically approached by senior officers who would dictate reports which Kitchener would type up. He attended political meetings both indoors and outdoors, mostly in Trafalgar Square, supervised by older constables or sergeants, who were impressed that he was able to jot down with great accuracy and speed what was said, despite the jostling crowd. Shorthand skills offered an officer the opportunity to record the exact wording. Furthermore, it could be difficult to take down speeches word-for-word amid the sound of hecklers; sometimes an officer had to concentrate only on the parts of a speech which had criminal implications.

Kitchener transferred to the Special Branch on 6 July 1912. Four days later, the Pethick Lawrences paid a visit to Christabel, whom the press had dubbed the 'elusive' Christabel. She and her mother had been staying in Boulogne to escape the hot Parisian summer. Still weak from hunger striking, the Pethick Lawrences were making their way to Switzerland. The group was faced with a predicament as the couple did not agree with the direction in which the WSPU was heading. They wanted Christabel to lead in London and were wary of the increasing emphasis the Pankhursts placed on the word 'war'. Christabel felt she could best direct the movement away from the grasping arms of the government. Aware of their differences in opinion, the Pethick Lawrences departed amicably and left for Switzerland the next day.

Events in July highlighted the sharper turn militancy was taking. Shortly after Kitchener's interview, Patrick Quinn represented the Metropolitan Police at the hearing of Katie Gliddon's brother, charged with grabbing Lloyd George and threatening him at a tumultuous Liberal meeting in South London. Women were not admitted so the male suffragists did the heckling instead, being thrown out on to the street, in one case bleeding and hatless. 'Charles Gray' was charged with grabbing Lloyd George on stage and pulling him to the ground. As a mêlée ensued, a side-wing, shaped like a tree, threatened to collapse. The magistrate did not accept the argument put forward by the lawyer instructed by Arthur Marshall's firm that Gray merely meant to touch Lloyd George on the shoulder and ask a question. As this was not Gray's first offence and similar events were happening 'constantly', and that ministers and others should be 'protected' by the law, a sentence was handed down for two months in hard labour, without privileges of Rule 243A.

The first major arson attempt was undertaken shortly after the Pankhursts' Boulogne meeting with the Pethick Lawrences. On 13 July, a night watchman prevented Helen Craggs and her accomplice from torching staunch anti-suffragist Colonial Secretary Lewis Harcourt's Palladian pile, Nuneham House. Like the Lympne trio, the women intrepidly took a boat to their destination. Among their arsenal were the following items: firelighters, a WSPU flag and 'The March of the Women' song sheets. 'They took care, however, not to endanger life,' said Kitchener on the WSPU in general. Yet, when affiliated members acted on their own initiatives, bearing the WSPU colours as they did so, there were some spectacular near misses which did not reflect well on the organisation. Helen was discovered in the estate's grounds, dressed in the colours, and was refused bail due to the severity of the crime: eight people were sleeping in the house.

When Christabel and her mother learnt that Emmeline Pethick Lawrence's lease on the WSPU's rented rooms at Clement's Inn was about to expire, Mrs Pankhurst secured flashier headquarters nearby. Lincoln's Inn House, on Kingsway, was an impressive Italian Renaissance-style, five-storey building which boasted a grand hall, an electric lift, tiled staircase, oak panels and arched windows. This opulence and enhanced functionality signalled the importance of the WSPU as an organisation of hard work and political muscle.

In spring 1913, in response to increasing suffragette militancy (which had included burning a church to the ground), Special Branch sent a memo to all police stations, requesting volunteers for the Special Branch who possessed a knowledge of French and shorthand. Walter Thompson, a PC from Paddington Green, sat the exam at 11 a.m. following his night duty. One early test for Special Branch recruits was the 'picking up-your-man' assignment. After studying a description of a man, new recruits were taken into a room in which thirty men were pacing up and down and they were given thirty seconds in which to identify the 'suspect'.

Thompson succeeded. Thompson became adept at getting to know a face by compartmentalising various sections, the left and right sides, the top and bottom half and from all angles. Nostrils could be stuffed with wadding or gum, cheeks could be blown out and suffragettes used fruit to plump out cheekbones, and moustaches could hide a man's features but, as Thompson learnt, eyebrows were hard to change while ears, which were unique, were a dead giveaway. Within his first few weeks, Thompson was stationed outside Lincoln's Inn, honing his skills of observation. He soon knew the key suffragettes by sight, particularly Mrs Pankhurst, and was recording their every move in great detail.

Kitty and Arthur Marshall were sent a subscription leaflet and a letter from Mrs Pankhurst, dated 16 October 1912, stating that the Pethick Lawrences were no longer working within the WSPU. No doubt watched and identified by Special Branch officers, the Pethick Lawrences had arrived on the doorstep of Lincoln's Inn House in early October. They were stunned to learn that there was no office space allotted to them, while staff moved around them sheepishly, refusing to speak to them. Mrs Pankhurst invited them to her room and gave them an explanation. She had reasoned that their wealth was becoming a liability as the threat of losing their estate might curb the organisation's militancy while sympathetic members would offer funds to help them, money which might otherwise have been given to the WSPU. Christabel advised them to continue editing *Votes for Women* but informed them the paper would no longer be the organ of the WSPU. The four later drew up separation terms in Boulogne. The Pethick Lawrences never fully recovered from the stinging experience, however, years later Christabel would resume contact with them. While the Pethick Lawrences kept *Votes for Women* afloat, Christabel founded the new WSPU publication, the *Suffragette*.

Having once been intended as a term of belittlement, the term 'suffragette' was now, according to the magazine's first edition of 18 October, a term 'of the highest honour'. Based across the Channel, Christabel's loyal team assembled the editions in London. Her subeditor was Geraldine Lennox, who had worked on *Votes for Women*, while Rachel Barrett, knowing nothing whatsoever of journalism, reluctantly took on the task of editing the *Suffragette* in the autumn of 1912. In mid-October, a new WSPU policy was announced at the Royal Albert Hall during a meeting at which the Pethick Lawrences were noticeably absent. After the swell of 'The March of the Women', Mrs Pankhurst, surrounded by women in white, argued for 'a unity of policy'. This display underlined the idea that the WSPU was an army, with one purpose, united behind one lady. As she hastened to add, the organisation's policy was not that of an ordinary army, bent on the death and destruction of its enemy. Rather, the WSPU emphasised that violence ran counter to the organisation's values; by instead targeting property and male-owned wealth, they would hit the government where it hurt.

By contrast, other suffrage campaigns continued to transmit messages of peace. Kitty was not much of a walker but the Beck sisters managed to persuade her to join them in the great five-week-long women's march from Edinburgh's Princes Street, to London in October and November. The event was organised by the Beck sisters' Sussex neighbour, Florence de Fonblanque, who was a member of various suffrage societies including the WSPU, the Women's Freedom League and the New Constitutional Society for Women's Suffrage. The marchers' motto was 'Co-operation and Good-will'. Kitty's group joined on the way. Wearing thick brown serge uniforms, green rosettes and brown hats with green cockades, they became known as the Brown Women. A covered van, bearing their petition, accompanied the ladies who carried a banner, 'From Edinburgh to London for Woman Suffrage'. Their belongings were pulled along by Fonblanque's mare, Butterfly. Initially, 300 women set out from Edinburgh; six of them making the entire journey but all the participants were heroes, averaging 15 miles a day. To the strains of 'See the Conquering Hero Comes', the walkers were met by thousands of sympathisers and headed to Trafalgar Square where Mrs de Fonblanque, much moved, told the crowd that their cause had support from friends everywhere. As usual, Asquith appeared to be unmoved by the women's hard and persuasive work.

On 5 December, Mrs Pankhurst opened the WSPU Christmas Fair at Lincoln's Inn House, unfurling the WSPU colour flag which flew on the rooftop of the building. Kitty had been in charge of Christmas decorations. As with the Prince's Skating Rink bazaar, Kitty oversaw the Farm Produce Stall, selling produce such as pickles and preserves, plum puddings and game, with donations from Princess Sophia Duleep Singh and Katie Gliddon. Christabel had announced that the aim of the WSPU policy of attacking letterboxes was to inconvenience the public into demanding that the government enfranchise women.

Arthur Marshall acted for two suffragettes convicted of pillar-box damage, Rosa May Billinghurst and Grace Mitchell. Both women conducted their own defence and in Rosa May's case, she related her reasons for the protest: she had witnessed the utter dejection of workhouse inmates and wanted to help change these women's lives. Grace was bound over to keep the peace while Rosa May went on hunger strike in prison. Her teeth were damaged and she sustained facial injuries. She was released after ten days. Incensed, Arthur told her that he would personally write to Basil Thomson to tell him of her experiences behind bars, but Thomson was not sympathetic to the suffragettes and not patient with those engaged in hunger strikes. While the suffragettes avowed not to assassinate cabinet ministers, Thomson nonetheless considered the suffragettes, with their arson attacks, property damage and window smashing, to be a more vexing problem than the Indian student agitation which had led to the murder of Sir Curzon Wyllie. And just before Arthur had defended Grace Burbridge who had poured phosphorus into a letterbox, Churchill was warning his wife to be wary of surprise packages.

9.

Infernal Machines

Early on the morning of 19 February 1913, Henry Elliott, a carter, drove past Lloyd George's holiday home, which was under construction near Walton Heath Golf Club, Surrey. It was 4.30 a.m. He saw a motor car leave and head in the direction of London. At around 6 a.m., there was an *éclat*, like the report of a large firearm. Half an hour later, James Gray, who was in charge of building works, turned up to work. The structure of the building had been completed and there was only the decorating outstanding. It was then that he saw that the night had swept away much of his work in an instant.

A servant's bedroom was the epicentre of the explosion. The walls were cracked and bulged outwards, the ceiling had given way and the window had blown out. Gray found an unexploded bomb packed with nails attached to a candle which would have burnt down and detonated the device. The candle had been lit, but theory had it that a draught from the explosion threw open the cupboard door, snuffing out the candle. Major Cooper Key, Chief Inspector of Explosives, concluded that the explosion was caused by black gunpowder. Special Branch detectives were put on to the case. Chief Inspector James McBrien (who would take over from Quinn as Head of the Special Branch in 1918) found a letter dated 10 January, which stated the potential defeat of the planned women's amendments to the Manhood Suffrage Bill meant that 'militancy was becoming more a moral duty and more a political necessity' and that 'if any woman refrain[ed] from militant protest against the injury done by the Government and the House of Commons to women and to the race, she will share the responsibility for the crime'. The handwriting having been verified, the letter would be used as evidence by the prosecution when Mrs Pankhurst was tried at the Old Bailey on 1 April.

McBrien and Quinn arrested Mrs Pankhurst on 24 February in Knightsbridge. She appeared in press snaps, Arthur Marshall by her side. The next morning, over a thousand local bystanders appeared outside Epsom Police Court to watch Mrs Pankhurst as she arrived in a closed car, wearing a motor veil and a thick, loose overcoat. Bystanders would have seen, but probably not even noticed, McBrien, the dark-haired man next to her who sported a moustache, who held her in custody. The pale-faced leader looked elegant in her mauve costume and black hat with its ostrich heliotrope-coloured feather. She accepted a bouquet of violets and lilies from Mrs Rosamund Massy, who had campaigned for the WSPU in almost thirty by-elections. Mrs Pankhurst was charged with 'counselling and procuring', and endorsing the perpetration of the bombing of Lloyd George's house, becoming 'an accessory before the fact to the commission of a felony by some persons unknown'. As she arrived, Mrs Pankhurst smiled at the many women in the court who wore WSPU colours. Archibald Henry Bodkin, a lean man and a known workaholic, prosecuted and Arthur advised Mrs Pankhurst who conducted her own defence. Arthur assured the court that Mrs Pankhurst would not undertake any further militant activity for a short duration of time. 'And not attend public meetings?' asked the magistrate. 'Oh, no!' Arthur tactically assured the Bench.

The next day, when Mrs Pankhurst arrived at court, there was a mysterious letter waiting for her addressed to 'The Magistrate for the Suffragettes', presumably a piece of hate mail. Arthur thought the missive was scurrilous and even Mr Bodkin suggested it be burnt. Mr Bodkin pointed out that to be guilty as charged as an accessory, Mrs Pankhurst did not need to have even been at the scene of crime. In his opinion, the explosion was serious: the lit candle was an inch from touching the shavings and would have exploded when the twelve workmen had arrived. Mrs Pankhurst questioned Charles Renshaw's reports of her meetings, therefore casting doubt on the evidence offered by the detective. Mrs Pankhurst was committed for a trial at Guildford's summer assizes. She refused to refrain from militant incitement and consequently was refused bail. A day after she threatened to go on hunger strike in jail, a date was hastily arranged for her trial at the Old Bailey on 1 April. Mrs Pankhurst agreed not to attend any more meetings and was released on bail until her trial.

Arthur was also working on the case of Olive Hockin, an artist who set fire to a pavilion at Roehampton Golf Club. Bodkin and Quinn attended her trial where it was revealed that inside the portmanteau she and her accomplice had dropped at the scene of crime were paraffin bottles, matches, hammers and a card with the inscription: 'Release Mrs Pankhurst – Refusing Bail to Mrs Pankhurst won't stop burning.' Arthur cross-examined McBrien who confirmed that he had never seen her before and had not associated her with the militant movement. Olive was tried at the Old Bailey on 4 April, charged with numerous offences, from damaging orchids at Kew to cutting telegraph wires and conspiring to set alight the croquet pavilion and furniture at Roehampton. She was found guilty of damage at Roehampton and was sentenced to four months in Holloway where she went on hunger strike and was moved to the First Division.

The case of R v. Emmeline Pankhurst commenced at the Old Bailey on 2 April. The air was stuffy, the court filled with balding men, constables, jury, and aldermen substantially dressed in scarlet. Bodkin and Travers Humphreys acted for the prosecution. Mrs Pankhurst's support group included Georgina Brackenbury, Annie Kenney and Rosa May Billinghurst, while Kitty's husband was at hand to offer advice from across the dock rail. Mr Justice Lush entered, dressed in scarlet. For two hours, Bodkin put forward his argument that the workmen might have been killed had the second device detonated. He also tried to show, through WSPU correspondence, that Mrs Pankhurst was not only in charge of the organisation but could incite or withhold militancy at her control. She pleaded not guilty to the indictment against her which was that she incited, counselled and commanded the destruction of the Walton Heath building. Transcripts of her speeches, in which she spoke of Josephine Butler as her childhood inspiration and drew parallels between the slave trade in the nineteenth century and the ongoing white slave trade in women and children, were submitted in evidence, complete with underlining to draw the prosecution's eye to guilty phrases. When asked why members of the WSPU had damaged Lloyd George's house, Mrs Pankhurst replied that, following the failure of the deputation of working women to rouse him to action, he needed to be shocked out of inactivity. Mrs Pankhurst accepted personal responsibility for the attack on Lloyd George's house and told her audience that the WSPU would not compensate him for the damage.

Detectives Charles Renshaw and Herbert Fitch, who had given evidence at Madan Lal Dhingra's trial, were present at a WSPU meeting at the London Pavilion on 27 January. In their report, they had underlined her words: 'Ours is guerrilla warfare.'

When she cross-examined the Special Branch detectives who had taken notes of her speeches, Mrs Pankhurst expressed her view that these were not accurate transcripts. She questioned the police and their methods of notetaking as being 'grossly inaccurate, and ignorant and ungrammatical'. The criticism, dealing a low blow with reference to the detectives' education and skill, was also intended as a slur on the police force's work, calling into question the validity of officers' testimonies. Charles Renshaw and his colleagues defended themselves ably. They answered that they had had training that gave them the necessary understanding of the difference between political and criminal statements and allowed them to use their well-honed discretion as to which notes to take. Not all words were included verbatim; only those that had a bearing on police procedure.

In her defence, Mrs Pankhurst spoke of unequal marriage laws, whereupon she was interrupted by the judge who was concerned with propriety and relevance of the information to her trial. In her speech, in which she pleaded not guilty because the indictment accused her of 'maliciously inciting', she claimed she was neither wicked nor malicious but had been motivated by noble ideals. Mrs Pankhurst was found guilty, with a strong recommendation to mercy and was sentenced to three years' penal servitude. Her response was thought-provoking, passionate and ominous. She considered herself to be a prisoner of war and, warming to her theme, told the court that she would stop at nothing to see justice done for women. The followers who had answered her call to arms *had* broken laws, she conceded. But they would not stop there. Even if she, the head of this writhing monster organisation, were to die, others would rise up to continue the fight. The authorities were facing a Lernaean Hydra, which it would be almost impossible to cauterise into submission.

In fact, her speech gave Mr Justice Lush the chills. He felt her crime would incite other groups and individuals to express their dissatisfaction through the destruction of property in acts in which others might be maimed or killed. He begged Mrs Pankhurst to reconsider her policy of incitement. On handing down his verdict, a large number of women shouted 'shame!' from the gallery to the court. They had to be ejected and Mrs Pankhurst was taken away by three wardresses. Lush ordered that in future, no more women would be admitted to his court without special permission. Supporters ordered taxi cabs to arrive at Holloway before Mrs Pankhurst, to cheer their leader as she disappeared into the prison. She would hunger strike her way out of Holloway.

The increasingly aggressive stance adopted by the WSPU alienated many would-be supporters and gave fuel to anti-suffrage campaigners. In April, Sir Arthur Conan Doyle told a meeting of the National League for Opposing Woman Suffrage that he felt that while there ought to be a distinction made between the constitutional suffragists and the 'female hooligans', the hooligans put women's suffrage back by two years. They would not see votes for women in a generation, he added, while Scotland Yard also took a dim view of Mrs Pankhurst's vow that she would fight to the bitter end. Indeed, the *Suffragette* was continuing to publish details of attacks on buildings and property, giving the crimes further publicity. Two 'suffragette bombs' were found in April and May 1913. The 'Milk Can' was discovered on 14 April, close to an entrance of the Bank of England at 3 p.m., when the area was particularly busy. No arrests were made, but the bomb was linked to the suffragettes by virtue of its hatpins which lay within a construction which was similar to other devices known to have been used by the suffragettes. On 8 May, Mr Harrison was cleaning the area near the Bishop's Throne in the chancel of St Paul's Cathedral, when he found a brown paper parcel, a ticking noise emanating from within. With alarming calmness, he took it to the Dean's Verger and on examination they found inside a Keen's Mustard tin which had been swathed in brown paper and editions of the *Suffragette*. Like the Milk Can bomb, it too was speedily submerged in water, the standard method of dealing with explosives.

While Mrs Pankhurst declared that no person was to be targeted, she could not guarantee that no one would be injured or killed. The act of conveying a bomb to a specified location put the public at risk. In 1894, the French anarchist Martial Bourdin tripped whilst carrying a device through Greenwich Observatory park, his death inspiring a scene in Joseph Conrad's *The Secret Agent* of 1907. On Majendie's recommendation, it was decided that London ought to have safe areas to which explosive devices could be brought and studied and, if necessary, destroyed. Duck Island in St James's Park received the go ahead and an office and dug-out were built. Although a handcart with rubber wheels had been designed for the purpose of conveying these devices, Kitchener remembered the devices being carried there by hand. The young man from Olney had not long been in the Special Branch when Superintendent Quinn drew him into the corridor and asked him to walk next to Detective Sergeant Lenehan to make sure that no one collided with him in the street. With that, Quinn re-entered his office. Kitchener quizzically looked at his colleague. 'It's all right, boy,' replied Lenehan, 'I have only got a bomb in my pocket to take over to the duck pond in the Park.' It was a device planted, his words suggest, by the WSPU, which had been found in a lavatory in Piccadilly Circus underground station.

'Cups of blood against a pale face.' This is how Sylvia Pankhurst described her appearance after she was forcibly fed. The image stayed with her for many years. By March, Reginald McKenna was under considerable pressure to revise the government's dealings with hunger-striking suffragettes whose crimes were severe; they could not simply be released. Forcible feeding was continuing to generate much negative press against the government, especially with the volume of published women's accounts of their experiences and their vulnerability.

An arrestingly intimate snapshot of a delicate Lilian Lenton in bed appeared in the press. The billowing pillows she lies on heavily support her frame. Too weak to sit upright, her body slides into the covers. Her hair is loose around her face and her gaze is turned pensively from the viewer, an image of Victorian female helplessness. Yet, together with 'Joyce Locke' (Olive Wharry's alias), she had entered Kew Gardens and had burnt down a teahouse. When the women were refused bail, Olive threw a book at the head of chairman of the Richmond Bench of Magistrates. Lilian Lenton went on hunger strike. Arthur, her solicitor, visited her in prison on the second day of her fast and was struck by her positive energy. A day later, she was forcibly fed, caught pneumonia and was speedily released.

Arthur Marshall fired off a letter to the Mayor of Richmond explaining the sudden illness which prevented Lilian attending her court hearing on

27 February. When Olive's case was heard at the Old Bailey on 7 March, a verdict of guilty was handed down. In her speech, she railed against the National Insurance Act which required working women to put aside three pence of their weekly earnings. Women had no say in the making of the law and ought not to be bound by laws and taxes, she maintained. She considered herself an outlaw and it was Asquith to blame for her actions, not Mrs Pankhurst. Olive was sentenced to eighteen months in the Second Division.

Scotland Yard kept a transcript of a speech George Bernard Shaw made against forcible feeding; as a sympathiser, he was being watched. Ralph Kitchener attended a meeting of the Men's Federation for Women's Suffrage on 17 March 1913 at the Memorial Hall, Farringdon, London. Senior surgeon at the London Hospital, Mansell-Moullin (his wife Ruth was a WSPU member), who had treated casualties of Black Friday, presided over the meeting and he put forward a measure to campaign for the immediate enfranchisement of women under equal terms to men. He felt that the government, with its broken promises, incited women to militancy and was to blame for the destruction caused. George Lansbury, who was on Scotland Yard's radar, praised Mrs Pankhurst's self-sacrifice: 'These women are entitled to adequate protection, and public opinion ought to compel the Government to use the Police in order to preserve order at public meetings. If that is denied, there is only one thing to do, and that is to arm ourselves.' Kitchener's report, stamped with Patrick Quinn's approval, was sent to the Under Secretary of State for his attention and subsequently housed at the National Records Office in Kew.

Arthur was concerned about Mrs Pankhurst, whose health was deteriorating rapidly. As soon as she was released on 12 April after serving nine days of her three-year sentence, Mrs Pankhurst went to stay in the nursing home at 9 Pembridge Gardens. She had been given a Special Licence under terms of which she was released for fifteen days, provided that she informed the police of her whereabouts. The 'Cat and Mouse' Act had not yet received the Royal Assent. Then, on 15 April, all WSPU meetings were banned in Hyde Park. As Nurse Pine was concerned that she might lose clients due to the noise and chaos caused by Mrs Pankhurst's stay, Mrs Pankhurst was transferred to Hertha Ayrton's home at 41 Norfolk Square. Hertha was profoundly affected by the image of Mrs Pankhurst laid out, virtually lifeless, on a white bed, with a silk handkerchief covering her head. Two sets of detectives guarded the house at the back and the front, which Hertha thought ridiculous as it was clear that Mrs Pankhurst was in no state to walk or to even be smuggled out with the help of a team to carry her. Two more police officers kept vigil outside the tube station across the road, more around the neighbouring houses. Whenever anyone emerged, a flurry of detective shadows would follow them. In Arthur's opinion, Mrs Pankhurst was not well enough to go back to jail when her licence expired on 28 April at 4.30 p.m.; if she was moved, she would die. Shouts of 'Murderer' greeted Patrick Quinn and Dr Smalley, Medical Inspector of Prisons, as they arrived on 29 April to assess Mrs Pankhurst's health. She was not re-arrested. When they left minutes later, the suffragettes shouted expletives: *Cowards, pigs, dogs, brutes, syphilis, gonorrhoea!* By the end of May, Mrs Pankhurst would be back in jail, arrested in Woking whilst attempting to travel by taxi to a meeting at the Pavilion and she would then be released again by the end of the month.

At Wormwood Scrubs Prison, Hugh Franklin, who had been caught whilst setting fire to an empty train carriage, was forcibly fed over 114 times. When he emerged, he was so emaciated he was almost unrecognisable. He never went back to jail. Reginald McKenna had believed that forcible feeding was not a suitable means of treating prisoners who were effectively political prisoners and had not been certified insane. But McKenna faced a dilemma: he could not set the arsonists free but he could not let them starve to death either. As the press-grabbing WSPU had stopped short of killing a member of the public and had therefore not given the government justification for treating them more harshly, the militants had to be handled with care and so they had to be kept alive.

Amidst cries of 'let them starve!', McKenna urged the government to pass the Prisoners (Temporary Discharge for Ill-health) Act 1913. Under the Act, which was referred to as a 'Cat and Mouse' measure, jailed suffragettes ('mice') were released under a licence – normally two weeks long – in order to recover sufficiently to be clawed back to prison by the police ('cats') to see out the remainder of their sentences. The Bill was passed with 296 votes in favour with only forty-three against. McKenna faced criticism from humanitarians for his measure against the women but had also received scorn from those who felt that hunger-striking suffragettes were subject to preferential treatment. Moreover, he could simply rile his contemporaries with his fact-driven, pedantic manner and an unflappable air of self-assurance. The swiftness of the Bill's passage through Parliament was not so much a panic-driven action against the police-slapping, house-burning women but a product of McKenna's calm persuasiveness and his successful presentation of facts and figures. McKenna's self-assurance was bolstered by a reluctance to ever admit he was in the wrong.

Hugh Franklin was the first 'mouse' to be released on 28 April under the 'Cat and Mouse' Act, after the Act received Royal Assent on 25 April. His licence stated that he was due to go back to jail on 12 May but could appeal to extend his recuperation time if he submitted to a medical inspection and satisfied the doctor. He was not to be absent from his address for more than twelve hours and could only change his address by telling the Commissioner of the Metropolitan Police one day in advance of the move. Franklin kept his release order, which had been publicly torn in half (and was subsequently taped back together), as a souvenir but had no intention of abiding by its terms. He fled to Dresden with Victor Duval's sister, Elsie, whose health was permanently weakened by her ordeals in prison.

A WSPU poster became representative of this government measure, depicting a suffragette mouse hanging from the mouth of a cat whose teeth cut into her limp, exhausted body. Christabel called on her readers to thwart the 'Cat and Mouse' Act, which, she argued, was a form of unending repeated torture, as Kitty herself had noticed. As she tells readers of her autobiography:

The 'Cat and Mouse' Act passed quite easily through the House of Commons, whereas the bill for giving votes to women had been before the House some twenty eight times … As the result of forcible feeding, the prisoner was so near death, that the government devised the idea of letting her out of Holloway and having her put in a nursing home or with friends until she was deemed well enough to be taken back to prison to finish her sentence. Meanwhile, two policemen were on guard to see that the wretched prisoner did not escape. That was the Cat and Mouse Act!!

The Act was a not just a cruel measure but a daft one too, as Kitchener points out: 'Personally, I could not conceive of a more naïve proposition being put forward, than to expect that women like the suffragettes, who were mostly educated women, would voluntarily return to prison at the expiration of their licence period.' Walter Thompson would rather not have to arrest Mrs Pankhurst; he found 'Cat and Mouse' arrests distasteful.

The mice would resort to all kinds of means to evade the clutches of the law. It was an offence not to declare one's current address. With that in mind, mice gave one address to the authorities and then flitted from one location to another, often finding a home with the tax-resisting Brackenbury sisters at 2 Campden Hill Square. Mrs Pankhurst also openly flouted the law by frequently changing location and keeping her whereabouts concealed from the authorities. Because she was the most famous mouse of them all, she required special treatment from both her enemies as well as her friends.

Even when the suffragette quarry was rediscovered at a different address, this caused further problems for the police. Kitchener's memoir shows up the flaws in this legislation from a policing perspective:

> Before very long many of the suffragettes were at liberty again and on the run; in a few cases where they could not get away from their addresses owing to our observation, or if they had been located by enquiries, all they had to do was to remain in-doors, for, although the Act gave police powers of arrest, it gave no right of entry, and the person concerned could be arrested only if found outside. Everything considered, it was not surprising that the Act soon became known as 'The Cat and Mouse Act.'

The Special Branch, which had been expanded to deal with protection duty, was now meeting the new challenge of enforcing the law in this manner. In the spring of 1909, Quinn had been in charge of thirty-four officers (minus those stationed at ports). In the month that Kitty had attempted to throw a stone at Gladstone's house at Littlestone, the Special Branch was boosted by sixteen men. With the passing of the 'Cat and Mouse' Act, Kitchener was given just under twenty new colleagues. By the beginning of the First World War there were eighty-one in Scotland Yard and thirty-three at the ports. The *Suffragette* was at pains to state that the WSPU did not bear a grudge towards the police. It was the government that was at fault. To spread the message of votes for women and to continue to reveal to the public what mice were undergoing, the WSPU encouraged donations to pay for copies of the *Suffragette* to be placed in institutions and libraries. Kitty as well as the Beck sisters were among those who subscribed.

10.

The Month of Flowers

Under hooded eyelids, Arthur Marshall regarded Ralph Kitchener who stood in the witness box, his observational skills put to the test. As Kitchener looked at Marshall, he would have seen a portly man in a crisp suit, a slight smile under his substantial moustache. Despite the self-assured look, under the desk Arthur's forefinger was nervously crooked inside his thumb, worrying at the skin. He had a lot on his mind. Kitty Marion described him as 'one of the bright legal lights in the movement in general and our own Solicitor, sort of legal Guardian Angel, in particular' and to Annie Kenney, he was 'that faithful friend of ours'. He had much to live up to. Archibald Bodkin also looked on as did Arthur Conan Doyle and Violet Asquith. The case in which this renowned suffragette lawyer and the young Special Branch detective had become involved would, as the papers mused, be a historic event in the fight for the vote.

In May and June, the Marshalls' Westminster home saw much activity. The year 1913 was distinctive not only in terms of the campaign for women's suffrage but of the Marshalls' own family history. Kinton Jacques and his new wife had two children, one of them a daughter who did not survive infancy. But in Brighton on 31 May 1913, just after the passing of the 'Cat and Mouse' Act, Norah gave birth to a boy. Kitty's half-brother, Arnold Kinton Rassam Jacques, was over forty years her junior. That month, too, suffragettes of Bow, Bromley and Poplar organised a spectacular procession and the old East End WSPU branches were amalgamated, separated from the WSPU and became known as the East London Federation of the Suffragettes (ELFS). Mrs Pankhurst would have issues with the name.

At 11 a.m. on 30 April, the police had pounced on the offices of the WSPU just as the next edition of the *Suffragette* was in process, barring the WSPU's staff from warning others by blocking the phones and standing many deep in the doorways. By 1 p.m., they had taken full possession of WSPU headquarters. Rachel Barrett, in charge of the newspaper's production, was arrested along with Harriet Kerr, the office manager (her architect father had designed homes on the separate spheres ideology); financial secretary Beatrice Sanders; Geraldine Lennox, the magazine's subeditor; and Agnes Lake, the business manager. These women, together with Flora Drummond and Annie Kenney, appeared at Bow Street Police Court.

As the WSPU headquarters were being raided, a teenager working in the office spotted some paper with Christabel's writing and correctly surmised that the slip of paper was Christabel's leading article. She surreptitiously hid the piece inside her blouse and later approached Grace with her find. Thanks to her quick thinking, Grace's success at securing £500 to pay the costs of the printer, which the team speedily found at the last minute, meant that the paper could go to press as planned, boasting Christabel's leader with the covering words: 'Raided!!' Grace went to see Mrs Pankhurst at Hertha Ayrton's flat and gave her a progress report. Mrs Pankhurst, who was very unwell, was thrilled to hear the news. But now the women needed to consider how they would continue to produce the paper themselves. Cicely Hale, who once attended the same French class as Violet Asquith, had to learn typesetting. Cicely had dived under the covers at the mention of Jack the Ripper, and now she had to face her fears and work late and walk home at night or in the early dawn light. Canadian Gertrude Harding would take the framed and typeset paper to various different locations for printing.

Before she set off across the Channel to see Christabel, Grace needed a disguise. Kitty gave her one of her fez toques and a heavy veil as accessories to go with what Grace thought of as the kind of 'racy' clothing which Kitty usually wore. As Kitty was much older than Grace, her disguise completely altered Grace's appearance. She did not seem to mind the clothing. It was preferable to the garments which the Actresses' Franchise League gave her to dress her either as a very old lady, so as to not attract suspicious eyes, or as a chorus girl whose clothing drew only the wrong kind of man. On that night, Arthur took Grace, dressed as Mrs Marshall, to the station, posing as her husband. Grace was wracked with nerves on her journey back from Paris. Her train at Southampton had been held up and 'tecs were looking for her. An older couple took pity on Grace, who looked travel-sick, and the elderly lady warded off the detectives when they put their heads into the first-class compartment. After avoiding the police at the station, Grace hailed a taxi and went straight to the Marshalls' home at 15 Gayfere Street, close to the Houses of Parliament.

The Marshalls owned at least two properties in Westminster where Arthur was registered to vote: one at 15 Gayfere Street and the other at 58 York Street. Evelina Haverfield, who was becoming disenchanted with the WSPU's increasingly violent stance and was no longer engaged in active service for the organisation, lived a few doors down at 51 York Street. Kitty and Arthur moved to Gayfere Street in 1913 and would keep their Gayfere Street address until the early 1930s. Number 15 was part of a smart, narrow and intimate street of Georgian flavour, formerly known as St John's Street until 15 June 1909. Until 1912, W.T. Stead had lived in Lord North Street which ran parallel to Gayfere Street. Had the Marshalls moved in before 1912, Kitty and Arthur and Stead would have virtually been back-to-back neighbours.

Still dressed as Mrs Marshall, Grace arrived at Gayfere Street. She would have seen that Kitty and her husband lived near the end of a row of short, terraced houses. Grace immediately noticed the home of a minister across the road, guarded by detectives. In her interview with Antonia Raeburn, she did not reveal his identity but it was highly likely that she was referring to Reginald McKenna. The Home Secretary, now in his fifties, was frequently seen striding home with a fleet-footed gait. He also had an athletic build, which he had acquired from his years on the rowing team at Cambridge. And his abode was located only a few doors down and on the opposite side of the road to the Marshalls' house near the point where Gayfere Street dramatically opened out on to Smith Square. Only a couple of years prior to Grace's visit, McKenna, the architect of the 'Cat and Mouse' Act, had commissioned Sir Edwin Lutyens to design 36 Smith Square. The substantial Neo-Georgian terraced townhouse with a red and grey brick façade, which fronts two roads, was designed to impress; in the 1950s, McKenna's home became a listed building. Directly opposite 36 Smith Square was the Queen Anne church of St John the Evangelist. Designed by Thomas Archer, St John's was one of fifty new planned London churches to be built as part of a commission of 1710 which recognised the needs of the city's growing population. St John's has been nicknamed 'Queen Anne's Footstool'. According to legend, when Archer consulted Queen Anne about the appearance of the church, the monarch impatiently kicked a stool upside down and instructed: 'Build it like that'.

Grace leapt out of the taxi and up to the Marshalls' door. She noticed that the downstairs lights had been extinguished but those upstairs were still alight. This meant that the Marshalls were still up but going to bed. Grace gave the danger knock then stood breathlessly on the doorstep, the 'upended legs' of St John's in the corner of her vision. Arthur ran down the stairs and opened the door. He was wearing his dressing gown and, seeing Grace, he looked about and assessed the situation. 'Oh, come in. I'll pay for the taxi,' he drawled nonchalantly. He paid the fare and shut the door as the cabman left. Once the door had closed, Arthur's tone changed dramatically. 'Grace Roe! There's a warrant out for your arrest!' Grace thought for a moment. She was, at least for now, safe within the walls of the Marshall home and she felt her confidence return. No longer tense with anxiety, Grace felt weary and travel stained. 'Well, I'll have a bath first anyway,' she calmly informed him.

Along with Annie Kenney, Flora Drummond and S.G. Drew, the manager of the printing company who had printed the *Suffragette*, the women arrested during the police raid on Lincoln's Inn House appeared at Bow Street Police Court on 2 May. Now in his eighties and suffering from ill health, Albert de Rutzen had retired. Henry Curtis Bennett took over as chief magistrate; Kitchener knew him as the Metropolitan Police magistrate from his Bow Street days. Bodkin was once again on the prosecution team. The police described the documents they seized, including 'Crime Record Books' which detailed which suffragettes had been arrested and when, a circular to the Young Hot Bloods as well as an incriminating letter found in Annie and Jessie Kenney's flat from Edwy Clayton, an analytical chemist and member of the Men's League for Women's Suffrage (this organisation was not militant but supported the WSPU and the WFL) and the Men's Political Union for Women's Enfranchisement who had plotted with the six women to set alight government offices, cotton mills and timber yards. Clayton had embarked on research on chemicals for explosive devices. Detective Inspector Hawkins of Scotland Yard had been to the flat where Annie and Jessie Kenney and Rachel Barrett were staying. By the time he arrived, Jessie had fled to Switzerland. Hawkins found a card in which Clayton reassured them that he was perfecting a chemical concoction. In it, Clayton asked his missive to be burnt. When Hawkins arrested Clayton, the chemist wrote to Arthur Marshall in, as Hawkins observed, the same handwriting as that which had appeared on the letter. Drew, the printer, gave an undertaking and the case against him was withdrawn.

Bodkin admonished the defendants for smirking in the court. Flora Drummond lamented his lack of humour. The police described the items they seized, including hammers and letters, and a suggestion from an engineer that the WSPU let loose a potent sneezing powder at music halls and theatres. It was Bodkin's musing over whether such a powder had led to an outbreak of sneezing at a recent Old Bailey trial that made Flora Drummond laugh, before she was ticked off. Annie Kenney was also distracted by Bodkin, but it was his appearance that fixed her attention. His head looked to her like an upturned egg and she tried to make sense of the placement of his ears and eyes. She felt that she could imagine the thoughts whirring around in his brain. Mr Bodkin reddened with annoyance as he spoke to Arthur. Annie was so absorbed in her thoughts and was staring at him with her blue eyes, abstractedly smiling at him, when Arthur whispered to her. 'Miss Kenney, Mr. Bodkin asks me to inform you that he does not appreciate your constant stare!' An anecdote in Kitchener's memoir describes Bodkin's dry sense of humour. Kitchener watched as a substantial constable laboured through a description of the material which was found at Lincoln's Inn House. Bodkin asked him about the whereabouts of a letter. 'In the vicinity of the desk,' he responded. 'Good heavens,' said Bodkin. 'The vicinity of the desk! You might as well say, "within the curtilage of the cupboard!"'

At noon on 8 May, the defendants entered the court, Harriet Kerr carrying a bouquet of flowers. Beasley read out transcripts of meetings from 21 October while Hawkins described the contents of seized letters suggesting mass pillar-box damage and the smuggling of a suffragette typist into the House of Lords to infiltrate the enemy. There were revelations that bottles of benzine had been found at Lincoln's Inn House. Kitchener and Detective Charles Hawtridge told the court whom he had seen entering and exiting Lincoln's Inn House in the last half of April. As this was happening, Arthur glanced from Kitchener to Flora Drummond, who was by then feeling decidedly unwell. Kitty's husband left the court and returned ten minutes later, informing the court that Flora needed medical care. The case was adjourned until a later date. At the conclusion of the trial on 15 May, all defendants were granted bail in varying recognisances and sureties, on the understanding that they would not undertake militant activities and would appear at the Old Bailey on 27 May.

The Suffragette Summer Festival was designed as a counterpoint to the trial, to show the public the softer face of the WSPU. A promotional scene, almost like a tableau from William Morris's *News from Nowhere*, greeted hot and weary Londoners. Women dressed in country clothes rode in on a flower-bedecked haycart, pulled by two horses, showering everyone who passed with petals. The publicity made a good impression. When the Festival opened on 3 June, it was well attended. Kitty had a starring role in the events. As before, Kitty had made requests for food donations, which met with a very positive response. The Lilley sisters gave their address as Holland House, Clacton-on-Sea and, after the raid of the WSPU offices, Kitty gave 15 Gayfere Street.

This was a serious fundraising activity to support the WSPU war chest and considerable effort was put into moving as well as enticing guests to part with their money. On entering, visitors saw a statue of Joan of Arc, her sword pointing towards a blue sky. Guests encountered a meadow in which stood a country barn, where chickens roosted in the beams, below them a lucky tub in the form of a bird's nest. In the barn Kitty, who wore a flowery muslin dress and replaced her mob cap with a wide 'picture-hat', sold farm produce, surrounded by flowers and soft music. Visitors then passed into a walled garden where they saw stalls. Gwen Cook's sweet counter was visible under a Japanese umbrella on the lawn. As well as being entertained by the Actresses' Franchise League, visitors wandered around the winding paths, overlooked by creepers, and could buy toys, trinkets and enjoy food such as shredded wheat, ice cream and strawberries, served by waitresses in period costume, with mob caps and flowers, while children dressed as elves and Brownies sold copies of the *Suffragette*. Kitty, known Suffragette General Provider, again garnered much praise. But against all this light entertainment lurked a darker plot. Emily Wilding Davison laid a laurel wreath under Joan of Arc's statue. She was also contributing to the suffragette fund, albeit privately, by putting into Kitty Marion's hand a small green chamois purse which contained a sovereign for 'munitions'.

The festival was overshadowed by Emily's accident at the Epsom Derby on 4 June and her subsequent death four days later. Christabel Pankhurst, who was faced with the challenge of incorporating her freelance act into WSPU policy, likened her to a religious martyr and spread the message that her death was a sign of how desperately women demanded the vote. The inquest at Epsom returned a verdict of 'death by misadventure'. Edith Garrud was not impressed by Emily's stunt: tying oneself to railings was too passive, but putting oneself in the path of a horse was downright foolish.

Sergeant Frank Bunn's notebook lists the items in Emily's jacket, including a helper's pass for the Suffragette Summer Festival. Bunn recorded her transportation, with kind assistance from a nurse, to a local hospital. The doctor's diagnosis of his unconscious patient was noted simply as 'concussion'. Mansell-Moullin operated on her brain but she died on 8 June, unaware of the hate mail that had been sent to her.

Greatly saddened, Kitty Marion used the sovereign which Emily had given her and purchased an arsenal with which to burn down the grandstand at Hurst Park Racecourse near Hampton Court on 8 June. When she was sentenced to three years' penal servitude, her supporters shouted 'No surrender!' and sang the 'Women's Marseillaise'. 'Guardian Angel' Arthur Marshall visited her in prison and he told her about other properties and venues which had been burnt down. This news cheered her up. Kitty Marion was released after serving solitary confinement, her tongue burning, yet still refusing the food and milk placed before her. She resisted when her fingerprints were taken and tore up her 'Cat and Mouse' licence, the pieces of which she sent to McKenna. With the help of a decoy, dressed and limping as she had done through weakness and pain of forcible feeding, she fooled police officers who were waiting outside what was known as a 'mouse hole' and made her way to Surrey. The term 'mouse hole' was inspired by the 'priest holes' in which clergy would take refuge during the reign of Elizabeth I when priests were often persecuted, tortured and killed. To frustrate searchers, sympathisers ingeniously built these tight spaces under stairs, in ceilings and behind panels. Kitty Marion was released on 8 July following a hunger and thirst strike. She would be on the run from the police again, looking for her own priest, or rather, suffragette hideout holes.

Grace Roe was in charge of planning Emily's funeral, which she attended in disguise, upset by the small organisational errors that only she noticed. The horse-drawn hearse was draped in purple, attendees wore the WSPU colours, interspersed with black and red, the latter being the colours of the funeral memorial leaflet. Two women who took part in the funeral procession were Ellen Dewar and her daughter Gladys. Ellen would join Mrs Pankhurst's elite group, the Bodyguard. Despite Gertrude Harding's efforts to protect her, Mrs Pankhurst was arrested as she made her way to the funeral. Her carriage, which followed the hearse, was empty. Mrs Pankhurst was only released again by the time of the appearance of the 20 June issue of *Suffragette*. She had begun a thirst strike.

In June, Arthur suddenly found himself in very hot water. Mrs Pankhurst, who was staying with Nurse Pine in Westminster, sent for Kitty. She asked her if she had seen the newspapers. Kitty had not yet as it was too early in the morning. Then Mrs Pankhurst showed her an account of the trial of a suffragette which featured a letter referring to Arthur and the sale of 'bombs' to the WSPU. As it turned out, the papers had printed a typo which should have read 'bonds'. Mrs Pankhurst urged Kitty to set about clearing Arthur's name and the newspapers duly paid £500 and costs. Arthur gave the money to Kitty which she, to great applause, donated to the WSPU at an Albert Hall meeting.

Edwy Clayton was sentenced to twenty-one months in Wormwood Scrubs, went on hunger strike and was released under the 'Cat and Mouse' Act. His reputation was forever tarnished. Rachel Barrett received nine months and found herself staying at the Brackenburys' home with nurses Pine and Townend in Pembridge Gardens, attended by Dr Flora Murray, assistant anaesthetist at the Chelsea Hospital for Women. Despite being watched by the Special Branch, Rachel Barrett slipped out of 2 Campden Hill Square on numerous occasions to speak at meetings, only to be re-arrested. Annie Kenney, who movingly referred to her modest upbringing and desire to effect a change in women's lives in her defence, was sentenced for three years. She told the jury that she would be out in three days.

11.

The Rules

All at once, she felt herself fly backwards. Her stockinged legs gave way and the ceiling tilted downwards rapidly to meet her eyes. A flash of white greeted her as she caught a glimpse of her gi and belt. Strands of hair came loose as her arm grappled instinctively in the unforgiving air for a hold but found none. Down she went, her body thudding on the quilted, horsehair canvas mat. Despite expecting the move, she gasped with the suddenness of it all. As the world righted itself, she looked around at the faces who observed her, some interested, others amused. Kitty was learning to take a tumble and Mrs Garrud, who guidingly had her arm, broke her fall.

Shortly after the 'Cat and Mouse' Act was passed, Grace Roe asked Gertrude Harding to form a protective shield around Mrs Pankhurst, known simply by the singular term, the Bodyguard. Sporty Gert was 24 and had travelled abroad by herself, showing bravery and initiative and she also demonstrated her commitment to the cause. When she was given the task of blowing up Leith Hill Tower in south-east England, Annie Kenney interviewed her rigorously to make sure that she was not a spy for Scotland Yard. The Leith Hill Tower job was abandoned as the risk of harm to others was considered to be too great, but Gert and Lillian Lenton instead combined forces to destroy orchids at the Royal Botanic Gardens at Kew. It was a highly significant move; in February, Charles Renshaw had looked up from his notetaking at the London Pavilion to see Mrs Pankhurst presented with a resplendent bouquet of orchids amidst applauding laughter in honour of the deed. The team Gert assembled brought a variety of skills to the table but first and foremost they were tested, as Gert was, on their loyalty to Mrs Pankhurst and the cause of women's suffrage.

Some Bodyguard members were more eager to spar than others and Mrs Garrud was not above grasping a reluctant individual's hand and challenging them to extricate themselves from her grasp. Although she had sufficient balance to swing a golf ball, Kitty was not particularly athletic, however, she could channel her anger for Dearest's sake. By contrast, Australian-born novelist Ida Wylie, who became the captain of the Bodyguard, simply adored physical fighting. Her womanising father had been a drunk with a mercurial temper rendering her childhood an unsure existence. To build herself up psychologically and physically she taught herself cycling, which strengthened her legs, and at 19 she sold her first short story. Despite her position within the Bodyguard and her antipathy towards detectives, Ida actually had quite a bit of time for the beat bobby even though she got a buzz from knocking off a policeman's helmet in a just cause. She had once asked a police officer how he would feel if he, like his female contemporaries, was regarded by a male interlocutor to be on a par with infants and lunatics. 'I wouldn't like it,' he responded, 'I'd black his eye for him.' She felt bobbies to be kind and well respected. British mobs, it seemed, treated women with less cruelty than in other countries, with impoverished Londoners often generously linking arms to protect women. After she and a friend threw stones, even sauce bottles and sardine tins, wrapped in messages of 'No Forcible Feeding' at Harley Street windows, they would run back to Edith Garrud's dojo, hide their equipment under the mats and don their gis. Officers would knock at the door and Mrs Garrud would tell them in a most indignant tone that they were disturbing a women's jujitsu class. This bought time for the stone throwers to gather their wits about them before an officer was eventually let in, seeing nothing untoward.

Gwendoline Ethel Cook, who had manned the sweet stall under a Japanese umbrella at the Festival of Flowers, thought of herself as a mouse of little consequence. After her father, a Birmingham doctor, had been declared bankrupt and had taken his own life, her mother died too and Gwen went to stay with friends in India. Her recollections would have interested Ida, who was writing novels set in India. Gwen travelled with her friends in the Himalayas for three months, unchaperoned and only accompanied by porters and servants. She discussed women's suffrage with her friends with contributions from the growling and squeaking macaques, the shadows of the great peaks gathering in the dusk. Votes for women had seemed a million miles away but here in Edith Garrud's dojo, the issue was up close, only a front punch away. Gwen, who gave the police the name Ethel Cox when she was arrested (her mother was called Ethel), was one of the youngest members of the Bodyguard but was lean and stood tall at 5ft 8in. She pulled a mean face, narrowing her blue eyes, when she was on the mat or if she grappled with a bobby outside Kingsway during her Bodyguard duties, tugging at his braces until his trousers came down.

The Bodyguard were to abide by a set of rules. They had to attend drill and were required to be present at specified meetings. Sometimes this consisted of standing outside a venue where Mrs Pankhurst was speaking and refusing to move, as Joyce Nettlefold, who would become the first female mayor of Cape Town in 1959, learned to do. The women grasped each other's arms and stopped police officers from entering which gave Mrs Pankhurst and the crew within time to get her out. When she was asked to become a speaker, Joyce jumped at the chance, as she considered this a step up from Bodyguard work – even when her hair was torn at meetings and she and her sister were threatened by crowds who tried to upend the wagon on which they stood. Joyce marvelled at the choreography of the WSPU and at the silver-haired Mrs Pankhurst who drew such enormous crowds with her fervent persuasiveness.

It was instilled into prospective suffragette jujitsuka that membership of the Bodyguard was an honour. When Kitty joined up, she was required to pay at least two pence a week for the privilege of putting herself in danger. The Bodyguard was split up into two streams with Company B being the backup team. Company A comprised an elite corps of women under 40 years old, women such as Lilian Lenton. Just as a member of Company B who showed promise and pluck could be promoted to Company A, if she was absent from drill for more than two weeks (as Lilian might be if she went on her many flights from the police), she could just as easily be struck off and relegated to Company B.

Known as the 'tiny, wily Pimpernel', Lilian Lenton aimed to burn two buildings a week and staged some daring escapes from the police. On one occasion when she was wanted by the police, 100 detectives were stationed outside the house in which she was recovering. Fifty heavily veiled women entered the house one morning and then rushed out of the front door. The police didn't know who to follow! Like other mice, Lilian sheltered at a house in Harrogate called 'Pomona'. To escape the clutches of the authorities, Lilian had to evade the beam of light that was trained on the house. Dressed as a boy, she dived into a coal chute, silently climbed a 5-foot wall, then entered the garden next door, only to find a detective standing about smoking and tapping his stick. Lilian was caught in the beam but her friend struck the detective which allowed Lilian to get away.

The little boy who lent Lilian his clothes was Leonora Cohen's son, Reginald. Leonora was surely the most famous Bodyguard, who would later be awarded an OBE for her social work. Just before her death, at the age of 105 in 1978, she commented that she was still an undischarged prisoner. Leonora was born just south of Leeds in 1873. Her father was an artist who died young and she felt keenly that, while her mother was hardworking, she was voteless and she suffered much prejudice as a result of being fatherless. She trained as a milliner and then married Henry Cohen, the son of Jewish immigrants from Warsaw who ran a thriving jewellery business. Like Arthur Marshall, Leonora's husband was at the ready with alibis, hot drinks and emotional support. Despite receiving threatening letters from anti-suffragists, Henry took her to meetings and kept an eye out for her while Reginald helped her sell suffragette publications and weathered taunts from his classmates.

When the Bodyguard met for drill and practice under the eyes of Edith Garrud, Leonora's success at the Tower of London was still relatively fresh in their minds. The women took lessons in the art of swinging Indian clubs against soft targets but Leonora proved that she already had an excellent sense of aim. On 1 February 1913, she set off for the Tower of London, armed, as any tourist would be, with a guidebook on the oldest surviving royal building in Britain. She was so nervous that she missed her tube stop. When she arrived, she bought some postcards to delay her planned event. She saw the White Tower, a statement of Norman supremacy, a shock of the new to Anglo-Saxon England. It would never become any easier for her, this process of steeling herself for an act of militancy.

As well as being an innovative royal residence, the Tower was also famously a place of torture, incarceration, execution, defence and a Fenian target. Leonora may have been considering the Tower's history and its symbolic significance when she affixed, using a purple ribbon, a luggage label to the iron bar which she was going to use to proclaim a new, feminist order: 'Jewel House, Tower of London. My protest to the Government for its refusal to Enfranchise Women, but continues to torture women prisoners – Deeds Not Words. Leonora Cohen.' On the reverse was written: 'Votes for Women. 100 Years of Constitutional Petition, Resolutions, Meetings & Processions have Failed.'

Leonora strode into the Jewel House and when she caught sight of a group of schoolboys, she pretended that she was with their group as their teacher. Then her moment came. Leonora, a tall woman, managed to throw a crowbar above their heads. The glass cabinet, which showcased the insignia of the Order of Merit of King Edward VII, smashed. 'Why did you do that?' demanded Yeoman Warder Ellis. 'It is my protest at the treachery of the Government against the women of Great Britain,' she informed him. Amidst this maelstrom, the Curator of the Armouries, Charles John ffoulkes, scribbled calmly in his day book for 1 February: 'Suffragette outrage in the Jewel House, one case broken. No damage in Armouries.' Leonora defended herself in court. She was charged with causing damage of more than £5 to the jewel case. Through their contacts, the Cohens found a cabinet maker who stated that it was possible to repair the case for under £5. Leonora was acquitted.

Like Leonora, Lillian Mary Dove-Willcox ran a guesthouse for recuperating suffragettes, hers boasting views of the Wye Valley. Lillian, who was five years younger than Kitty, had found it impossible to eat when Mrs Pankhurst was hunger striking. Bristol-born Lillian was already a widow by the time she joined the WSPU in 1908. She soon became involved in a series of arrests and releases until her pro-suffrage father-in-law manipulatively wrote to *Votes for Women* to shame his daughter into ceasing her militant activities as she was giving the cause a bad name. The WSPU backed her up, stating that while hunger striking was not officially espoused by the movement, his mere sympathy with the cause would be ineffectual.

Helen Crawfurd would become the representative of the Communist Party and the first woman councillor in Dunoon in the 1930s. The daughter of a master baker, she was born in the Gorbals in 1877, the fourth child in a family of seven. She saw her older brothers practise boxing with their father, following the Queensberry Rules. After marrying a clergyman, she began preparing for missionary work, where she encountered the writings of Josephine Butler who had campaigned tirelessly and successfully for the repeal of the Contagious Diseases Acts. Helen joined the WSPU in 1910 and was moved to militancy when a meeting that she attended was broken up by students setting fire to pieces of paper, which provoked an outbreak of sneezing. While the scene caused some amusement, Helen was furious. She wanted to help any way that she could and took part in the window-smashing campaign in March 1912. If Mrs Pankhurst came up to Scotland, she would be ready to protect her.

Not only were the Bodyguard on the run from the police, but they, like other women, could receive unwanted attention from the criminal underworld or even just the ordinary man in the street. The Bodyguard knew of the many risks they took in traversing the streets of London at night. In 1887, there had been the case of young seamstress Elizabeth Cass whose arm was grabbed in the darkening streets by a policeman as she attempted to buy gloves – no respectable woman would be seen without them. He told her he had been watching her and now she was under arrest. PC Bowden Endacott had mistaken her for a prostitute. The case became a cause célèbre and was almost the undoing of Endacott's career. Importantly, the surly judge who presided over her case ominously sent a warning out to every woman to know her place. Peering through his spectacles, he informed her that no respectable woman walked Regent Street at 10 p.m. and stopped to exchange words with a gentleman. The implication was that if Miss Cass found herself in Regent Street, charged again for behaviour considered suspiciously indelicate (even if this just to ask a male pedestrian the time), she could be fined or sent to prison.

John Ruskin had advised houseproud middle-class women that they were better off in the home, which they ought to beautify while their husbands braved the temptations and dangers of the world. But such visions of Victorian and Edwardian womanhood were mythical and outdated given the numbers of women who worked and lived in cities undertaking a wide variety of jobs as, for example, tour guides, underground conductors, Salvation Army representatives, milliners, typists, guides who helped women find their way around London, and shop workers. Now that the women were engaged in criminal activities, the police, it seemed, could look for any excuse to arrest them, even, as they had often done before, cite difficulties in discerning 'respectable' women from prostitutes as their clothing styles could be similar. But early detective fiction showed that intrepid women might not be kept back by clothing. In 1864, in *Revelations of a Lady Detective*, Mrs Paschal infiltrates a secret society and does not think twice about discarding her crinoline in order to climb down into an underground passage. Anything was possible, as was demonstrated in the figure of Richard Marsh's lip-reading jujitsuka detective Judith Lee, who was taking the *Strand Magazine* by storm. As women dressing for the coronation parade had learned, Mrs Garrud's School of Jujitsu, at 8 Argyll Place in London's West End, was strategically placed near Regent Street, conveniently very close to the famous department store Liberty's, a woman-friendly space in the city, famous for its luxurious fabrics. Her Bodyguard would be out at all hours, buying gloves and beating bullies.

Detectives could also show chivalry and have an amicable interaction with their quarry. As Kitchener learnt, trailing a suspect was not as exciting as was commonly represented in crime thrillers. During lengthy observations, a detective, often working by himself, had to be extra vigilant whilst following the unpredictable movements of quarry who may suspect that they are being watched. Kitchener became skilled at identifying which individual in an interaction was the key one. Wardrobe mishaps entertained him on particularly dull shifts. Kitchener was trailing a newly recuperated mouse down Euston Road whose licence was due to expire.

> She reached the halfway point across the busy road and had stopped on an island when an updraught from the underground railway swept through the ventilator underneath her by a passing train. The result was what might be expected; this was, of course, before the days of mini dresses, and the upsurge of air from the grating at once took charge of the lady's skirts and held them suspended like an open umbrella during the passage of the train. Fashions in ladies' underwear have certainly changed since then! Two or three other persons besides myself could see what was happening and were greatly amused, but the suffragette herself seemed to take no notice and stood there quite unperturbed until the roadway was clear for her to continue her walk.

On another occasion, Kitchener's mouse had just slipped into an office and as Kitchener waited, an elegant lady began to cross the Strand. As she came up to the traffic island, she too suffered an unfortunate wardrobe mishap:

She was approaching the refuge in the middle of the street when part of the white undergarment began to show below the bottom of her dress; she stepped on to the refuge in the middle of the street, and as she did so she noticed that something was restricting her movements, and glanced down at her feet. At this point the undergarment fell completely to the ground and the lady saw what was amiss. She obviously had a keen sense of humour, and with a smile turned around to see if anyone else had noticed what had happened, but no one appeared to have taken any notice. She therefore stepped daintily out of the obstructing piece of attire and continued her walk still smiling, leaving whatever it was behind her on the refuge. By chance, almost at the next moment, a street cleaner came along with his barrow; he at once noticed the piece of material and stooped to pick it up. As he opened it out and found what it was, he too glanced around to see if he had been noticed, and he, too, thought he was unobserved. Hurriedly he then rolled the article up, opened the box at the back of his barrow, placed the garment therein and continued on his way. As far as I could see, no one of all the persons passing either way at the time, had paid the slightest attention to either the beginning or end of the episode.

The incidents show the plucky ways in which women might react to the embarrassments and inconveniences of their clothing in the public space.

As Kitty had herself found out, the marital home was not a 'queen's garden'. If the law could and would not protect women in their own homes, women, it seemed, would have to find their own form of self-defence. Edith Garrud choreographed Cecil Armstrong's playlet, *What Every Woman Ought to Know*, which was enthusiastically received in 1911 in London's East End. The play tells the story of Liz who overpowers her costermonger husband Bill, telling him: 'When you're drunk, I'll always be a match for you.'

Ellen Dewar and her daughter Gladys knew about the risks of the metropolis. Like Kitty, Ellen joined the Bodyguard in middle age. Ellen Dewar brought her unique skillset to the Bodyguard: she could offer disguises. Her husband Fred was a Paddington 'court hairdresser' who inherited his business from his father. His work involved tending to the hair and beauty requirements of members of the court, aristocratic families who lived nearby, and politicians. The props he provided were surely a match for Scotland Yard's makeup department and in fact, his premises were raided at least once. Fred was sympathetic to the cause and supported his wife, involving himself on at least one occasion in a protest at the Royal Opera House when Ellen and others showered the audience below with suffragette literature.

Disguise was not only a popular Edwardian and pre-war pastime; makeup and make-believe were also vital tools in the Bodyguard's box of weapons. Suffragette mice could dress up as men or, as in Lilian Lenton's case, as Leonora's son, but a certain amount of acting was necessary; Ethel le Neve was caught out by her display of affection towards Crippen. But the correct props were needed, too. Kitchener encountered a mouse clad in a man's clothing, heading for St Pancras Railway Station. The giveaway for him had been the lady's umbrella that the 'man' was carrying.

Of average height and build, Ellen acted as a decoy for Norah Dacre Fox. Ellen would stand up to speak and then be erroneously pursued by the police while the real speaker got up to address the crowd. Ellen's daughter, Gladys, was born in 1897 and was what she described as 'a junior suffragette'. Eerily, Ellen knew of a case of a girl called Angela who was a victim of the white slave trafficking trade. The girl was going to visit her aunt but did not reach her destination of Marble Arch. The police found no trace of her. Ellen wrote to Mrs Pankhurst who, within a few days, traced the bus on which she had travelled, the conductor telling her that a lady and a gentleman had suddenly alighted just before Marble Arch because their 'daughter' was taken ill.

The author Elizabeth Robins had concerned herself with the subject of white slavery. In 1907, she had famously written the play *Votes for Women!* and its accompanying novel, *The Convert*. She also offered her Sussex Backset Town house as a place of recuperation for suffragette mice. Published in the year of the Bodyguard, her international bestseller, *Where Are You Going To ...?* (published in America as *My Little Sister*) details the narrator's fruitless search for her abducted sibling, Bettina. Robins had confided in her diary about the challenges and dangers that women faced. She had written in her curling hand that men often attempted to take liberties with her, stalking her across street crossings and lonely beaches. At one point during her acting career, Robins, who was the first actor to play pistol-wielding Hedda Gabler in an English adaptation of Ibsen's play, even went to bed with her own gun under her pillow. Robins' fiction warned women; asked them to look for signs of danger; to read the features, clothing and demeanour of those around them; and to reconsider getting into a cab or accepting a drink from a stranger. She encouraged women to use their intuition. Kitty Marion, also a suffragette and actor, was approached by an elderly couple posing as theatre producers. They became strangely testy when she refused their generous offer to take her to Paris, dress her in finery and make her 'a woman of the world'. But she listened to her instinct and backed away. When the narrator of *Where Are You Going To ...?* approaches the police, the inspector offers to circulate an enquiry and to watch various houses. His blunt pencil is a symbol of his impotency while the girl realises that even Sir Edward Henry, the 'man with the sword', in all his fine regalia, whose likeness she spots at the police station, cannot help her. When she was given the title of Commandant, police officer Mary Allen made it her life's work to track down and bring to justice the likes of traffickers who haunted the top decks of buses, armed with hypodermic syringes. However, Angela, like her fictional counterpart Bettina, was never seen again.

12.

Dancers in the Dark

Rachel Barrett was determined to put up a fight. To make her yield, the male warder inserted his own fingernails under hers, right down to the quick. The prison team kept her elbows below the table and tried to bring the paper to her finger to make it easier to extract a print but she made it impossible for them to roll the balls of her inked fingers across the paper. The only satisfaction she could glean from the ignominious experience was that, judging by their expressions, the results were less than perfect. Kitty Marion, who had been arrested for burning down the Hurst Park Racecourse, struggled so much that the prison staff only managed to extract an indistinct mark. Her accomplice was Clara (Betty) Giveen who was visited in Guildford Prison by Arthur Marshall. He managed to talk the staff out of taking her prints.

During the militant suffrage campaign, memoranda were sent to all prisons giving orders on how to compile dossiers on newly arrested women. One of these memos advised that 'agitators' for women's suffrage convicted of criminal offences (not minor ones such as obstructing traffic) be photographed on entering prison and have their prints taken. Force could be used, particularly if they were likely to hunger strike and be released under the 'Cat and Mouse' Act and authorities could erase the restraining arms of wardens and fill in the spaces with white, grey or black pigments. Mary Richardson, who was sent to Holloway for striking a policeman, had her prints taken and her photograph was snapped just before she had a chance to cover her face. The wardresses held her by the arms. When it came to obscuring their faces from the photographer, suffragettes used scarves and motor-veils to excellent effect. To try to catch an individual suffragette, the prison employed a photographer with a special lens from Scotland Yard and waited for her to approach a specified area, surreptitiously marked by a few crumbs. Arthur Barrett was engaged to take snaps of the militants. Concealed in the police van at the entrance yard, Arthur duly took photographs of suffragettes as they shuffled about in the prison yard, too tired to put up their hair, and exchanged news with each other. The arrangement was so secret that a codename was adopted for his telephone conversations with Basil Thomson. If, using his lingo, Thomson required Arthur to photograph some suffragettes outside Scotland Yard then he would request that 'Banjo' should 'photogram' the 'wildcats' outside 'New Varsity House'!

On 14 July, Annie Kenney, a slim figure clad in white, made a surprise appearance at the Pavilion, together with birthday girl Mrs Pankhurst, whose voice quivered with weakness as she told the audience that 'a defi-ant deed is worth innumerable thousands of words'. Annie gave a speech in which she challenged the police to arrest her. Mrs Pankhurst praised the WSPU for carrying on the fight, despite the government's attempt to break their spirits by raiding Lincoln's Inn House. 'I would rather be a rebel than a slave,' she emphasised. 'I would rather die than submit; and that is the spirit that animates this movement. ... Kill me or give me my freedom: I shall force you to make that choice.' Fights broke out in which umbrellas and sticks were used. The Bodyguard knew that their own vulnerable points were their neckties and long hair and these were in a dishevelled condition when they arrived at the police station. Annie was forced into a cab amidst shouts of 'shame' and 'cowards' from the police. The attention focused on Annie, Mrs Pankhurst managed to slip away to Ada Wright's flat off Little Smith Street and Great Smith Street, round the corner from Kitty's Gayfere Street home.

At a subsequent meeting, Annie managed to fool Charles Renshaw, whom she described as 'my own special detective'. She was dressed as an elderly lady, complete with elastic-sided boots and an ebony cane, with plums in her cheeks to fill out her face. She auctioned her licences and was arrested again. After a stay at 2 Campden Hill Square, which overlooked an immaculately maintained private square – this key location, the home of Hilda Brackenbury and her daughters, had by now earned its famous sobriquet 'Mouse Castle' – she arranged to be delivered to an address near the Pavilion and to have two baskets ordered for her, one marked 'Marie Lloyd, Pavilion. Luggage in advance.' The first one was directed to a City of London office and acted as a decoy while the labelled one was to contain Annie herself, stuffed in alongside wads of paper. The transportation of the baskets was overseen by a sympathiser, disguised as a workman. Thus Annie, presumed to be stage paraphernalia, was carried on to the stage of the Pavilion by unsuspecting, sweating, cursing couriers who bemoaned the supposedly selfish actress for the weight of her luggage.

The police had been on the lookout for Annie. It was rumoured that she would be clad either as a widow or as a man with a moustache. But they were in for a surprise when she suddenly appeared on stage. Ida Wylie and the Bodyguard held the fort for five minutes to allow Annie to say a few words. When Annie was recaptured, they went back home to recuperate before preparing for sentinel duty outside Holloway where she was now residing. A sympathiser lent the WSPU rooms opposite the prison where the sentinels could change and rest as they alternated watch duty every four hours. Observing the prison by day was often uneventful, but by night, rowdies would come to the area and threaten the women and so they had to do guard duty in groups of four, watching in trepidation as mobs crept towards them in the darkness.

At midnight on Saturday, 19 July, there was a constant stream of male and female visitors dressed in evening attire to Great Smith Street where Mrs Pankhurst was now staying. The police kept their eyes trained on the location. A taxi pulled up outside the entrance to the flat on Little Smith Street, which lay at right angles to Great Smith Street. Two women entered the building, shortly afterwards accompanying a frail, veiled lady outside, intending to guide her to the taxi. When officers drew in, there was a scuffle, shouts, cheers and the sound of police whistles, but the lady was seized and driven off to Holloway. The taxi proceeded several hundred yards down the road before the police realised that they had arrested the wrong woman. Mrs Pankhurst had in fact walked behind the veiled lady, slipped out through the crowd into a back street and was driven off. No one knew where she had disappeared to and repeated enquiring knocks at the house were met with silence and darkness within.

Kitty and Arthur were chuckling to themselves. Mrs Pankhurst had escaped under the light of the moon to Theydon Bois. To Kitty's relief no one seemed to perceive the suspiciousness of the sound of the taxi cab as it came up their hill. But precisely which hill was this? Kitty does not say and despite many enquiries and archival research, the exact location of the Marshalls' house, the romantically titled 'Kenilworth', has not yet surfaced. This was indeed an excellent hideout, swallowed up by history. Having earned a break, Kitty, Arthur and Mrs Pankhurst spent a relaxing Sunday lounging outside in the garden on deckchairs, amused by newspaper reports which claimed that Mrs Pankhurst had been arrested.

On Monday, they drove by car early in the morning with a veiled Mrs Pankhurst to the Pavilion for the usual WSPU meeting. But she did not even make it to the stage. Detective Inspector Riley, who was in charge of the police, was 'severely handled'. Emily Diana Watts' *The Fine Art of Jujutsu* had featured a manoeuvre which started out with the jujitsuka putting their right arm on their partners' waists, giving the deceptive initial appearance of being a waltz. At the Pavilion, Kitty was not engaged in a sedate turn around the ballroom; her dance was more frantic in nature. Kitty spun around in a scrum with Riley, gripping on to the detective's tie with one hand whilst holding a small suitcase in the other. The dance only finished when she allegedly slapped him across the face. Mrs Pankhurst quickly instructed Kitty to make an announcement at the meeting, expressing the leader's regret at not being able to attend. A young man came to help Mrs Pankhurst's protectors and the whole group was shoved into a room in which there stood a table with suffrage literature and badges. Then the lights went out.

Kitty heard a table overturn. The young man was cut on the head by an officer brandishing a stick in the dark. Kitty did not have the chance to make her speech for Mrs Pankhurst as she was taken to Vine Street. A considerable number of uniformed constables – 150 – poured into the hall behind Mrs Pankhurst. Hatpins were allegedly used by the suffragettes. Police officers were stationed outside the Pavilion to keep the pavement clear. As Mrs Pankhurst was taken to Holloway, the crowd roared *Cowards! Assassins! Murderers!* Members of the WSPU followed in hot pursuit. Outside the prison, Mrs Pankhurst bid her adieu, waving a handkerchief. Within a week, she would be back at Great Smith Street and back on the stage at the Pavilion, wheeled in on a bath chair, in need of a blood transfusion.

Although the police had been requested to tread with more care when it came to arresting women so as to avoid bad press, some self-defence situations were so extreme that these codes of behaviour were mutable, particularly so in the dark where the normal rules might not apply. Cecil Bishop's description of another fight at the Pavilion offers a sense of the panic and confusion Kitty and others felt in the darkened room, albeit from a different perspective: '[W]hen you have an umbrella point sticking in your eye, and a wooden chair is about to descend on your head you cannot worry about the sex of the combatants!' Just as Kitty and Grace Roe wore cardboard armour, officers sometimes considered home-made solutions to self-defence problems. As Bishop was a detective and not a constable, he did not wear a helmet but instead had crafted a reinforced, padded cap for himself which he wore to the Pavilion and his many confrontations with the suffragettes. The headgear protected him when he was assaulted with music stands when a fight with the WSPU broke out in the Pavilion's orchestra pit.

On the day of Kitty's trial, 22 July, Nina Boyle of the Women's Freedom League hired a launch and pulled up alongside the terrace of the House of Commons just as tea was served. Mr Muskett, who presided at Marlborough Street Police Court, commented that Riley had been subjected to such violence and lynching that he was gasping and almost 'in a state of collapse'. Kitty's team was charged with obstruction and a Major Henry Francis Fisher was arrested for assaulting Riley and Detective Sergeant Cox. Kitty's lawyer argued that she was trying to maintain order. Muskett said that he would discontinue her trial if she agreed not to commit the same crime again. Kitty was not prepared to cooperate. Pleading guilty to a technical assault, she was fined 20 shillings or twenty-one days in prison. Just as she was contemplating undertaking a hunger strike, her fine was anonymously paid, much to her annoyance.

Four days after Kitty's hearing, the participants in the Great Pilgrimage converged on Hyde Park. The 'Brown Women' march in which Kitty had taken part was an inspirational precursor to this ambitious six-week NUWSS propaganda trek, starring Mrs de Fonblanque. Pilgrims travelled in various modes from destinations in four corners of England and Wales, resolutely eschewing the purple of the WSPU. Instead, they wore tidy dark-coloured skirts, white blouses, cockleshell badges, and sashes and rosettes with the NUWSS colours, red, white and green. The accompanying Hyde Park rally was so enormous that Millicent Fawcett was unsure how she would be able to climb on to her wagon and speak to her audience. Then a man made a path through the crowds for her. She wondered who he was. 'Plain-clothes officer, ma'am,' he replied quietly, in answer to her thoughts. The whole event left her in a wonderful daze.

Ramsay MacDonald and Reginald McKenna both felt that the Great Pilgrimage had assisted the campaign for women's suffrage and Asquith agreed to accept Millicent Fawcett's delegation in August; the Great Pilgrimage was new evidence for the support for women's suffrage. Millicent Fawcett suggested to Asquith to put forward another Representation of the People Bill, adding, 'Well, women are people, aren't they?' 'I suppose so,' he replied doubtfully. 'At least it is another very ingenious suggestion, and deserves consideration.' What a concession! This was probably the closest anyone had come to winning over the arch-opponent of women's suffrage.

Meanwhile, Arthur was involved in his own campaign for justice. He applied for the money, in the form of postal orders and cheques amounting to almost £300 taken during the raid, to be restored to the WSPU in Mrs Pankhurst's name. However, witnesses came forward to testify that the WSPU was an illegal organisation and that this money ought not to be given to it. Furthermore, the police had stated that the cost of the prosecution would be greater than this seized money.

The Bodyguard had been given an assignment to protect Annie Kenney at the London Pavilion on 6 October 1913. Cecil Bishop, Ralph Kitchener and Inspector Parker and their colleagues had checked the premises beforehand. The speakers that afternoon were Flora Drummond, Marie Naylor and Norah Dacre Fox who shared the stage with Annie. Kitchener noticed Dulcie West who was wanted under the 'Cat and Mouse' Act. They arrested her and put her screaming into a taxi. McBrien ascertained that the woman on the stage was Annie Kenney and, on Patrick Quinn's instruction, Cecil Bishop, Ralph Kitchener, Detective Inspector Sandercock and others closed in. Flora Drummond had just finished her speech and was sitting down when Annie got up. 'There are detectives all round,' said Annie, eyeing the room, 'so I had better start.'

While she spoke, it appeared to witnesses that the police were appearing from all sides and they watched as she was being dragged off the stage to Holloway. Her dress was almost torn. Among those arrested was Lillian Dove-Willcox, who tried to puncture the tyres of the taxi taking Annie to prison. Bishop prevented McBrien from being struck over the head.

As it was, he emerged with two injured fingers, minus a hat and stick. Sandercock's waistcoat was ripped and he also lost his hat. Police headgear could be a lucrative find for suffragettes keen to secure more funding for the WSPU. Mrs Dacre Fox offered two hats and a stick for auction which had been lifted from the detectives who arrested Annie. 'I learned afterward that the suffragettes auctioned the "trophies" in the shape of hats and sticks taken from detectives and added quite a sum to their fighting fund. I supposed they needed money, but in my experience their biggest fighting fund was in their nails and teeth!' quipped Cecil Bishop. Bishop amusedly speculated that his colleagues' hats and helmets eventually found their way into the drawer of 'some elderly lady whose children would be shocked beyond measure if they knew of the excesses to which their mother went to win the vote – which she doesn't use!'[24]

Flora Drummond appeared at Bow Street. She did not agree to refrain from militant activity, but as Arthur pointed out, her ill health stopped her from engaging in it anyway. She was granted bail and her case was remanded until 23 October. Meanwhile, three women, one of whom was Ida Wylie, paid Holloway a visit on Saturday, 11 October. The strong and heavy sjambok in their possession resembled the whip that Kitty's uncle, William Baldwin, had made from rhinoceros and sea-cow hides. Dr Forward, who had overseen the forcible feeding of Rosa May Billinghurst a year earlier, was Ida Wylie's target. As he scurried towards the prison entrance, he was grabbed by the collar. 'You are torturing our women, Dr Forward and you ought to be forcibly fed yourself instead of thrashed,' informed one voice with frightening softness. Then, he was struck. The impact broke the sjambok in half. Hatless and gasping, Dr Forward got to his feet and scurried off and the women who attacked him got away.

With the passing of the 'Cat and Mouse' Act, Sylvia Pankhurst, who was dodging the police, was sometimes defended by a boxer named 'Kosher' Hunt. Norah Smyth assisted in drilling Sylvia's People's Army of men and women, which offered courses in self-defence and training in Victoria Park by Sir Francis Vane, a peer with left-wing sympathies. The recruitment poster for the People's Army, which was signed by Sylvia, announced that the government aggression could only be matched by armed resistance. At the Bow Baths meeting on 13 October, Sylvia's friend, Zelie Emerson, amused the audience with her description of Dr Forward's attack outside Holloway. She recommended her audience knock off the helmets of the police officers standing on guard outside and she felt that a good form of protection against 'McKenna's pups' was offered by the 'Saturday night', a type of life-preserver, or weighted cudgel, formed out of a rope, the knot of which was strengthened with lead to render the weapon heavier.

One of these 'pups' was Cecil Bishop, who was ordered to patrol the front entrance and to break up the meeting. 'We managed to break up the meeting all right and the suffragettes saw to it that everything else was broken up, too!'[25] While the *Suffragette* reported police officers using chairs, Bishop stopped a crowd hurling chairs from the gallery on to those on the ground floor. His younger colleague, a new police recruit, was apprehensive about fighting women which seemed 'not right' but Bishop assured him that they were there to make arrests, not to fight. He was promptly knocked over the head by a woman wielding a chair; she turned out to be his aghast fiancée. With the aid of brandy, he came to. No serious injuries were suffered by anyone at the Baths and only a few officers were scratched. Bishop succeeded in taking one of the ringleaders outside but she bit him and this was when he dunked her in a barrel of rainwater. Heavily defended by sympathisers, Sylvia made her escape but she was arrested the next evening in Poplar Town Hall.

In October, Glaswegian Margaret Skirving slipped between two constables during the royal procession down the Mall for the wedding of Alexandra, Duchess of Fife to Prince Arthur of Connaught on 15 October 1913. She reached the king and had one foot on the step of his carriage. As she lifted her hand, in which there was a bundle of papers, including a petition to the king, her wrist was grabbed and she was arrested. In court, the judge reminded her that: 'The police were there to prevent anyone from approaching the royal carriage.'[26] Her behaviour had been 'rude', insensitive and ill-timed. This comment was more than a slap on the wrist. In March, King George I of Greece, the Queen Mother's brother and uncle to King George V, was shot whilst out walking, months before his golden jubilee, and only a handful of years earlier, in 1908, King Carlos of Portugal had been assassinated as he travelled in an open landau to Lisbon. The event was embedded in Harold Brust's memory. Before he joined the Met, Brust had been a personal attendant to Sir Francis Villiers, British Ambassador to Portugal and was given the job of delivering correspondence in person to King Carlos. Brust prevented an assassination attempt by a Portuguese revolutionary and he shared his misgivings over the quality of the Portuguese detectives and his own plans to join the Met and become a royal bodyguard with his friend Crown Prince Luís Filipe. This was the last conversation he had with the heir to the throne; he could only watch as King Carlos was shot dead and his son was mortally wounded while his younger brother, Manuel, was shot on the arm. His mother, the sole uninjured member of the family, struck out at the assassins with the only improvised weapon she had to hand – a bunch of flowers. Following the assassinations, Luís's younger brother, King Manuel, was overthrown in 1910 and came to live in London. Ralph Kitchener was engaged in surveillance duty outside the king's Richmond home. Kitchener shared this duty with Harold Brust. Brust was on duty in Twickenham, near King Manuel's home, when he spotted a shifty man nearby and acted on his well-honed instinct for imminent danger. He cornered the man, overpowered him and arrested him. 'I thought it was a perfectly legal thing to do,' ventured Margaret Skirving at her hearing. The judge showed a remarkable degree of leniency towards her, given the potential seriousness of her actions. Cecil Bishop reflected that the British police force and government had in general demonstrated patience towards the militant suffragettes who, he felt, would have been threatened with firearms in any other country.

This was not the case with Mrs Pankhurst when she arrived at Ellis Island in the same month as Margaret Skirving's approach to the royal carriage. However, the American authorities were very cautious and detained this mouse, whose licence had expired, at Ellis Island for further questioning. She was faced with the threat of deportation on the grounds that she had committed felony 'involving moral turpitude' but Woodrow Wilson (the president's daughters lobbied him about female suffrage) intervened and allowed her to set foot on American soil, provided her stay did not exceed five weeks. She was treated to an ovation from the waiting crowds. Mrs Pankhurst told her New York audience that she had always wondered why citizenship was so jealously guarded by men. 'We are neither superhuman nor are we subhuman,' she said. 'We are just human beings like yourselves ... We know the joy of battle ... And so we are glad that we have had the fighting experience, we are glad to do all the fighting for all the women all over the world.'[27]

The Ladies Aeolian Orchestra were due to perform at the Great Women's Demonstration on 4 December at the Empress Theatre in Earl's Court to raise money, galvanise support and welcome Mrs Pankhurst back home. Stewards, who were to enter the building through the Lillie Road entrance for the meeting were organised by Olive Bartels. Also arranged for the same date was a Christmas Sale at Lincoln's Inn, opening on 4 December. Jane Terrero took over the Farm Produce Stall from Kitty who was doubtless busy with other commitments.

Chief Constable Sowerby of the Plymouth County Borough Police was warned by the Home Office of Mrs Pankhurst's arrival on the White Star liner the *Majestic* in Plymouth on 4 December. Gwen Cook and the Bodyguard were among the thousands of supporters who gathered around the town to welcome Mrs Pankhurst. Sowerby was one of the first chief constables to recruit women to Special Constabulary to help discourage young women and girls from entering brothels and he had assisted survivors of the *Titanic*. He launched an extensive operation, utilising all night and day officers to keep order as Mrs Pankhurst was returning with her American friend Rheta Childe Dorr with whom she had compiled her memoir, *My Own Story* (1914). The ship dropped anchor at Plymouth Sound, and Sowerby, in a tug, sped towards the *Majestic*, accompanied by Detective Inspector Hitchcock of the Metropolitan Police, two policemen and a wardress. Two drenched suffragettes sped close by in a fisherman's dory. 'The cats are here, Mrs Pankhurst!' they warned. 'They're close on you—.' Mrs Pankhurst heard their voices fade into the mist. A nervous boy approached her and told her that the purser requested her appearance below. She refused.

By sailing out to meet the ship, Sowerby reached her before the Bodyguard, whom Sylvia called 'a plucky band of women armed with Indian clubs'. He was successful in outwitting her defenders who had been standing in the drizzle at the dock gates. 'Who are you? Have you got a warrant?' Mrs Pankhurst enquired and Sowerby told her that he did not need one to arrest this famous mouse. Sowerby allowed Rheta to accompany her friend to Bull Point, a government landing stage, where Mrs Pankhurst was then conveyed to Exeter Prison, in the presence of Scotland Yard detectives. Those on board the *Majestic* were shocked to see the delicate lady carried off like a common criminal. A timber yard was set alight in protest. Suffragettes waited outside Exeter, braving the inclement weather, until Mrs Pankhurst's release on 7 December. She was cheered by a crowd ten deep at Paddington Station, leaning on

Mabel Tuke's arm and that of her nurse as she passed down the rows of the Bodyguard who maintained a watchful silence at her salute while others cheered. A cavalcade, headed by her ambulance, pulled up outside Lincoln's Inn House. Flora Drummond coordinated the movements of the Bodyguard whose members saw to it that Mrs Pankhurst was safely admitted to WSPU headquarters.

Mrs Pankhurst soon left for Paris to see Christabel and was conveyed by stretcher, watched on the platform by Patrick Quinn. Sufficiently rested and ready for the next round of re-arrests, she arrived at Dover on 13 December. Inspector Buckley and Inspector Edward Parker entered her compartment. Peering at her face, Inspector Parker thought that she looked remarkably well given police reports were describing her complexion as 'sallow'. The officers reminded her that she had failed to inform the authorities of her change of address. She would be taken into custody. Mrs Pankhurst knew what she had to do. Hunger striking always commenced at the point of arrest and so she disposed of her nourishment, throwing her as yet unbrewed tea out of the carriage window.

The officers travelled in the compartment next to her and her two friends from Dover to avoid bad publicity at Dover Town Station. Mrs Joyce, a police matron, accompanied them. Mrs Pankhurst then asked Nurse Pine and Dr Ede to witness her will, which she told them she was being deprived of signing during her arrest. 'The Government is making cowardly brutes of you,' she told the police. As the train approached Victoria Station, she was asked to stand up but refused: 'You will have to take me by force.' A great crowd waited for her at Victoria Station, including her Bodyguard, but her arrest was effected in a dimly lit part of the platform which had mainly escaped the attention of the crowd of sympathisers who had been cut off from the entrance platform. She was taken, groaning (Inspector Parker had a suspicion that she was playing to her audience), by Buckley and the matron, who carried her under each arm and put her in a police motorcar and she was driven to Holloway, amid some shouts of 'Bravo, Mrs. Pankhurst'. At Holloway, it took three wardresses to persuade her forcibly out of the car.

The year ended with a bang. Or rather, two. Outside Holloway Prison. Just after 9 p.m. on 18 December, two very loud explosions were heard across Finsbury Park and Camden Town. Local polices and those who lived in the neighbourhood rushed to the scene, some fearing an earthquake. Many panes of windows smashed. One boy's arm was cut from the shattered glass as he lay in his bed. Despite the loud reports, there was not much to see apart from two large holes dug at the base of the walls of the gardens backing on to the prison. In one of the gardens where suffragettes on picket duty rested, Quinn, McBrien and Major Cooper Key deduced that dynamite had been used and that this action was the work of the suffragettes. The parallels of the Fenians' bombing of Clerkenwell's House of Detention in 1867 were not lost on the public.

13.

Shadow Play

Kitchener had been following Kitty Marion for months. He even shadowed her during Emily Wilding Davison's funeral. Sometimes, he was instructed to overtly let a suspect know they were being watched by sidling up to them at a shop front or by sitting next to them on a bus. On 6 January 1914, the situation came to a head. Kitty Marion was met at Charing Cross station by a WSPU member who telephoned the headquarters to inform them of her safe arrival. Kitchener had been watching the exchange. Waiting outside the phone booth, Kitty heard a man say 'Hullo, Katie' in a mild North London accent. His quarry put up a fight. Did the detective, standing on her right, see that she had passed incriminating evidence to her friend on the left? She was only too glad to be accompanied to the station master's office if it meant creating distance between her friend and the burden she was carrying and the detective. So, as she put it, she 'moused off with the cat'.

Kitchener brought reinforcements from the Yard, who confirmed who she was, and bundled a resistant Kitty Marion, who kicked the cab's glass window, into a taxi which took her to Holloway. The mouse and the cats were crammed into the tiny space. Those who did not fit inside hung off the edge of the vehicle. Despite this, the group discussed votes for women. The officers agreed with female suffrage but told her that if they refused to arrest her, they would lose their jobs. It was back to Holloway, hunger striking and forcible feeding.

In her cell, Kitty Marion soaped 'No Surrender' on the wall. As the daily dust settled, the words took on a colour that not even whitewash brush could eradicate. Like an ancient palimpsest, which was scraped after use but retained faint and often readable remains of previous work, the writing surface offered by the prison wall would continue to bear the markings of Kitty Marion's resistance. The arsonist and actress mouse was sent to Nurse Pine to recover. Kitty's nail-scratched and bruised body was so wasted that it was felt that she had aged in appearance by thirty years. Flowers from well-wishers – Mrs Pankhurst sent an azalea – crowded her room. Dr Flora Murray examined the patient. She thought that a suspicious rash on her neck and positive pathological tests suggested that Kitty had been drugged. As Mrs Dacre Fox warned, drugged women behind bars were at the mercy of men.

McKenna confided in the Bishop of London, who had interviewed Kitty Marion, that there was no alternative to forcible feeding, however, he maintained that the blame lay on the shoulders of the women who chose to hunger strike. But, like the soapy, waxy words scribbled on Kitty Marion's cell wall, the evidence of drugging at the hands of the authorities could not be ignored or covered up by shifting the blame of drug-taking on to the women and their sympathisers. During her temporary release, she was taken to a new location, followed by the CID. Her friends performed a 'shadow play' – reminiscent of a style of puppetry performed against a strong background – of looking after an invalid in a well-lit room. Behind the scenes, Kitty Marion was escorted to the back of the house and driven off on a motorcycle.

Mrs Pankhurst's escape from well-heeled 2 Campden Hill Square, between Notting Hill and Kensington, was a triumph for the Bodyguard. The house at Campden Hill Square had a balcony which was ideal for Mrs Pankhurst to make a speech as it was now almost impossible to secure a hall. Working from received intelligence, Scotland Yard had been watching the square for a few days and sent a large number of plain-clothes men to the area in anticipation of the next sighting of Mrs Pankhurst. As Kitchener eyed the crowd, which was growing into the hundreds, he realised that an effectively large group of bobbies and detectives were necessary. He knew that the Bodyguard had been meeting for Indian club practice and was ready for them and their clubs which they kept suspended from their skirts.

The WSPU made it known that she would give a speech so that plenty of people would turn up to see her take to her stage at 8.30 p.m.

on 10 February at the only lighted window at 2 Campden Hill Square. Mrs Pankhurst told her audience that while the government fought for property rights, the women were fighting for human rights. She told them that she would never ever, come what may, serve her three years in jail. 'I am coming down now,' she informed the audience.

The announcement was intended for Kitty. She speedily took off Mrs Pankhurst's coat and her small toque with its white feather and put them on Florence Evelyn Smith. In return, she gave Mrs Pankhurst a substantial, soft beaver felt hat and a veil. Kitty liked veils because they made the job of identifying the wearer very tricky. Mrs Pankhurst's new coat was now a mackintosh. Ralph Kitchener watched as the Bodyguard formed a protective screen and he saw Kitty and Florence emerge from the house. Together they proceeded down the garden path. All the while, Kitty was thinking how alike Florence and Mrs Pankhurst looked. She was also aware of the men and suffragettes who gave them support as well as the sheer numbers of police present and the rowdies ready to taunt the women. It was going to be a rough ride. They made it 20 yards down the road, when Kitty loudly called out in the most persuasive voice she could muster: 'Mrs Pankhurst, friends, don't let her be arrested.'

Around twenty women started to swarm protectively about them, including Princess Sophia Duleep Singh and her friend Ada Wright, but Kitty and Florence were trapped. Florence heard voices behind them. 'There she is. That's Mrs Pankhurst. Now come on, boys, now!' They felt a great push from behind and fell. Florence was knocked on the head and toppled face forward to the ground. As it turned out, her hat protected her from worse injuries. Someone sat on her back, winding her. 'God, have mercy on me,' whispered Florence into the mud before she lost consciousness, hearing words, and feeling breaths scented with alcohol. She was lucky to have lost consciousness, Kitty thought. Kitty's dress was torn, she lost a fur-trimmed hat and an old French paste buckle heirloom, perhaps one of the numerous items of jewellery which Caroline Augusta had left to her daughters to divide amongst themselves, but worst of all, her ribs were being crushed. In this collision of bodies, she thought she was going to die. Kitty began to pray.

All at once, six large policemen came over to them and formed a protective circle round the two women. Kitty continued to keep up the ruse, demanding for help for 'Mrs Pankhurst'. Kitchener saw Kitty struggle.

The veiled woman was hefted like a sack of potatoes off to the nearby police station in Notting Hill. Kitty felt that this arrest helped her cause. Onlookers could see 'Mrs Pankhurst' being propelled away with such energy which kept up the deception that she was the great leader and that the cats had got her. Meanwhile, Mrs Pankhurst, supported by two laughing young women, made her way out of the building, took a left turn and hopped into a waiting car to a safe house before the police officers could agree with themselves whether or not they had arrested the right woman. Kitchener was impressed with Mrs Pankhurst's stealthy escape. Further adventures awaited the leader in the form of pouring rain, punctured tyres and toothache. She finally arrived at her secret destination at 4 a.m. whereupon she went to bed. Kitty would spend the next few days in bed, in pain.

Florence remembered being examined under a street lamp, her veil torn from her. She was then dragged into a police waiting room, where she huddled, semi-conscious, on a bench. Kitchener had rightly guessed that she had been wearing the same clothes as Mrs Pankhurst and he saw too that the arrested lady was the same build as the leader. She recalled an aggressive grey-haired man whom she presumed to be Riley who came in and confirmed that she was not Mrs Pankhurst and slammed the door. What bothered her most of all was that this was the treatment that would have been meted out to Mrs Pankhurst, actions which could have killed her. She later gave her statement to Arthur at his offices in Mark Lane.

When asked by Keir Hardie if Florence would receive compensation, McKenna maintained that Florence and the police were felled to the ground by the pressure of the crowd. There was no proof of police culpability and hence no grounds for compensation and while a doctor certified that Florence was too ill to appear in court on the following day, she was well enough to attend a WSPU meeting a few days later – which in his mind mitigated her claim of having suffered significant injuries.

The WSPU's annual report for the year 1914 contained two pages in which both the Special Branch and the Bodyguard feature:

Police Methods. – The past year has seen an important and dangerous development of the Political Police force which was created by a Liberal Government in 1880, and has been by the present Government very much extended mainly for the purpose of dealing with the militant

Suffrage agitation. The Political Police force has lately been recruited by men of a low type, prepared as it would seem to put their hands to any scandalous method of coercion which the Government may prescribe. This force principally consists of plain clothes detectives who wear no mark of identification such as, for the protection of the public, is worn by the ordinary uniformed constable, and they are therefore able to commit unchecked, and do commit, serious acts of violence against Suffragists with whom they are deputed to deal.

The Women's Bodyguard. – A women's bodyguard, destined it would seem to expand into a veritable army, has been formed in order to protect Suffragists in danger of arrest and torture. Before the year ended, the Bodyguard had achieved two conspicuous victories, and in both cases were successful in preventing the arrest of Mrs. Pankhurst. An important characteristic of the Bodyguard is that it consists entirely of women and makes no appeal to the aid or protection of men. It is increasingly felt that the Government, so long as they see women relying, even where physical conflict is concerned, upon the aid of men, will not realise the true seriousness of the Women's Movement, and will continue to hope that they may subdue it by dint of terrorising or in some way buying off the men connected with the movement. Experience proves that Suffragists will, politically speaking, never stand on firm political ground, until they are able, whether on the platform or on the militant battlefield, to make themselves independent of the help of men. Apart from this, the fact that a Bodyguard consisting entirely of women can hold its own against the police is an education to women in general, and perhaps even more to men.[28]

In this piece, the Bodyguard's display of political fitness through physical capability demonstrates the team's pivotal role in tackling the 'Political Police', a branch whose history and development is here linked to a Liberal government which continually showed itself hostile to the suffragettes' cause. To reinforce this message and introduce an extra level of propaganda, the *Suffragette* printed a series of articles on what it called the 'Political Department'. Based on unsubstantiated sources, the pieces compounded negative impressions of the Special Branch by asserting that two Special Branch officers were German, a foretaste of the anti-German sentiments that Christabel and Mrs Pankhurst would elaborate on during the war. Accusations such as those that Special Branch officers drank whilst on duty could be rebutted, but the complaint that the Branch interfered with civil liberties was valid. In the late 1890s, the Special Branch was tasked with observing members of the Legitimation League, which had espoused inheritance rights for children born out of wedlock. It was the League's connection with anarchists which attracted the Special Branch's attention. George Bedborough, editor of the League's publication, the *Adult*, was prosecuted for publishing Havelock Ellis's work on homosexuality, *Sexual Inversion* (1897). The League collapsed. Yet, the pieces printed in the WSPU annual report asked readers to consider that 'white slavers' could dress up as detectives who were not required to show proof of their identity to make an arrest; anyone could pose as an officer.

14.

Under the Fig Tree

For Kitty, the battle at Glebe Place was undoubtedly Mrs Pankhurst's most impressive escape. She had been told to arrive at Glebe House on Friday, 20 February to prepare again to escort Mrs Pankhurst's decoy. Meanwhile, Gladys Schütze followed orders and made sure she had plenty of food in stock, in case Mrs Pankhurst's escape went wrong and the Bodyguard was forced to stay over the weekend. All at once, there were a great many aspects to consider. Her housemaid, who was dating a policeman, had to be kept indoors. Gladys also had to cancel a game of bridge she was hosting and, more awkwardly, forestall a visit from a staunch anti-suffragist. She felt that she had a lot to prove to herself. Very early in Gladys's writing career, H.G. Wells told her, in his high-pitched voice, that she would never make it as a professional writer. Gladys would, in his opinion, always be an amateur. At the same time, Christabel Pankhurst made clear that she did not rate Gladys as a vital player in the suffrage campaign. The rebuff had stung.

Just before the government banned the *Suffragette*, Gladys had been asked to take messages to Christabel in Paris. This involved wearing notes tucked into her curls and hiding missives which had been sewn into a suspiciously badly fitting coat. She was terrified on the journey that the awful coat might attract the attentions of a detective who might engage her in conversation. On one occasion, she dropped her bag and when a man picked it up for her, she made herself scarce. Shaken, Gladys arrived at Christabel's apartment and received a frosty and distracted welcome. Gladys felt that Mrs Pankhurst appreciated the sacrifices that members made but Christabel did not rouse such any inspiration in Gladys. To her, the great lawyer who had impressed courtrooms with her wit and perspicacity was a cold, lofty and self-important figure. At least Ethel Smyth acknowledged this tired traveller and attempted to make small talk with her about Germany and music, but to Christabel she was irrelevant. Made to feel like a piece of jettisoned luggage that had appeared on Christabel's doorstep, Gladys was understandably hurt.

Around forty-eight hours before Mrs Pankhurst's expected visit to Glebe Place, Gladys's phone rang. It was a WSPU organiser. 'Your house has a balcony, hasn't it?' she was asked. She replied in the affirmative. Her housemaid was dating a policeman, she let slip. 'Get rid of her at once. You oughtn't to have such people in your house,' came the voice down the receiver. She couldn't just get rid of the maid, Gladys responded. 'Well, you can keep her in. Keep everybody in until Mrs. Pankhurst has left the house.' Mrs Schütze was then instructed to procure enough food for an imminent siege but not from her usual shops. And she was to carry it in herself, disguised in parcels. The organiser asked if she had a long cape under which she could hide the parcels. She did? 'Good.' The line went dead. In the aftermath of this terse exchange, Gladys came to realise that she had been entrusted to sort out the essentials and must on no account slip up.

While she was making her arrangements for Mrs Pankhurst's visit, Bodyguard members began to appear. Gladys saw a millworker, a dressmaker, two shop assistants, two teachers, two clerks, three domestic workers, a children's nurse, a society lady and several ladies like Kitty – whom she thought came across as middle-class women of leisure – walking into her house. She found the twenty women some accommodation space and was impressed by their orderly queue to use their two bathrooms, one of which was fitted with a state-of-the-art hot-water 'geyser' that delighted the Bodyguard members. 'Yes, this is a lovely house. So old. And with all this wood about – what a place for a job!' echoed Lilian Lenton's words.

Mrs Pankhurst arrived at 3 p.m. and was thrilled to see them all. She made friends with the Schützes' dog and praised their cook, Mrs Duckett, who was a strong supporter of the movement. Mrs Pankhurst and her hosts stayed up late into the night. The drawing room, with its Huguenot connection and fig tree, made a favourable impression on her. As she watched the Bodyguard making camp, she admiringly observed the tree's indomitable branches twisting tenaciously up around the room all the way to the ceiling. Mrs Pankhurst's heart, too, was tough and strong. This is what Dr Schütze confirmed in his examination. Now she could show the government, too chary of forcibly feeding her and hiding behind the excuse that her heart was weak, a report that she was well enough to undergo the procedure, if the prison authorities, too frightened of creating a martyr, dared. Mrs Pankhurst was enjoying herself so much that she and her hosts stayed up chatting about Australia and married life until almost midnight, long past the hour at which Mrs Pankhurst ought to have gone to bed.

The next morning, the WSPU announced that Mrs Pankhurst would speak from an address at Glebe Place at 4.30 p.m. through advertisements in the press on the morning of the planned appearance. A poster parade set off in the rain from Lincoln's Inn House to Chelsea just a few hours beforehand, drumming up support and interest. By 3.30 p.m. crowds of between 500 and 1,000 people had already gathered in this normally quiet street. Half the Bodyguard had spent a hectic night under the fig tree in the drawing room at the back of the house. After a brief introduction, Mrs Pankhurst stepped on to the narrow balcony from the French windows to great applause. She was watched not only by the crowd in the street but by the residents in neighbouring houses. At her side were other women and the group received a mainly sympathetic response, coupled with some noises of disapproval. Among those in Mrs Pankhurst's entourage was the tax resister Princess Sophia Alexandra Duleep Singh, the daughter of Maharaja Duleep Singh, the man who, as a result of his defeat during the Anglo-Sikh Wars of the 1840s, had been forced to relinquish the Punjab and hand over the Koh-i-noor diamond to Queen Victoria, Sophia's godmother. A trip to India heightened her sense of injustice and radicalised her and she learned from first-hand experience what the police were capable of when unchecked. Then there was silence. It was clear to see that among the audience was a considerable number of police and what looked to be plain-clothes officers. Of course, Ralph Kitchener made up their number.

'Tools of the Government' was what Mrs Pankhurst called Kitchener and his colleagues as she perched on her balcony above the men. These were men, she added, who were only earning their bread and having to follow orders; it was the politicians who were the enemy. Mrs Pankhurst kept the audience engaged for forty-five minutes. Certain parts of her speech affected Kitty directly. She opened by referring to the police's treatment of Florence Smith, the would-be Mrs Pankhurst, at Campden Hill Square:

> This happened at night, and, you know, on a dark night 'accidents may happen', and how convenient it would have been, friends, to have got rid of a militant leader by an accidental blow on a dark night! The Government would have expressed great regret, some man would have been dismissed for excess of zeal, and there would have been an end of Mrs Pankhurst.

The speaker knew that she was taunting the crowd. 'How convenient it would have been to have got rid of one of the leaders of this movement by an accidental blow,' Mrs Pankhurst ominously concluded. Kitty's nervousness grew with the memory of the event. She and the decoy were almost crushed to death. They had at least fooled the detectives who were scratching their heads, arguing amongst themselves whether or not the lady they had in their custody was really the fabled Mrs Pankhurst. But how often would they be able to trick the police? Kitty doubted that they could pull off that same stunt again.

Mrs Pankhurst reminded the audience of the impact of venereal disease on women's and children's lives. Mrs Pankhurst said that she was the wife of a lawyer and learned a lot about the law through him. 'I am the wife of a lawyer, and when you are associated with the law, you hear a good deal that the ordinary outside does not hear.' She related the story of a judge who could not take his seat on a court bench as he had been caught in a house of ill-repute. 'You have broken the laws,' interjected a member of the audience, 'why don't you take your punishment?' The lady, who had been released half a dozen times under the 'Cat and Mouse' Act and had served twenty days of her prison sentence, responded: 'I tell you it would take far less courage to accept the punishment than it does to resist it.' She mused that it might take hundreds of years to serve the full term of her sentence if the 'Cat and Mouse' cycle continued. She reminded the audience what this was all for:

> We are fighting for a time when every little girl born into the world will have an equal chance with her brothers, when we shall put an end

to foul outrages upon our sex, when our streets shall be safe for the girl-hood of our race, when every man shall look upon every other woman as his own sisters, when Love shall be lifted to be the noblest thing in life. When we have done that, we can rest upon our laurels, assured that we have passed on to future generations an inheritance worthy of the great human race of which we are humble members.[29]

As the meeting drew to a close, the Bodyguard team members checked their equipment. A group of heavily veiled women, a dozen or so strong, emerged from the gate which protected the front door on to the street. They were shielding 'Mrs Pankhurst' and, when later questioned, claimed that they did not know that they were guarding a decoy; at the very least they ought to have suspected this to be the case, given that the ruse was tried at Campden Hill Square. Kitchener looked on as one Bodyguard member aimed her club at a policeman who had another woman in charge. The intended blow missed him and struck the other suffragette and an Indian club was bloodied, much to the horror of witnesses.

By 6 p.m., the police had cleared Glebe Place of any onlookers who now gathered in the King's Road. The Schützes told the police that Mrs Pankhurst had escaped, but they remained unconvinced and two cordons of officers were stationed at either side of Glebe Place in wait. The real Mrs Pankhurst stayed behind and until the next day, the press was uncertain whether she had made an escape or not. Kitty doubted the police would be fooled again so soon after the Campden Hill Square escape. She was right. As Kitchener recalled: 'This time, however, Mrs Pankhurst did not get away. The subterfuge of the veiled woman had been expected, and after it had been made certain that she was not Mrs Pankhurst she was not arrested, and her leader had to remain in-doors.' The press informed readers that Glebe House had no back entrance so Mrs Pankhurst was effectively trapped. By Sunday evening, the formidable force which had guarded Glebe Place was much reduced to a small collection of detectives. This was a tactical mistake.

On Sunday night, Kitty's phone rang. Against the backdrop of Arthur's displeasure, Kitty heard that she was to pick up four suffragettes in a taxi and to follow a blue car which would be waiting outside a Knightsbridge shop. They were to follow this car to Glebe Place. She did not know what to tell the taxi driver so she told him that they were not sure of their address and asked him to follow the car. Kitty was not adept at bending the truth but she salved her conscience by tipping him well and she also promised him a return journey if he was happy to wait, which he was.

It was late in the night when the blue car stopped outside the home of Peter and Gladys Schütze. Inspector Buckley, who was in charge of plain-clothes officers stationed outside Glebe House, saw Kitty and her fellow Bodyguard members spring out of the car and attack the small group of policemen and detectives who guarded the front of Glebe House. They were joined by Bodyguard reinforcements in the taxi behind them. Other Bodyguard members poured out of the house, shouting 'Charge, girls!' as they came forth from Glebe House. Kitty launched herself at a large officer with a mackintosh cape, tipping his helmet over his face. It was a distraction which enabled Mrs Pankhurst to rush up the basement area steps with two other women. When they tried to enter a taxi, an officer blocked their path. As Mrs Pankhurst recounted in undisguisably excited tones:

> The police were between two fires. While the battle raged, I, with two others, dashed up the area steps and into the car. The big detective stood at the area door and was trying to block the car, and a girl engaged him single-handed with an Indian club; he had his umbrella, and she kept him off until I was away. All I regret is that I saw so little of the fight, being otherwise engaged myself. ... As for our fighting women they are in great form and very proud of their exploits as you can imagine. The girl who had her head cut open and would not have it stitched as she wanted to keep the scar as big as possible. The real warrior spirit![30]

Just at the point at which Mrs Pankhurst was ushered into the blue car and was speedily driven away by a chauffeuse to a secret location in Colchester, Kitty spotted an inspector running after the car to get its number plate. She knocked his helmet off and he was so busy trying to find his hat that he missed the number as did his fellow officers. Kitty's contingent drove back to Piccadilly Circus to debrief. Pleased with their evening's work, they all went home for a celebratory rest.

The Bodyguard members were praised for their valiant efforts by Mrs Pankhurst and in the pages of the *Suffragette*. In particular, Gladys was thanked for arranging for Mrs Pankhurst to speak at her home. This was overdue praise given how she had been treated in Paris. The date on which Gladys received this recognition by the WSPU proved a rather eventful Sunday in the history of Smith Square. Half an hour after the end of the service, at 9 p.m., there was an explosion which could be heard 200 yards away. Kitty's neighbour and Smith Square resident, Reginald McKenna, ran to the scene at St John the Evangelist and gave the alarm. A photograph appeared in the press of Canon Wilberforce surveying the destruction. A dozen seats were wrecked, the glass window in the chancel swelled out against the wirework and a small window was smashed. A chunk of cornice had fallen near the pulpit. From the destroyed pews, which were covered in white dust, experts deduced that gunpowder had been used. A cannister was found and a half-burnt candle which had been lit at the end of the service. Literature found at the scene suggested the explosion was the work of the WSPU. Another consequence of the successful Glebe Place escape was that Mrs Pankhurst was more determined than ever to organise a deputation to the king. But first, she was embarking on a lecture tour of Scotland.

15.

The Battle of Glasgow

Mrs Pankhurst's car rebelled. The tyres burst and the lights failed. Neither of the two women with whom she was travelling across the Scottish countryside could find the house in which they had planned to shelter so they spent the night in the car. An automobile might have been a luxury for the time but as the women's predicament showed, car travel was not necessarily comfortable. When it was light, a confused farm labourer roused them with a knock on the window. Eventually the group managed to locate their safe house, a Scottish manse. As she settled down into the bed covers the following night, warm from the attention she was receiving, Mrs Pankhurst began a delicious meditation on what was about to unfold in Glasgow. She thought about the Scottish Bodyguard and their willingness to protect her at all costs. If she got away, Westminster would be laughed at; if she were arrested, the public would be up in arms. It seemed to Mrs Pankhurst that whatever happened, the government could not win the forthcoming public relations battle.[31]

Meanwhile, Basil Thomson, Assistant Commissioner for the Metropolitan Police and head of the CID since June 1913, had seen an advertisement which stated that Mrs Pankhurst was due to speak at St Andrew's Hall, Glasgow. He immediately made contact with Chief Constable James Verdier Stevenson of the City of Glasgow Police. Thomson had long coveted the job title he now held. The work brought him an extra £400 in salary and he was keen to undertake reforms and to tackle the issue of the suffragettes. He told Stevenson that Mrs Pankhurst was shirking jail under the 'Cat and Mouse' Act. Under the terms of the

Act, no warrant was needed to arrest a person who failed to comply with the terms of their licence. Stevenson also did not need a warrant to enter St Andrew's Hall and arrest her. Although her photograph had been circulated, Thomson sent two men up from London to identify Mrs Pankhurst. Together with three inspectors and seven sergeants, there were to be 159 police officers deployed, 109 of them in uniform (under directions from Inspector Walker) and 50 in plain clothes. Both Kitty and Kitchener are disappointingly silent on their thoughts of what happened in Glasgow. Were they even there? It is unlikely but the events did however mark a change in suffragette and police relations which in turn pitched detectives and the Bodyguard further into battle.

On the platform on the evening of the 9 March were members of Mrs Pankhurst's Bodyguard with whom Kitty was acquainted including Lillian Dove-Willcox and Olive Bartels. Flora Drummond was there. Helen Crawfurd, one of the Scottish Bodyguard members, stood on stage and was admiring the efforts of the organisers who had spent the day decorating the stage with tissue paper, muslin, flower pots and the colours of the WSPU. St Andrew's Hall could accommodate 3,000 people who passed under the caryatids, shafts of columns carved into female figures, high up above the atlas statues who guarded the entrance. The sounds of organ music warmed up the considerable crowd. Then, Mrs Pankhurst emerged from the group of women on the platform, threw off her cloak and hat and strode over to the chairperson. She was a motivational speaker, and a magician too. Helen Crawfurd was stunned. She was mystified. How had her leader got there? In fact, she had taken a taxi with two women to a nearby street, and striding unobtrusively past the 'tecs, had submitted her ticket as if she were an ordinary visitor, entered the hall, walked round the gallery and got to the platform. The police were caught off guard as they thought that they had covered all entrances to the building. Mrs Pankhurst, now holding a bouquet of flowers, was a tiny figure on the stage but her voice, as ever, projected across the hall. Her speech was widely reported:

> I have kept my promise and in spite of His Majesty's Government I am here to-night. ... [I]f there is any distinction to be drawn at all between militancy in Ulster and the militancy of women it is all to the advantage of the women. Our greatest task in this women's movement is to prove

that we are human beings like men, and every stage of our fight is forcing home that very difficult lesson into the minds of men … You get the proof of the political injustice.

She managed to speak for about three minutes. Helen watched aghast as police officers emerged Trojan-horse style from their hiding place under the platform, their truncheons drawn. 'Here's the police!' called a male steward as thirty uniformed men and twenty plain-clothes men rushed into the hall. Inspector G. Walker and the uniformed police divisions waited in the basement. At 8.05 p.m., Walker was given the order by Superintendent Douglas, whose task it was to direct the arrest, and led the police into the fray.

The officers were in for a nasty surprise. Glaswegian teenager Cecilia Russell had helped with the laying of barbed wire under the decorations in preparation for Mrs Pankhurst's speech. These fortifications dictated police procedure: police officers had to remove the wire before attempting the platform just in case one of them fell over back into the barbs. As Walker was assessing the injurious mesh before him, one of the women struck him on the head with a chair which knocked him down and he tore his hand on the barbed wire. He was aware of a woman falling off the platform. He got up, baton in hand but did not use it. Helen and her friends threw plants, water bottles, water and tables at him and his officers in the area below. One woman found herself in the way of a plant pot missile and was sent crashing into the piano. To Cecilia's horror, the barbed wire had only surprised the police but had not kept them back. As soon as the wire had been dismantled, she saw officers dash on to the stage, waving their batons. Helen Crawfurd was terrified that the lights would suddenly go out and people would be killed in a stampede that was becoming increasingly violent.[32] A Bodyguard member, who was wearing a light blouse, was splattered with blood as she was caught by the throat and thrown down the stairs.

Mrs Pankhurst, when awaiting her trial at the Old Bailey on 1 April, had held another WSPU meeting at St Andrew's Hall on 13 March 1913. When a group of students became rowdy as Janie Allan was introducing Mrs Pankhurst, muscular male stewards stepped in to put out the disturbers. This time, Janie, the granddaughter of Scottish shipping magnate Alexander Allan, went prepared with a pistol, a *Scheintod*, meaning 'apparent death'. With her fingers around the distinctive skeleton motif on the grip cartouche, she fired two blank shots into the face of a constable. The idea was to scare and stall but not to injure the officer on duty. Although these 'gas pistols', as they were sometimes known, were non-lethal, they were designed to project a type of pepper spray, which explains why one of the officers, Constable Ross, was blinded. Detective Dickie wrested the Scheintod from her grasp and fired her blank rounds into the ceiling but was struck on the head with sticks.

Helen and the Bodyguard swarmed round Mrs Pankhurst and reached the stairs just as Walker and PC Millar caught up with them. Chief Constable Stevenson, who instructed Superintendent Douglas to organise the arrest, knew that they had to effect the arrest quickly. This explained why observers saw the police rush towards Mrs Pankhurst. If he delayed arresting her until after she left the platform, there would be an even stronger resistance and heightened confusion, allowing the suffragette leader to get away. Born in Athlone, County Westmeath, Ireland, Stevenson had joined the Royal Irish Constabulary in 1884 and in 1902 had applied for the post of Chief Constable of Glasgow, beating the other ninety-three applicants. He was earning £1,000 a year and was made a CBE and Member of the Victorian Order. A year before he met Mrs Pankhurst at St Andrew's Hall during the Battle of Glasgow, he was awarded the King's Police Medal. He had a reputation for good service to keep up.

Walker and Millar lifted the WSPU's figurehead to her feet. Detective Lieutenant John Trench, who was the recipient of the King's Police Medal for gallantry and worked on unsolved murder cases, taking up the cause of Oscar Slater who had been suspected of killing an elderly lady in 1908, confirmed: 'Yes, that is her.' Walker took her by her left arm and escorted her down the stairs. A member of the crowd wrenched his baton from him but, rather than wrestle for it and lose his grip on Mrs Pankhurst, he was forced to let it go. He was met at the entrance by a baton-less Sergeant Millican, who ran up the stairs and took Mrs Pankhurst by the waist, partly carrying her to the taxi, assisted by Trench and another detective. Onlookers saw what they felt was Mrs Pankhurst being mishandled. To Cecilia, it looked as if Mrs Pankhurst was not being led but dragged and thrown into a cab by what she could only describe as 'muckleloons' (burly policemen) into a cab bound for the Central Police Station.

Mrs Pankhurst was offered a seat in the taxi. 'No,' she replied simply and took up a position between Inspector Parker and Trench. As she lay on the floor, she looked up at the officers crowded above her on the seats. One nervously attentive female attendant, Mrs Isabella Russell, stood next to her. Mrs Pankhurst made an assessment of her contusions and the damage to her belongings. She noticed that her coat was torn off, her fountain pen was gone, a velvet band round her neck was damaged. Her bag and gloves were no longer with her and her necklace was cut into pieces. Peter Schütze examined her on 15 March and noticed that her bruises confessed the level of violence to which she had been subjected. Walker returned to the basement until the end of the meeting as Flora Drummond and Barbara Wylie, who were surrounded by earthenware debris, crushed flowers, broken tables and dismembered chairs, tried in vain to calm the audience, now livid at Mrs Pankhurst's treatment. Flora was cornered by the police and was taken to a room. Her coat had been torn off, her gloves and bags were missing and she was bruised. Stewards came to her aid and she got to the platform where she attempted to restore order.

By playing the role of a martyr, Mrs Pankhurst could be perceived as a saint. Her suffering, and embellished performance of it, would be reinterpreted as the militants' unjust treatment, their collective pain. Cecilia and her friends were furious and began looting properties along Sauchiehall Street to the Central Police Station where Cecilia and a now loose-haired and hatless Helen Crawfurd, whose jacket was now devoid of buttons, smashed the building's windows. She and Cecilia were joined by 6,000 others in their vigil outside the Central Police Station where Mrs Pankhurst was spending the night. Helen had treated accounts of police violence with a proverbial pinch of salt but was now disgusted by what she had seen and it seemed to her that the public was also on the women's sides as she saw from the angry letters sent to Glasgow's newspapers. Using a poker, Helen Crawfurd broke two large windows at the Army Recruiting Offices, Gallowgate, demanding Mrs Pankhurst's release.

The day after the Glasgow fracas, Mrs Russell, who had accompanied Mrs Pankhurst to her cell, was to work a long shift. In the morning, when Mrs Pankhurst refused to walk to a taxi, Stevenson saw to it that she was carefully placed on a stretcher, the process watched by Mrs Russell who also accompanied her in her railway carriage all the way to London as Mrs Pankhurst lay on a seat. Inspector Parker was with them while the other officers remained a discreet distance apart in other train compartments. Two ladies joined them and Parker allowed one enthralled friend to speak to Mrs Pankhurst for a few minutes. Lillian Mary Dove-Willcox had managed to outwit the police and caught the same train as Mrs Pankhurst so that she could be close to her leader. Mrs Russell then took Mrs Pankhurst by taxi to Holloway at 7.30 p.m., dodging the crowds picketing the main London stations at which the WSPU leader might be arriving. Mrs Pankhurst shook hands with Mrs Russell. She had no complaints to make about the police who were only doing their duty but next time, she warned, it would take a regiment to arrest her. Behind bars, she breathed a sigh of gratitude to her valiant Bodyguard.

Keir Hardie asked who had given orders to the police to arrest Mrs Pankhurst on the platform and whether Mrs Pankhurst had been invited to give herself up. Chief Constable Stevenson's response was that the WSPU leader knew full well that she could be arrested and it was obvious from the resistance of her Bodyguard and the vast collection of weapons employed, that she and her supporters were clearly aware that they were flouting the law. A photograph of the seized items appeared in the press, including six Indian clubs, barbed wire, police batons, a revolver containing discharged cartridges, wire cutters enrobed in green cloth and an ominously named 'skullcracker' (an elasticated leather strip weighted at one or both ends with lead and also known as a 'life-preserver'). These weapons were received by the committee before a deputation of women arrived on 12 March and so the tone had already been set and the committee unanimously found that there was no cause for complaint against the police.

Scotland Yard had already sent word to galleries and museums, advising that they take extra care. If they were not doing so already, they ought to request that visitors leave muffs and parcels at the galleries' entrances. And then Mary Richardson struck a retaliative blow with her famous attack on Velásquez's 'Rokeby Venus' at the National Gallery. Despite the Scotland Yard memos, which argued that caution should be taken with women with muffs, she had smuggled a meat cutter into the gallery, hidden in a wrap. The foot-long meat cutter slashed the painting seven times, cutting Venus's back and defacing her buttocks. Mary had chosen the paragon of feminine attractiveness in order to highlight the physical destruction that was being done to Mrs Pankhurst, a living symbol of justice in the modern age, whose own soul radiated beauty. It was an attack on the male artist's controlling eye, on the objectification and sexualisation of women. How did Kitty, an artist, consider the attack? She does not say. But perhaps Mary's point of view is representative. When cornered, Mary claimed that paintings were ten-a-penny; Mrs Pankhurst was one in a million. Mary, once an art student herself, said that while she loved art, she valued justice more. Although Kitty does not mention Mary Richardson's deed, it is likely that she sympathised with the act being one of a defence of Dearest and the fight for social progress she symbolised. After all, Kitty was responsible for organising posthumous likenesses of Mrs Pankhurst, uniting art and justice.

As a result of the slashing of the 'Rokeby Venus', art galleries and palaces across the country were closed but attacks continued. On 4 May, Mary Wood attacked John Singer Sergeant's portrait of Henry James at the Royal Academy, creating clefts across his temples, right shoulder and lip. To Mrs Pankhurst, these attacks struck a blow to the tourist industry and further disrupted the British way of life. In the wake of these incidents, the National Portrait Gallery received Gwen Cook's photographic 'portrait'. The use of photographs, a cost-cutting measure, was a response to other measures which had been tried and tested by galleries. Gwen's image was amongst those taken by Scotland Yard and widely disseminated. The Wallace Collection requested further copies from Scotland Yard which could be placed in the mess room. It was felt that a cursory look at the photographs would not suffice to imprint the women's images on attendants' minds. They needed to be on constant display. Gwen's mugshot was juxtaposed with that of Mary Wood who had attacked Henry James' likeness, while Gwen was described as being capable of damaging anything.

Armed with photographs of known suspects, the attendants of the National Gallery were unprepared for a visit from 'Anne Hunt' on 17 July 1914. She set her sights on Sir John Everett Millais's portrait of the National Portrait Gallery's founder, Thomas Carlyle. The seated figure, his body turned towards the viewer, his claw-like unfinished hands resting on a walking stick, could not fend off the attacker, whose cleaver hacked at his imperious face. When the assailant was stymied in her attack, a halo of cracked glass radiated from Carlyle's white hair and beard. He had his revenge when some of the splinters cut the hand of his assailant and drew blood from her finger. Anne Hunt (whose real name was Margaret Gibb) was protesting against the treatment of Mrs Pankhurst by the police. As she ambled into the court at Bow Street, her hands, one of which was bandaged, were in her pockets. 'We value pictures as much as anybody, but we value human life more,' she said, echoing Mary Richardson's sentiments. She attempted to escape from the dock during her trial, her face bathed in perspiration. Three police officers restrained her and her bandage came undone, blood running down the dock. The *Morning Advertiser* was frustrated:

> What did Carlyle do in his life-time that his portrait in the National Gallery should have roused the anger of a fury? We do not remember that he ever wrote anything calculated to invoke the maledictions of women. On the other hand, his writings have proved an inspiration to brainy women. It is the brainy women who are most insistent in obtaining the vote, we are told. And they exhibit their braininess by slashing the portraits of great men like Carlyle. Are not the militants ... acting in such a manner as to persuade many people that they are unworthy of the vote?[33]

Anne Hunt, who was probably not aware that Mrs Pankhurst was one of the 'brainy women' referred to in the paper, admired the works of Carlyle, and likely just attacked the portrait at random. Struggling against the wardresses in court and stamping her feet when her arms were immobilised, she announced that, years later the painting's historical value would be raised by the attention it had received from the suffragettes. It was also an argument which Christabel had used in relation to Mary Richardson's destruction of the 'Rokeby Venus'. Perhaps in some ways, both women were right.

16.

Their Last Gasp

Kitty found herself involved in one more battle and, indirectly, in a final scandal as the stakes continued to get higher. Christabel's gravitation towards Christianity was evident in editions of the *Suffragette* and she used religious imagery to work supporters of the WSPU into a greater frenzy. The Easter edition of 10 April 1914 features a barefoot suffragette taken to her place of torture, against a background of the Cross. She is to be crucified on the cell slab or in the prisoner's chair. Within, Ida Wylie's piece 'Resurrection' declares that:

> We stand now before the greatest resurrection which the world has seen since Easter day nigh on two thousand years ago – the resurrection not of a nation but of two-thirds of humanity, of a whole sex. ... No other period of apparent death has been so long, nor the awakening so long tarrying.[34]

Having sacrificed herself over and over again for the cause, Mrs Pankhurst was now saving her strength for the deputation to Buckingham Palace on 21 May to see King George V. Where Margaret Skirving had failed, Mrs Pankhurst would surely succeed. Three days before the deputation, the WSPU hired a large empty house overlooking the royal abode. Kitty was in the thick of events inside the WSPU's building, watching suffragettes entering alone or in pairs, some disguised as servants. Any perceptive and patient bystander in the street would have noticed that none of these visitors were leaving. The vast house accommodated around

200 women. Among them was Mrs Pankhurst. Then, on the morning of 21 May, the papers carried the advertisement revealing the nature of these goings-on: a deputation would walk along Grosvenor Place and the virtually flat Constitution 'Hill' to reach the Palace for 4 p.m. *The Times* reassured its readers that the police had arranged for the approaches to the Palace to be sealed off. One thousand police officers formed a cordon around the Palace and more were seen within the courtyards, greatly augmenting the normal levels of protection.

Then the women emerged from the house. Kitty, Mrs Pankhurst, Rosa May Billinghurst and Gladys Schütze took part in the march which included women from across the country. The deputation, which walked in groups of eight, two policemen at its head, formed at Grosvenor Square, Mayfair. When the deputation reached the Wellington Arch the trouble began. The women saw a large police contingent and a number of mounted officers. Arch gates were closing as they arrived but Mrs Pankhurst, slight as she was, managed to slip through. She looked back in horror as more women tried to push through, throwing themselves against the gates to prevent themselves from being shut out. Mrs Pankhurst could not help admiring the determination of these bleeding and bruised women in what appeared to be a tough fight, of hundreds against thousands. Women were trampled by horses' hooves and those who, like Kitty, grabbed the reins, were struck by truncheons. Kitty had brought a pair of secateurs from her garden in Theydon Bois and succeeded in dismantling three bridles which caused a necessary distraction as the officers, who attempted to strike her with their batons, had to dismount to assess the damage.

Kitty found herself squashed against the railings by a horse's hindquarters but was not kicked. She was impressed by the self-sacrifice of the women shown, given that they could be killed at any instant, while the police were 'the roughest men' she had ever encountered, hitting and even throwing the women. Kitty was thrown several times. A police officer shoved her into a crowd, who in turn pushed Kitty down Constitution Hill. This time she was kicked. Thankfully, a small group of men clasped hands and formed a cordon around her, seeing her into a taxi. But Kitty did not go home. She and another woman returned to the scene, telling her former attackers that she was not afraid of them. The spirit of her uncle, William Baldwin, lived on in her; she persevered resolutely with her secateurs, marching straight forward as far as she could go.

Rosa May Billinghurst watched Kitty and other women cutting the bridles. Her carriage was being overturned when Ellen Dewar, who, with her Bodyguard team, had been tasked with helping Mrs Pankhurst reach the Palace, spotted her and came to her immediate assistance. Ellen was arrested. Her collar bone was broken and she also had broken ribs but she was released by a sympathetic sergeant. Kitty and Rosa May blamed plain-clothes officers for the violence. It was as if they were attempting to break the suffragettes' morale, picking off the weaker targets. Rosa May was squirted with green paint and struck on the arm by an inspector before she and her vehicle were thrown into the paths of a bus which managed to stop in time. When she recovered, a policeman punched her in the chest.

It is likely Kitty drew her Indian club as others were doing. Some women threw red and green paint over the policemen. Gladys Schütze was horrified by what she experienced and witnessed. As she stood against the railings at Constitution Hill, a mounted officer on a grey horse struck her on the head with his truncheon and backed his horse into her. The animal kicked her in the lower abdomen and her already weakened hip which meant that she was too incapacitated to work. She overheard a constable tell another to grab a woman by the breasts. Janie Allan, who took part in the deputation, noticed that the police guarding the Wellington Arch were particularly aggressive. To Mrs Pankhurst, this was Black Friday all over again. Kitty agreed. Her statement of what she saw was published in the *Suffragette*:

> Most of the mobbing seemed to be instigated by plain clothes men. It seemed as if they were out to terrify us and break our nerve down. I was out on Black Friday, and have been on several deputations, but I have never seen women so disgracefully treated before, or our women so inspiringly courageous – the elderly ones in particular.[35]

Over sixty women and three men were arrested. The temporary police station within the Arch's wall, where a collection of the women were locked up, was raided, furniture and glass smashed. At their trial at Bow Street, shoes, oaths and a bag of flour were lobbed at the magistrate, Sir John Dickinson. Mrs Pankhurst and Mrs Duckett, who had been marching close to Kitty, had managed to make their way down Constitution Hill and through the police cordon at the bottom of the hill before Mrs Pankhurst was spotted. Mrs Pankhurst was feeling very pleased with herself until an inspector took hold of the WSPU leader and carried her into a waiting taxi, two detectives springing in after her. 'Arrested at the gates of the Palace. Tell the King!' Mrs Pankhurst called to press reporters.

Captured at various angles, the confrontation outside Buckingham Palace between the delicate rebel woman and the stocky figure of authority became a symbol of women's metaphorical struggle against patriarchy. Silhouetted against the pale background, her elegant high-heeled shoes float mutinously off the ground, her ankles crossed, hinting at the unyielding stiffness of her body as she resists and twists painfully in the officer's sure-footed grasp. One of her shoes falls off. Yet throughout the tussle, she exudes a sense of elegance, like, as Christabel felt, a queen at her coronation. Close by, a plain-clothes detective in a boater hovers, a concerned expression on his face as he supervises the officer and testily directs words in the direction of his colleague's recalcitrant cargo. She reassured Ethel Smyth that she had young bones and withstood the hug but Sylvia Pankhurst noticed that in truth it was causing her great pain.

Her 6ft 4in captor, whose 'huge', 'herculean' and 'burly' build fascinated journalists, has passed into the history books with barely a mention of his name but at the time the incident and its aftermath made him nationally famous. Chief Inspector Francis Henry Rolfe of A Division was known for his tough and healthy physique and 'plucky' character, while the slight Mrs Pankhurst famously made it known how weak she had been made by her numerous encounters with death. Yet, in a matter of months, this mighty man, with an equally large personality to ensure his popularity among the force, was himself struck down with a sudden illness.

Chief Inspector Rolfe had dealt with the suffragettes on numerous occasions, one memorable event being the smashing of eighteen panes of McKenna's doorway and windows at his Smith Square home. The protest was made early in the morning of 14 March in response to the sudden arrest of Mrs Pankhurst at St Andrew's Hall. The six window smashers, one of whom described herself as 32-year-old 'Boadicea', appeared at Westminster Police Court. Gwen Cook also took part in the raid. Rolfe witnessed the attack and appeared in court to give evidence of the weapons brandished by the women, which included 7lb sledge hammers and life-preservers. Constable Bolter, stationed in Gayfere Street, saw most of the group emerge from a taxi and steal towards Mr McKenna's house.

Brindle St James.

Stained-glass dedication to Frances Mary Buss, St Mary's Theydon Bois. (Photographer Hugh Meteyard)

Three Ladies Window, Brindle St James.

Kitty's playing cards. (Museum of London)

The 'E.P.' pews at St Martin's, Ongar. (Reproduced with kind permission from St Martin's Chipping Ongar)

Falmouth Harbour. (Reproduced with kind permission from Judy Ford)

Waltham Abbey, circa 1920s. (Reproduced with kind permission from Judy Ford)

Hulls Mill, also known as Maplestead or Hovis Mill, on the River Colne. At the time of painting, this mill was the smallest and much prized mill of the Hovis breadmaking company. (Reproduced with kind permission from Chris Ripper)

Corfe Castle. (Reproduced with kind permission from Chris Ripper)

The Fig Tree Room at 63 Glebe Place as it is now. (Reproduced with kind permission from Sandra de Laszlo)

The exterior of Glebe Place. Photograph taken during the heatwave of 2022, in sharp contrast to the damp February night which witnessed the Battle of Glebe Place.

Front of 63 Glebe Place.

The magistrate of Westminster Police Court declared that he had never heard such a deplorable story and sentenced them all to two months' hard labour.

'Tripped over a Rope', 'Police Inspector's Death Sting', 'Fatal Gnat Sting' ran the news when describing Rolfe's death. He was policing the Royal Agricultural Show, Shrewsbury on 2 July when his heel caught on a 2ft rope and he landed on his elbow. He died of meningitis following blood poisoning – not a gnat bite as the press had first asserted – at St Thomas's Hospital on 19 July, leaving behind his wife Ellen and seven children. Among the many mourners attending his funeral at Wanstead was Sir Edward Henry himself. The newspapers printed his photograph, alongside that of the one in which he featured with Mrs Pankhurst, his legacy being intertwined with the woman in his grip.

When Kitty had some time to rest, she resolved to embark on further militancy. It was hard to find stones in Central London and so she broke a cabinet minister's window with a cricket ball. Kitty was arrested but her fine was paid by an unknown supporter. It was the sixth and last time that she was arrested. Grace Roe was also apprehended after the Buckingham Palace incident, in a raid on WSPU offices on Saturday, 23 May. McBrien ordered a complete search of Lincoln's Inn House and found clubs similar to those used during the Buckingham Palace demonstration. When the WSPU took possession of Lincoln's Inn House around a month later, there had been much damage, with torn and scattered clothes and photographs strewn about. A few days later, during a service at St Paul's, a suffragette cried: 'Christ is being crucified in Holloway!'

On 24 May, Kitchener took part in the dramatic re-arrest of Sylvia in the East End's Victoria Park, which is shaped like a kicking Wellington boot. As she walked to Victoria Park from Old Ford Road, which glances off the heel and ankle of the park, she was chained to twenty men and women who were cleverly fastened using padlocks in a line on either side of her. However, Kitchener and his team managed to uncouple her from the others. He was taken aback by the anger of her self-defence when she was put into the vehicle. While her friends aimed at them with their banners, Sylvia thrust a particularly lethal-looking hatpin at him.

The day after the deputation to the king, the *Police Review and Parade Gossip* published a piece entitled 'The Appointment of Policewomen'. The paper reported that the employment of women police officers had met with varying success abroad and contrasting responses from within the British police force. Scotland Yard did not feel employing female constables was worthwhile, as women were already employed in vigilance work and that related to women and children and to female prisoners. Mrs Dacre Fox's reply, which charts how WSPU attitudes had shifted since the Princes' Skating Rink ballot of 1909, was included:

We, of course, think the idea is excellent. There should be no specialising between men and women; the community should have the pick of the best of both sexes. The doctrine of physical force and the sex question apply less in this respect than in any other, as Policemen only exist by the moral force behind them, which would be equally behind Policewomen. In any case, in the natural order of things the spheres of activity of Policemen and Policewomen would automatically adjust themselves to circumstances, and where women were most useful thither would their energies be directed.[36]

The *Police Review and Parade Gossip* felt that the best people to ask about whether women should join the police were constables themselves, and invited correspondence. But the editor believed that women's and men's skills would complement each other: '[H]ow pleasant upon the long beat might such co-operation prove!'

Grace Roe felt as if she were losing consciousness as she stood in the dock. She wanted to tell the court about her ordeal in remand. Six days of hell, her hands were scratched from fights with seven wardresses, and three doctors were required to pour liquid into her body. Judging from the sunken temples, which were so obvious to her friends as they watched her, her body had not absorbed the nourishment. For some reason, she could barely move. The words that would have expressed themselves through her blue lips came out as tears running down her bruised face.

Also bearing battle scars on her body and clothes was Nellie Hall, who had been charged with the possession of window-breaking equipment; she attempted a whisper and fainted. The magistrate was unsympathetic. Grace's and Nellie's fluctuating physical states, from near inertia to rage, would characterise this long drawn-out trial.

'Women have been tortured until they are nearly dead. ... I refuse absolutely to listen to anything you have to say. ... I won't be tried. ... Put my feet down. … I won't be tried. … How would you like to have tubes put down your throat? … Nobody who has not been forcibly fed knows what it is,'[37] Grace told the court on one occasion. Nellie, whose hair was disarranged from struggling with the officers who kept watch on her cried: 'You are all devils, you beasts.'

Nellie and Grace were removed and then brought back again but did not stay long due to their protests. The magistrate requested Arthur Marshall to exert a restraining influence on the women.

Nellie's mother and sister were released on bail. Hilda Burkitt, a mouse whose licence had expired, and bookkeeper Florence Tunks (represented by Arthur) were on trial for arson. They had been forcibly fed thrice daily while on remand. The raid of the WSPU premises made Arthur's job of locating relevant documents harder. Dr Flora Murray, who had accompanied Grace in court, had her suspicions confirmed when traces of bromide showed up in Kitty Marion's samples. Since Kitchener had arrested her, she had been forcibly fed 232 times. By the time of her release in April, she had lost over 2 stone and looked many years older than her age. Grace Roe, who was barely consciousness during some of the Conspiracy Trial, was also probably being drugged, Dr Murray stated.

Arthur went on holiday on 29 May, leaving the managing clerk of Messrs Hatchett Jones, Bisgood, Marshall & Thomas, Arthur James Barnett, in charge of his work relating to the Holloway prisoners he was representing. But Arthur's holiday was not to be a restful break. During the Conspiracy Trial, it emerged that Barnett had disgraced the firm through actions of which Arthur had no knowledge. On 6 June, Bodkin initiated proceedings against Barnett. Bodkin showed that, on Arthur's instigation, the firm had been acting for Grace Roe. She had vomited severely several times following the feeds and on 26 May, wardress Miss Cann found a paper-wrapped packet containing a tube of pills of a powerful emetic. It was a dangerous drug to take, particularly by someone in Grace's fragile state. The purpose was to make her so ill that she would be released early. On the note accompanying the pills was written:

I have had great difficulty in getting these. The person I saw was very loth to give them. Remember, you must never take more than one at a time. Ask to see Marshall again at once. I will send you in some. Say you must see him about your private affairs if you have difficulty. I hope it will be all right. We were glad to get news of you yesterday. Our friends were delighted with your protest in court. Everything is going splendidly. This feeding is horrible and it shows that they are at their last gasp.[38]

While Arthur Marshall was on holiday, Grace wrote to him. Her letter was passed to Arthur Barnett who met a 'Miss Cunningham' who gave him a letter to take to Grace. Armed with Grace's request for Arthur's or his representative's presence in jail, Arthur Barnett visited Grace on 30 May, the letter from Miss Cunningham in his hand. Holloway Prison rules stated that he had to sign a declaration that he was visiting her for professional purposes and to defend her. He signed the document and was admitted. His meeting with Grace took place in a room with a glass window. A prison official, a Miss Cann, watched them closely and spotted him passing something to her. Miss Cann immediately approached Grace and took the item out of her hand. It was a packet containing six tablets of even more potent apomorphine hydrochloride, with an accompanying message which was reprinted in various versions in the newspapers:

> I only got your note late last night. There is nothing more drastic to be had. You may take three at a time, and if that is not effective four at a time, but on no account more. Four is a little risky. Ask to see Mr. Barnett again to-morrow. ... I cannot dare think what you and Roberts are suffering. We must get you out. We are doing all we possibly can.

On the back of the missive was the request: 'Destroy the note.' Grace was sent back to her cell but Arthur Barnett, despite flouting the regulations, then went to see Nellie Hall.

Bodkin thought it deplorable that a professional man or one linked to a professional man (such as Arthur Marshall) abused this position of trust. Arthur Barnett had brought banned items into prison and now Barnett would himself be on trial. It was a slap on the wrist. As Ethel Smyth remembered:

> For years Mr. Arthur Marshall had looked after the legal business of the W.S.P.U., on lines usually adopted by fairly well-to-do people who served the Union; that is, there was more love about the transaction

than money! Also a grave risk. This fact I only learned many years later, and possibly Mrs. Pankhurst never realised it. If she had, the thought would have been brushed aside ... these things were inevitable! ... And indeed to one who expected prison matrons and police constables to throw up their jobs rather than bully Suffragettes, the possible effect on a solicitor's career of rendering services to law-breakers was all in the day's work ... part of the price that had to be paid for the enfranchisement of women! Yet she was much attached to both the Marshalls and had no more devoted friends.[39]

Bodkin also wanted to dispel any rumours circulated by the *Suffragette* that women were being drugged in prison, deliberately put into a drowsy state so that forcible feeding could be an easier process. He wanted to show that it was not the prison that was doing the drugging but the suffragettes and their legal advisers. Yet through their physical condition, not just weak from hunger but also, disquietingly, merely semi-conscious at points, Nellie and Grace provided a visual rebuttal to Bodkin's claims that his side was on the moral high ground. They were being drugged and, as far as Grace was concerned, she felt she needed to take drugs to make her vomit and undo the results of forcible feeding.

At her trial, Nellie Hall, very likely buoyed by the female audience and press reporters, interrupted Bodkin. 'Stop talking. We all want to hear what Miss Roe has to say.' She stood up for Arthur Barnett: 'We hear that a man has been summoned for giving a drug to women in prison. It is a lie.'

'Why, instead of raiding a clean and wholesome place like Lincoln's Inn House, did not the police raid the West End brothels?' protested Grace. Detective Lenehan attempted to give evidence, amid further shouting from Nellie. Grace and Nellie were sentenced to three months on 9 July.

At his trial on 13 June before Mr Bros of North London Police Court, Barnett claimed that he did not know that the packet contained pills. He pleaded guilty to conveying a letter to Grace Roe, contrary to regulations. Mr Muir, who defended Barnett, said that it was his client who had abused his position in the firm. 'Neither Mr Marshall nor any member of Mr Marshall's firm will act again for this Union in connection with any part of its business, legitimate or otherwise.' This was damage limitation and it worked in that the magistrate did not extend the punishment to Arthur's firm; Arthur Barnett was fined £10 and was ordered to pay

5 guineas in costs and then the case was dismissed. Clearly, Mr Bros did not believe the clerk when he claimed that he did not know what the prison regulations were. Whilst sympathetic to the WSPU's campaign, Arthur did not like the direction that the militants had taken the fight.

On the evening of 19 June, the Special Branch stepped up the search for mice. The officers found one, namely schoolteacher and mouse Arabella Scott, at the flat of a Miss de Pass when she was out. They also found some chains and paperwork. Homes of sympathisers were to be searched. The housekeeper of Glebe House asked for a warrant, but she was not allowed to see it. Then eighteen or nineteen men came into their hall and searched the whole house including the bedrooms. Officers trespassed on one of the two studios next to the house, pulling down a curtain and taking two address books and stamps, none of these items belonging to the Schützes. A previous houseguest of 63 Glebe Place, Kitty caused some animosity for her show of solidarity with her fellow suffragettes during a six-town Red Cross Cup competition held on 5 July at Copped Hall, Epping, close to Theydon Bois. The owner, Ernest Whytes, had inherited the eighteenth-century mansion from his elder brother and his father and had carried out significant remodelling. Although Kitty had gained her St John Ambulance medal a few years previously, the campaign for female suffrage now took up most of her time so she could not attend many lectures.

However, she was still involved with the Red Cross as a member of the 58th Essex detachment. In the morning everyone marched in long rows for inspection. Major Freeman and his colleagues impressed Kitty with their neat uniforms, helmets and white feathers and their medals. They were accompanied by a formidable-looking head army nurse. When they came to Kitty, they had rather a surprise. Unlike her fellow competitors, she was not wearing her Red Cross badge but instead had brazenly affixed the famous WSPU prison badge with the broad arrow on the Westminster portcullis under which sat the ribbon of the WSPU colours. Kitty wanted to draw attention to their campaign. Despite her convictions, she felt herself turn as scarlet as the major's uniform under his gaze as he scrutinised the medal with his eyeglass. The other contingents, curious as to the delay in proceedings, craned their necks in her direction. A rumour spread that Kitty had lost her detachment three points for her choice of badge. One of her party threatened to wrench it from her, but clearly Kitty's Bodyguard training gave her the confidence to say 'Come on then' and the woman shrank back.

After the lunch break, the competitors were asked to treat 'patients' who bore labels on them describing their wounds. Kitty's task within her group was to note their names, ages and religion. The same major again paid special attention to her, commenting on her writing and neatness. The commandant of the 58th detachment, a Mrs Gerald Buxton, shuffled her group into order and they were surprised to hear that they had won the cup. Kitty was elated not just for the win but for so much attention being paid to her badge and the cause it symbolised. The major was so impressed by the 'plucky little woman' and her badge that he would give her group the cup.

Rachel Barrett had successfully escaped the clutches of the authorities that summer. However, she was effectively imprisoned as, being responsible for bringing out the *Suffragette*, she barely went outside and her movements were restricted to after dark. After venturing out to have a confab with Christabel in Paris, Rachel returned to England in June and went to live with her lover Ida Wylie in Edinburgh with Ida's unsuspecting aunt. Jessie Kenney brought her material for the *Suffragette* which she assiduously printed once a week. Then, on 4 August, the British government declared war on Germany.

17.

Broken Hearts and Hammer Toes

Mrs Pankhurst had reminded Peter Schütze of his Australian mother, Caroline, a capable woman, just as able to asphalt a garden as she was able to talk about cultural matters or craft a Christmas dinner. A warm personality, she adored Peter and he adored her. It was why Gladys never forgave Mrs Pankhurst, whose pulse Peter had taken and whose speech he and Gladys had hosted, when she told him that people with German-sounding surnames had better keep a low profile. Mrs Pankhurst was making an observation of the brewing situation: police forces were having to cope with the growing threat of widespread anti-German riots.

Gladys's best-known novel *Mrs Fischer's War* (1930), prefaced by an impressed John Galsworthy, would have prejudice and alienation as the main themes, the wife of a husband with a German name who is disowned by pacifists and patriots alike. Unlike her soldier son John, Mrs Janet Fischer refuses to anglicise her German husband's surname by dropping the 'c'. Gladys, writing as Henrietta Leslie, dedicated the novel to her husband, with the inscription: 'You and I will lovers die.'

Mrs Pankhurst was a staunch Francophile and her anti-German sentiments dated back her school days at the progressive Parisian École Normale de Neuilly, where she made friends with Noémie Rochefort, the daughter of a Republican and swordsman, Henri Rochefort, in prison for his part in the Paris Commune. The École's walls were still pockmarked by bullet shots from the recently fought and lost Franco-Prussian war and the impact of the loss was evident as she and her friend walked the Parisian streets. 'Vive la France!' she called to her New York audience on 14 July 1918, her adopted birthday, a date which she shared with Arthur Marshall.

When war was declared amidst the warm and unsettled weather, a group of some thirty suffragettes took position across the road from 10 Downing Street, willing to serve their country. As far as Basil Thomson was concerned, the country had bigger problems to deal with than window-smashing suffragettes and so a truce was called and imprisoned women were released in the hope that they would be useful to the war effort. Kitchener, who had been deeply impressed by the suffragettes' show of loyalty, encountered a former mouse in a railway station and was struck by their exchange: 'Her smile of recognition when she saw me showed no sign of animosity, but, on the other hand, seemed to say, "Hello – we are on the same side now!"'

Christabel had begun to embark on her numerous anti-German motivational speeches to encourage women and men to join in the war effort. She had not suddenly become an apologist for the government against whom she had been so staunchly campaigning. Rather than fighting for the government, she was campaigning for the interests of the British people and Britain's friends, she argued. Standing alone on a stage at the Royal Opera House, surrounded by bouquets of lilies and roses, flags of Allied forces surrounding her, Christabel told her audience:

French civilisation is one of the finest civilisations in the world. … France is the land of ideas and ideals. … [T]hat country in which women's position is lowest and most hopeless, is Germany. Therefore, if the women of the world are to preserve and to increase the liberty they already enjoy, this country of ours must be victorious in the present war. The world domination that Germany seeks to win would mean the abasement of women, would mean a disastrous check to women's progress towards equal citizenship.[40]

Looking on with approval was Mrs Pankhurst. Sylvia was also in the audience, but not sitting next to her mother. Sylvia despaired, particularly when she thought of her father's own campaigns for international peace where he had been helped by her mother. Christabel had been concerned that Adela was planning to form an organisation with Sylvia to rival the WSPU.

Mrs Pankhurst, feeling that Adela also needed to find an outlet for her campaigning energies, encouraged her emigration to Australia. Like Sylvia, Adela was a pacifist and was campaigning against the war in Melbourne. The WSPU leader would never see her youngest daughter again.

Christabel Pankhurst renamed the *Suffragette* magazine *Britannia*, adopting a strident patriotic and anti-pacifist tone, in contrast to Sylvia's *The Woman's Dreadnought*. From Mrs Pankhurst's speeches, it is clear that Germans and Bolsheviks were the enemy, the former threatening the state and women's potential opportunities for future political liberation, while the latter, through encouraging class war and strike action, threatened the smooth operation of the military-industrial force and Britain's chance of winning the war.

Indignation at the Belgian atrocities further mobilised hatred towards Germans or Britons with Germanic connections. In the days before the First World War, Special Branch detectives had been keeping their eyes on known German agents and suspected spies. When war broke out, activities were naturally stepped up and Quinn issued the men with not one warrant but multiple warrants for arrest. On one occasion, Kitchener and his colleagues were sent to Victoria railway station to try to catch a manager of German spies in Britain.

Kitty Marion could see both the German and British viewpoint, but was convinced by the news of the Belgian atrocities to sympathise with the latter. However, despite her sympathies, she learnt that the police were after her as a suspected German spy, and when registration for all was made compulsory, Kitty Marion could no longer keep under the radar. She did not want to be deported but she did not want to get others in trouble for abetting her in her bid to remain obscure. Christabel told her to approach Quinn at Scotland Yard. Kitty Marion regarded him as 'quite a friendly enemy'. Obviously, he knew of her suffrage past with the WSPU, which was now loyal to the government in its time of need. Could she become a naturalised citizen and be exempt from deportation? A statement of her travels abroad and her movements was taken while Quinn and a colleague listened sympathetically. Bingham applied to the Home Secretary on her behalf but her application was denied. The Home Office did allow her to go to America, no doubt happy to shake off this problematic ex-mouse.

Special Branch men were in demand with some going off to work as liaison officers for navy and police. At the outbreak of the war, Kitchener was sent to Grimsby which he did not like as he preferred the variety of work offered in London. The chief constable did not appreciate the appointment of this outsider and, unusually for Kitchener, the local police were unhelpful in finding him accommodation. There was little work around the docks of the Humber to keep him active. Quinn told him to bide his time. In the winter of 1914, Kitchener married his girl from Olney, Helen (Nellie) Hoddle. Her father, Alfred, was a butcher and Nellie was born in Market Place, next door to what would become The Cowper Memorial Museum and Library in 1900, soon known as The Cowper and Newton Museum. Ralph Kitchener and Nellie were married in Grimsby which is where their first son Joseph was born.

Kitchener's work soon picked up pace. In May 1915, he arrested spy Ernst Gustave Waldemar Olsson who was working as a first mate on board the *Zeerand* which travelled from Grimsby to Rotterdam. Olsson had tried to bribe a marine store dealer into giving him information about the navy or military at Grimsby or the Humber defences. The papers mentioned Ralph Kitchener by name, revealing that he had found, amongst other items, diaries in Olsson's possession. A postcard belonging to Olsson bore official information which ought not to have been disseminated to anyone outside the British service. Olsson was found guilty of looking for information that might be useful to the enemy and, falling foul of the Official Secrets Act 1911, he was sentenced to penal servitude. Kitchener's arrest of Olsson put him in good stead with the local chief constable.

In September, Kitchener was put on to a case at least equal to the account of the fate of the *Demeter* bearing its evil load, which runs aground off the coast of Whitby in Bram Stoker's *Dracula*. Kitchener would never have believed all that was reported in the papers had he not seen the aftermath of 'The *Noordzee* Horror' with his own eyes. In mid-September 1915, a Norwegian cargo ship caught sight of a dilapidated Dutch herring lugger, its hacked sails flapping. The *Noordzee* docked in Grimsby and Kitchener was one of the first officers on deck. There was one mast and some rigging, but the nets, compass, lifeboat and gear were missing and the donkey engine had been thrown overboard. Not only had the sails been axed but the wheel had been attacked. In the cabin, the slaughterhouse stench was unbearable. Kitchener saw immediately that there was blood everywhere, and chunks of skull were embedded among the ship biscuits and strewn rice.

It transpired that the crew of a dozen members, which included two boys, had succumbed to a form of religious mania, exacerbated by strong alcohol. An enormously sized crew member insisted that he had just risen from the dead and was under instructions to find the Devil in the ship. Three crew members were killed – one was decapitated – and the men wrecked the ship to destroy the Devil's supposed hiding places while the two boys hid below. The crew were sent back to Holland and the men were found guilty of murder. Ruminating on the terrible nature of the crimes that had been committed, Kitchener concluded that an evil spirit of sorts had indeed been on board.

There were further dangers up the east coast. In December 1914, three German warships pierced through the morning fog and shelled Old and West Hartlepool, Scarborough and Whitby, killing and injuring over 120 people, including women and children and damaging Scarborough's iconic Grand Hotel.

Anyone caught making sketches or working on paintings near sensitive sights or the coast came immediately under suspicion. It was this sense of wariness and not just the German lettering on Kitty's bag that led to the police officers approaching the Marshalls on their sketching tour of Ipswich. Kitty, who was a Red Cross nurse, could be called up at any time, therefore, the Marshalls decided to stay local and go on an English walking holiday. She did not like to take her exercise in the form of walking, preferring any kind of vehicle to travelling on foot, but she was persuaded by the prospect of doing some sketching. Her Austrian rush bag had *Schultasche* written on it and she thought nothing of the matter. Having trekked across the countryside, covered in dust, the Marshalls were spotted by a curious local on a bicycle who reported them to the police. They were then approached by a sergeant and a group of constables in a field on their route from Ongar to Ipswich. The sergeant opened the conversation with: 'Enquiries have been brought to us about suspected German spies.' Kitty showed him her sketch and instructed the men to telephone Scotland Yard where her file was kept. Apparently, the officers were convinced by her identity and expressed admiration for the suffragettes.

The attack on the coast from Zeppelins, which looked like silver cigars, highlighted women's vulnerability in war. As she was filling in her American immigration application form, Kitty Marion witnessed one pass over the streets of London, and felt both pride in German technology and horror at the use to which it was now being put. When Mary Allen saw her first Zeppelin over the skies of Hull, she felt a stab of fear as she watched the machine hover overhead in silent dominance. Ida Wylie saw a Zeppelin hanging from a rooftop across the road from her home. When it broke up into flaming pieces, she was horrified and satisfied at the same time. Dazed and angry, she sheltered on the staircase, the safest place to take refuge during an airplane raid, and, through the window on the landing, glimpsed searchlights seeking out victims. After an attack, special constables and Boy Scouts on bicycles sounded their bugles to signal the all-clear. While some were relieved it was over, others had trouble processing what had happened. Mary Allen saw victims of aerial bombings displaying signs of shock, with one lady hurriedly wheeling out a canary inside a pram, absent-mindedly leaving her infant grandchild at home.

Women of all backgrounds were doing their bit for the war effort. Despite St Paul's exhortations that women should remain silent in church, during wartime, they started to read the lesson. But there was much debate over whether they could speak in front of a mixed audience or, indeed, where in the church this daring break with convention was to take place – surely not in the pulpit, where the vicar usually stood? Other women flouted bans, venturing into the front lines to transport the wounded in motorcycles, while knitting circles raised funds for soldiers' provisions and some women caused amusement in West End gentlemen's clubs when they served them their whisky and soda. Brewing tea was now seen as an important activity as women volunteered in soldiers' recreation tents, offering home comforts and organising wholesome British forms of entertainment.

Gladys Griffiths took part in the Right to Serve march which took place on 17 July 1915 amidst bad, windy weather. A crisis in shell production was blamed for the failure to break through the Western Front but there was a labour shortage in munitions factories. The march was a WSPU event that Lloyd George had asked the Pankhursts to organise. There were 20,000 women of all classes marching, flourishing red, white and blue, instead of the colours which they had sported during their suffrage demonstrations and marches – which themselves had been good practice. Mrs Pankhurst and Annie Kenney walked behind a pageant in which Belgium was represented by a barefoot woman in torn clothing, mourning her children. Along the route there were fifty tables at which women, moved by the spectacle, could sign up.

The overwhelmingly female workforce who were creating shells in armament factories were especially vulnerable Home Front targets, as were the women police who were sent to watch over them as well as oversee their behaviour, steering these newly liberated women away from perceived bad influences. Assisted by suffragette Nina Boyle and then Mary Allen, Margaret Damer Dawson's Women's Police Volunteers (later renamed the Women's Police Service) trained women in first aid, jujitsu, drill, espionage and police court procedure. Martial arts skills were highly useful: a shell-shocked veteran, who was preparing to bayonet an escalator of oncoming and panicked commuters whom he believed to be German soldiers, was stopped in his tracks by a jujitsu hold.

While her mother and oldest sister were spurring on the recruitment drive, Sylvia Pankhurst launched a fight against poverty and malnutrition, transforming a neglected East End pub into a mother-and-baby centre. Mrs Pankhurst, too, felt she ought to do her bit and she adopted four 3-year-old 'war babies'. She decided that a fresh start would be best for them and had their past remodelled. The girls' birth certificates were destroyed and new birth dates were invented. Kitty Marshall tried to reason with her, thinking she was taking on too much. 'My dear, I wonder I did not take forty,' Mrs Pankhurst responded. Kitty thought that Mrs Pankhurst was kindness itself. Not all of Mrs Pankhurst's old followers agreed. Mrs Pankhurst, who normally received funding from the loyal WSPU, was disheartened by the lack of support and funding for her project. To support them, Mrs Pankhurst gave lectures in Canada, accompanied by Catherine Pine, whom the girls called Aunt Kate, but eventually came to the realisation that she could not keep all the children.

Kitty put her skills as a Red Cross nurse to use, working for Dr Flora Murray and Dr Louisa Garrett Anderson. As Kitty appreciated, Louisa's mother had overcome tremendous obstacles to enter the medical profession and now Flora and Louisa had to deal with the prejudice of the British government. So, they successfully approached the French embassy. The Women's Hospital Corps (WHC), which bore the motto 'Deeds not Words', transformed the newly constructed Hôtel Claridge in Paris into a hospital, using the ladies' cloakroom as an operating theatre and

the grill room as a mortuary. Despite having been denied adequate training in treating men, female doctors gave orders, inspected, studied and
operated on frequently shattered male bodies and minds. They still had
to put up with the usual comments. Cicely Hamilton, who went to work
in a woman-run hospital during the war, was amused by a Frenchman's
attitude that the women who worked there must have had unhappy love
lives: 'I was rather tickled by the idea of curing your own broken heart
by removing someone else's hammer toe, but the man was perfectly
serious.' Impressed patients passed bullets to each other across the beds,
exclaiming that female surgeons had extracted them. Even a visit from
Mrs Pankhurst perked up the patients, some of whom had converted to
the cause. Another WHC hospital was set up at Château Mauricien in the
Channel coast holiday town of Wimereux. There, a wounded policeman
recognised a suffragist. She told him he had arrested her. 'I wouldn't have
mentioned it, Miss,' he replied with embarrassment. 'We'll let bygones
be bygones.'

At the beginning of 1915, wounded soldiers were evacuated to Britain
for treatment. Flora and Louisa were offered the opportunity to run a
hospital in London which attracted former Bodyguard member Joyce
Nettlefold as well as Kitty, who had volunteered at an auxiliary hospital in Theydon Bois. The site, which received 26,000 patients and was
chosen as the location for the Endell Street Hospital, was the St Giles
Union Workhouse in Bloomsbury, said to have inspired the setting in
Dickens' *Oliver Twist*. Louisa, Flora and their teams dismantled many
of the grim paraphernalia associated with the building's former func-
tion including the unloved bric-a-brac belonging to the Guardians and
some ghoulish restraints which they found in padded rooms. The hospital opened in May 1915. While there were other organisations run by
women, Endell Street Hospital was the only overtly militant suffragist-
run military unit.

The hospital's central London location meant that thirty to fifty soldiers arrived in Kitty's care suddenly, often at night, swiftly taken up on
custom-built lifts. Surgeons often performed twenty operations a day.
Endell Street staff pioneered prosthetics and experimented successfully
with new substances that reduced the number of dressings required.
Soldiers marvelled at the 'flappers' who conveyed them to the wards with
their colourful bedding, the scent of flowers in the air. The seventeen

wards were unofficially given the names of female patron saints, a bridge between the spiritually and physically palliative images of women with which the soldiers were familiar and the scientifically intrepid and capable real women in whom the men now placed their trust. Each ward was proud of its surgeon. There was a recreation area, which boasted a green room, and a stage which bore the motto 'Deeds not Words'. Over 1,000 artistes performed at the Endell Street Hospital. Other activities included basket-weaving, which Kitty enjoyed. The hospital was entirely staffed by women, from the doctors to the orderlies, but as Kitty noticed, men were still called in to take out the bins!

The hospital also cared for women, such as officers' wives, and continued to operate until 1919. After the war, a number of the orderlies, who had escaped the machinations of brothers, fathers or other male figures to stop them from working at Endell Street, had to return home, unemployed, to live once more under patriarchal rule. Only a small number pursued successful careers in the medical profession, but one of the major achievements associated with the hospital was that women were permitted to treat male patients and practise military medicine.

Most of the casualties treated at Endell Street were British, but after the Gallipoli Campaign, the hospital saw an influx of ANZAC troops. Kitty's brother, Lieutenant Francis Augustus Jacques of the 14th (King George's Own) Ferozepore Sikhs of the British Indian Army, was drawn into the Gallipoli conflict. He had been involved in various imperial campaigns including the suppression of a rebellion near Afghanistan in 1897, and China (during the Boxer Rebellion), both campaigns earning him medals. He was made Lieutenant Colonel in 1913 and countered a Turkish offensive at the Suez Canal at the outbreak of the First World War before proceeding to the Dardanelles.

By the end of 1914, fighting on the Western Front was at a stalemate. Commonwealth and French forces decided that the war could be shortened if a new front was opened at the Dardanelles, a strategically important 60-mile-long, thin strip of water, dividing Europe and Asia. The plan was to knock Germany's ally, the crumbling 'Sick Man of Europe', the Ottoman Empire, out of the war, thereby securing British interests in the Suez Canal. Churchill thought that this goal could be achieved using outdated British ships and he underestimated the determination of enemy forces and the harsh terrain.

Just a couple of days before the first Allied landings at Gallipoli, Kinton Jacques fell into a coma. Kitty's father was 77 years old and living with Norah in Hove. Despite his failing health, he continued to preach in the diocese of Chichester until a month before his death. He died near the end of April and was laid to rest next to Caroline Augusta in Brindle. The Allied landings, which were set in motion only days after Kinton Jacques' death, were the first of a series of unsuccessful attempts to conquer the peninsula. Francis Jacques was sent to the Dardanelles, leaving behind him a young family and his wife Olivia Katharine – whose maiden name had also been Jacques. Francis thought of Olivia and the girls when he knew that he would not make it out of the advance alive, but he drew strength from the fact that they would be looked after. Francis died on 4 June on an advance on the Gallipoli Peninsula. After many failed advances, British troops were evacuated in January of the next year. Francis was buried in the battlefield at Gallipoli. His name appears on the Helles Memorial on the tip of the Gallipoli Peninsula. Its 30-metre-high obelisk is visible from ships sailing through the Dardanelles. In Brindle church, a plaque was hung close to the names of his mother and father. 'Thy way, not mine, Oh Lord', reads his inscription.

Kitty probably did not see Mrs Pankhurst very much during the war. Unlike her daughter Sylvia, Mrs Pankhurst did not want Russia to leave the war and accept peace on German terms. Lloyd George supported her planned visit to Russia. Her former bodyguard, Helen Crawfurd, was furious. She felt that Mrs Pankhurst had not stood up for exploited workers and was not a suitable representative for all British women. Mrs Pankhurst and Jessie Kenney arrived in Petrograd on 18 June. Mrs Pankhurst found herself among a group of admiring women and met Commander Maria Botchkareva (or Bachkarova), who led the Women's Death Battalion, formed by Alexander Kerensky to embarrass soldiers into fighting. Two-thirds of the battalion were killed or injured, sometimes going over the top of the trenches before the male soldiers. Once the Bolsheviks came to power, the battalion were told to return home and don women's clothing. Jessie Kenney and Mrs Pankhurst toured Moscow, meeting Elizabeth Robins' brother Raymond. When they returned to Petrograd, Jessie and Mrs Pankhurst were advised to wear peasant costume so as not to appear bourgeois but Mrs Pankhurst refused, stating that she was not too scared to walk among the people. When a frightened maid came to tell

Mrs Pankhurst to get changed quickly as there was fighting in the streets and the hotel needed to be evacuated, Mrs Pankhurst replied that she was not leaving until she was properly dressed.

Wartime called into question the system of voting. In order to vote, a man needed to be resident for a certain amount of time. Now men were going to the trenches for unspecified durations. This situation prompted the idea that voting qualifications needed to be shaken up. And if the rules were due for an overhaul, might this not be a good time to introduce women's suffrage? Mrs Pankhurst and her friends launched The Women's Party on 7 November 1917, the year in which Bodyguard Gwen Cook married Daniel O'Brien. Mrs Pankhurst was the Women's Party treasurer, Annie Kenney its secretary and Flora Drummond took on the role of chief organiser. *Britannia* became the organ of the Women's Party. Among its pledges, the party advocated equal pay, equal marriage and divorce laws, the raising of the age of consent for girls, equal parental rights, better housing and support for mothers and mothers-to-be. On the negative side, the party also advocated a punitive peace for Germany, rationing and naturalisation laws to prevent Germans from acquiring British citizenship. Mrs Pankhurst felt that there were German sympathisers living in her midst, bent on harming British interests.

The House of Commons passed the Representation of the People Bill with a majority of 385 to 55 and the Royal Assent for the Representation of the People Act was given on 6 February 1918, six days before Elizabeth Wolstenholme Elmy died. Some women now had the vote. But the celebrations were muted by the war. Edith Garrud's 24-year-old son, Lieutenant Owen Henry Garrud of the Post Office Rifles, died in August 1918, and was buried in Croisilles, France, only months before the Armistice. A family photograph captures a proud Mrs Garrud, her thick wavy hair parted in the centre, chin cocked up slightly, proudly close to Owen who is next to his sister Sybil. The women are smiling, but he has been captured in mid-sentence.

18

Twinkle, Twinkle, Little Star

By 1918, Kitty and Arthur had moved to Chipping Ongar, just west of Chelmsford. Jane Taylor, who wrote the lyrics to what became known as *Twinkle, Twinkle, Little Star*, was buried within the hall of Ongar's Congregational Church. David Livingstone lived in Ongar in 1838 prior to becoming a missionary and proceeding to Africa, where he eventually met Kitty's uncle William Baldwin. Livingstone is said to have frequented the Royal Oak and got lost on a walk to London. Kitty became the local representative of the anti-slavery Universities' Mission to Central Africa, which was founded in Livingstone's honour. Right across the road was The Old House, where Kitty and Arthur lived. Dating from the 1600s, The Old House sits in a long and narrow plot, which mirrors the contours of the motte-and-bailey castle behind the town, discernible through its undulations in the ground. The home is set back slightly from its neighbour, behind a row of bushes, the walls plastered with pargetting and the living room, with its fireplace and seventeenth-century timber beams and low ceiling, peeps out on to the High Street. Here, Mrs Pankhurst felt at home, a comfortable nook where she talked about politics and people to her close friends.

Women of the age of 30 and over who satisfied property qualifications or who were university graduates or wives of men who met the criteria were now given the parliamentary franchise. However, many of the younger women who had worked in key roles in the war, such as in munitions factories, were shut out of this new legislation, which benefited predominantly middle-class housewives, like Kitty. While she was over 30, Lilian Lenton, with neither property nor husband, was disappointed to be shut out of the legislation. Millicent Fawcett felt that there was more work to be done. The NUWSS changed its name to the National Union of Societies for Equal Citizenship while Christabel stood as the Women's Party candidate for the industrial Birmingham constituency of Smethwick in the 'khaki election' of 14 December 1918. She lost her seat by a narrow margin of 775 votes, which was devastating for Mrs Pankhurst. With the dwindling away of the Women's Party, Mrs Pankhurst went to the United States and Canada in September 1919, determined to campaign against Bolshevism.

When American Nancy Astor became the first MP to take her seat, Mrs Pankhurst was also disappointed: she hadn't been one of the WSPU's trailblazers. Lady Rhondda, who would not live to see the Peerage Act receive the Royal Assent and therefore would never have the chance to take her seat in the House of Lords, founded the Six Point Group to tackle inequality in the areas of politics, education, morality, society, economics and the law. Lady Rhondda's mother, Sybil, was also busy with Kitty, as joint honorary secretaries of a Testimonial Fund which had been set up in 1919 to provide support for Christabel and her mother. By November 1922, they had raised just under £3,000, a fraction of the £10,000 they were hoping to collect. After her bills were paid, Arthur presented Mrs Pankhurst with the remaining money which went towards a house in Westward Ho! but the restless Mrs Pankhurst was unable to maintain the property financially and the house was let and then sold at a significant loss.

In the year in which the Six Point Group was formed, Arthur Marshall became a Freeman of the City of London, joining The Worshipful Company of Basketmakers. Arthur joined mainly for networking and to engage in charitable giving. He joined 'by redemption', that is, he paid a fee, as opposed to joining through an apprenticeship or through his parents. The fellowship to which Arthur belonged was established in 1569 and the Company Arms bear the motto: 'Let us love one another'. After banquets and dinners, the toastmaster announced, 'The Prime Warden bids you all a hearty welcome, and drinks to you in a Loving Cup.' The vessel which contained spiced wine was passed round. Arthur stood up, as the man next to him presented him with the Cup. They bowed. Arthur lifted the lid and his neighbour took a sip from the Cup. It was important that Arthur used his right hand, a demonstration that he did not mean to attack his neighbour with the sword that was normally carried in this hand.

Kitty frequently sketched out and about in Ongar and Mrs Pankhurst was also on the move, becoming a Canadian citizen in 1923, lecturing widely in Canada on venereal disease, sexual promiscuity and Bolshevism. While selling the *Birth Control Review* in New York, Kitty Marion saw Mrs Pankhurst and Nurse Pine, who both pointedly ignored her, which Kitty Marion felt to be on account of her German connections. Before long, Mrs Pankhurst found that she was struggling with the bitter Canadian winter. Moreover, her finances were dwindling and she realised she could not support her family, and so she and Christabel made the hard decision to relinquish two of Mrs Pankhurst's war babies and return home. Mrs Pankhurst turned down Lady Rhondda's offer to work for the Six Point Group and felt that the spread of Bolshevism needed her attention.

Indirectly, Kitchener's involvement in the Campbell Case of 1924 had a bearing on Kitty Marshall's future activities. Kitchener was asked to arrest John Ross Campbell, editor of *Workers' Weekly*, who was charged with incitement to mutiny for printing a piece which encouraged soldiers to stand side-by-side with workers in industrial disputes and to unite with other workers and other armed forces to smash capitalist oppression. Under influence of backbenchers, Prime Minister Ramsay MacDonald's Labour government did not proceed with his prosecution and the Liberals and Conservatives won a vote of no confidence against MacDonald. Parliament was dissolved and the general election in 1924 saw a landslide victory for the Conservatives under Stanley Baldwin and the demotion of Herbert Asquith's Liberals to third-party status.

It appeared that the Communist Party's policies were at odds with British law, bringing about the 'Dictatorship of the Proletariat' by illegal methods. Kitchener felt that no government could turn a blind eye to such propaganda; Mrs Pankhurst could not have agreed more. Kitchener was aware that dire poverty could push people to further ends of the political spectrum. On the orders of Basil Thomson, Kitchener was told to visit the family of one arrested man. He had his colleagues bring in food for the family, a gesture for which the husband was grateful – the movement had not provided his family with support while he was jailed, but the police had looked after them and he therefore changed his mind about taking part in further action.

By 1926, Kitchener and Mrs Pankhurst were doing their bit to chip away at the General Strike. Now a senior detective inspector, Kitchener was asked to interview a supporter of the General Strike who advocated that the armed forces use their weapons and join the strikers. Kitchener gave him a friendly warning and presented him with a verbatim account of his speech. He then toned down his speeches. Mrs Pankhurst offered Mary Allen her services and went to areas of deprivation, organising concerts for strikers' wives, attempting to assuage some of the bitterness. Baldwin's wife, Lucy, collaborated with Mary Allen to provide transport for children to school, women to places of work and patients to hospitals. Mrs Pankhurst was impressed by the new government and she stood as the unlikely Conservative candidate for Whitechapel and St George's in a bid to stop the spread of communism among working-class women and their families.

In contrast to Mrs Pankhurst's uncertain success in her chosen political field in the East End, Christabel's career was blossoming. She was now a sought-after writer on religion, and a preacher, speaking at her old haunt, the Free Trade Hall, and at one point sharing a platform with Lloyd George at a Baptist service. For Christabel, Christianity offered world peace and inner peace; through the bond of religion, Christabel and the Pethick Lawrences were able to come to terms with their past difficulties and move forward. Christabel was sometimes asked to lecture to the Christian Police Association. 'I said I would come, because it is a Police Association.' She added playfully, 'You see, there was a time when we – well, when we worked together.'

The Marshalls arranged for Mrs Pankhurst to occupy a set of rooms in Whitechapel, a base from which to visit tenements and pubs and to speak to potential converts at open-air meetings. But Kitty and Ethel Smyth sensed that their friend looked exhausted, so the Marshalls took her to Gibraltar. They arrived back in England in the spring of 1927, Mrs Pankhurst's health much improved. During her campaigning, Mrs Pankhurst stayed with the Marshalls from time to time, tending to the flowers in the churchyard of the brick and flint St Martin's, Chipping Ongar's oldest surviving building, dating back to the eleventh century. In April 1917, Arthur had been appointed sidesman which involved helping the church warden, taking the collection and showing congregants to their places. The Marshalls were both present at a meeting in 1918 and in that same year the rector himself proposed that sideswomen be elected. The proposal was passed by nine votes to two. In 1918, Kitty became one of two sideswomen. These new appointments were a reflection of the changing world, with women's greater role in church and politics. Shortly afterwards, Oxford lecturer and women's suffrage campaigner, Maude Royden, became the first woman to preach inside a Church of England church, despite the Bishop of London's misgivings.

Then suddenly, Mrs Pankhurst heard what Christabel and Ada Goulden Bach had been keeping from her: Sylvia had given birth out of wedlock at the beginning of December 1927. A photograph of Richard Keir Pethick Pankhurst appeared in the press. His father was Silvio Corio, an Italian anarchist. Sylvia's mother and sister never forgave her for sullying the Pankhurst name and whenever Sylvia called, Mrs Pankhurst would lock herself in her room. Despite Sylvia's appeals, Mrs Pankhurst refused to meet her grandson, who went on to write and edit over forty books on Ethiopian history, influenced by Sylvia's support for Ethiopian independence. Richard later received an OBE in recognition for his services to Ethiopian studies while his wife, Rita, and their children, Helen and Alula, became noted writers and activists. In the run up to Easter of 1928, Mrs Pankhurst went back to Ongar with the Marshalls, her health even more fragile. It was at the Old House, on Easter Sunday, that Mrs Pankhurst learnt of Sylvia's confession piece in the *News of the World*. 'I shall never be able to speak in public again,' wept the lady who could face up to Poor Law Guardians, the police and hooligans. Offering her shelter from the media, Kitty had once again been Mrs Pankhurst's bodyguard.

Mrs Pankhurst ceased her campaign for the East End seat. Arthur secured a quieter set of lodgings for Mrs Pankhurst in Wapping and eventually she went to a Wimpole Street nursing home. Mrs Louisa Baldwin sent her a letter, thanking her for all her efforts for the women's cause. Her husband would be known as the premier who was true to his word and saw to it that women would be equally enfranchised. The letter meant a lot to Mrs Pankhurst. Despite her estrangement from Sylvia, the suffragette leader was at peace with her past. 'After all, I have had a wonderful life,' she told Christabel. In her final moments, it rained outside while Christabel read the Twenty-Third Psalm. Just as the sun came up, Mrs Pankhurst died on 14 June 1928, a month before her seventieth birthday and two weeks before the Representation of the

People (Equal Franchise Act), 1928 became law. The Marshalls put up a garden seat by their porch door in her memory.

Arthur's firm handled communications while flowers were sent to the adjoining chapel of a mortuary in Cambridge Place in London's West End where Mrs Pankhurst laid in state in a room draped in purple, on a catafalque which was surrounded by candles. Hundreds of mourners came to pay their last respects and to look on her face one last time, her pale features and silver hair against the background of the dark pillow. Her body was then taken to St John's Smith Square, very close to Kitty's home, where a vigil was kept. That weekend, Amelia Earhart became the first woman to fly across the Atlantic, a feat she and her crew achieved despite driving rain and fog. Leaving Newfoundland on Sunday, her plane, the *Friendship*, which was running out of fuel, was coming to land in the direction of South Wales just as Mrs Pankhurst's funeral, held the next day on 18 June, began. The church was full and those who could not get admittance stood quietly outside. Among the famous mourners were Mrs Stanley Baldwin, Viscountess Astor, Lady Rhondda, George Lansbury, the Pethick Lawrences, Charlotte Despard, Commandant Mary Allen and her colleagues in the uniform of the Women's Auxiliary Police Service, and of course, Kitty and Arthur Marshall.

Many of the women who attended wore either NUWSS or WSPU colours. A substantial laurel wreath in WSPU colours inscribed with the word 'Victory' hung near the coffin, which was topped with a wreath of violets. Poignantly, Herbert Jones, the jockey who was knocked off his horse when Emily Wilding Davison was killed, also laid a wreath, bearing the words: 'To do honour to the memory of Mrs Pankhurst and Miss Emily Davison.' The air was heavy with the scent of flowers. Around the church, women carried pennants in the colours, WSPU ribbons or badges. One of the mourners wore a badge with the inscription 'Demonstration, 1910', an allusion to Black Friday. Nellie Hall and Miss Elfrida Acklorn carried the Union flag and the WSPU banner, 'dipping' them at the chancel. Then the choir and clergy entered. Reverend Hugh Chapman, who had been a friend of Mrs Pankhurst, read the burial service. In his address, Reverend Dr Geikie-Cobb said of Mrs Pankhurst: 'She had fought her fight – nobly, consistently, graciously, and success had crowned her warfare.' Mrs Pankhurst's favourite hymns, including 'Sun of My Soul', 'Thou Saviour Dear', were played and

'Abide with Me' closed the service, followed by Chopin's funeral march. One man in the audience was heard to say, 'I didn't hold with her ways, but the women wouldn't have got it without her.'

More than fifty cars followed the hearse to Brompton Cemetery, watched by pedestrians packed tightly into the pavements. On the arrival of the coffin at the Fulham Road entrance to Brompton Cemetery, Flora Drummond gave the order: 'Women! Rally for the last time!' Her voice boomed as she led the cortège from the Fulham Road entrance of Brompton Cemetery to the grave site, her followers' prison medals jangling, Kitty naturally wearing hers. Minnie Baldock walked in front of the cars, carrying a flag of WSPU colours, followed by the two Union flag and WSPU flag bearers and the pallbearers. The ten pallbearers, who included Kitty, were Harriet Kerr, Marie and Georgina Brackenbury, Marion Wallace-Dunlop, Marie Naylor (an artist and Royal Academy student and skilled speaker), Mildred Mansel (like Kitty she had taken part in the '108 Deputation' to the House of Commons in 1909), Rosamund Massy (who was Kitty's age and had supported Mrs Pankhurst's Whitechapel election campaign, despite their political differences), Ada Wright and Barbara Wylie who had been present at the Battle of Glasgow. Mrs Pankhurst's adopted daughter Mary was found standing by herself, crying. She was approached by a stately 50-year-old lady, Miss Bevis, who told her that she was to be her guardian. Mary would call her Madre.

To the last, Mrs Pankhurst was involved in disorderly scenes, with the police force called into play. When the pallbearers and mourners had reached the grave, there was very little room for them. Some onlookers had climbed on to neighbouring gravestones to get a better look. Jostling for space, the mourners, pallbearers and clergyman were almost pushed into the green grave, which had been lined with laurel, ivy and privet, but the police restored order and made way for them. Christabel, Sylvia and Enid Goulden Bach's mother, Ada, who was said to bear a striking resemblance to Mrs Pankhurst, watched as her coffin was being lowered into the ground at the same time as the House of Lords was passing the final measure for equal suffrage.

19.

Firestarter

Kitty, Rosamund and Lady Rhondda were hatching plans over crème caramel. Most of Mrs Pankhurst's pallbearers agreed that a statue ought to be erected in Mrs Pankhurst's honour. And so the Pankhurst Committee Memorial Fund met up and got to work. Lady Rhondda was the honorary treasurer while Kitty and Rosamund Massy, who had organised tickets for the funeral, were joint honorary secretaries. But Kitty was the prime mover, pushing buttons. The fund set up an appeal for £2,500 to pay for a statue, a headstone for Mrs Pankhurst's grave in Brompton Cemetery and a portrait by Georgina Brackenbury. The committee members achieved their goal, with £200 to spare.

For the statue project, Kitty directed her attention towards Sir Lionel Earle, Permanent Secretary of the Office of Works. Exuding confidence, she did not ask *if* she could erect a statue but *how* it was to be done. Earle asked Kitty which site she wanted. She had a couple of sites in mind but she particularly liked Victoria Tower Gardens. It was a good choice. Sitting snugly inside rows of trees, and offset by the expansive Thames to one side, this is a special space in the heart of Westminster. Even on an overcast day, the vista, which sweeps across the vast lawn towards the Gothic-inspired Houses of Parliament, creates an effect that is calming, elevating and even cosy. When looked at together today, the features in this public park reflect the causes that had interested Mrs Pankhurst, namely the fight against slavery in all its forms, the spirit of French resistance and the promotion of safe places for children. In the middle of the park stands the gloriously Gothic-styled Buxton Memorial, built in memory of the anti-slavery campaigner Thomas Fowell Buxton. It was moved from Parliament Square to Victoria Tower Gardens in 1957. Just as Mrs Pankhurst and Christabel were lecturing on the threat to French liberty from the German war machine, a cast of Auguste Rodin's 1889 sculpture *The Burghers of Calais* was erected in the park, without ceremony due to the war. The work commemorates the self-sacrifice of six prominent members of the town who, it is said, offered themselves and the keys to the town up to King Edward III's besieging force in return for the safety of the townspeople. While the burghers would eventually be spared, thanks to the influence of Edward's wife, Philippa of Hainault, Rodin's piece captures the burghers' expressions of resignation and determination as they walked to their deaths, nooses around their necks, the punitive sackcloth covering their careworn figures. And lastly, a feature, lighter in tone, was introduced at the opposite end of the park in 1923. The enormous sandpit was designed as a central London substitute for Margate or Southend-on-Sea, offering a space for all children whose parents could not afford seaside trips to enjoy waterside air and build sandcastles. Today, Horseferry Playground offers a sandy area, albeit much smaller in size, which is situated next to a set of dance plates whose atonal chimes drift casually in the light evening breeze.

Kitty certainly made an impression with her determination. Privately, Lionel Earle found Mrs Marshall somewhat irritating and his colleagues smirked at the Latin which the committee had initially chosen to inscribe on the statue. Earle portrayed the militants as warmongers, and persuaded his correspondent to agree that a statue of Mrs Pankhurst, this leader of feminist warriors, would be inappropriate. Yet, when it was revealed that Prime Minister Stanley Baldwin would be unveiling Mrs Pankhurst's monument, the Office of Works became more responsive and Kitty was asked to submit a photograph of Walker's maquette. Ethel Smyth admired Kitty's spirit: 'It takes faith combined with love both deep and pertinacious to set in motion things far more immovable than mountains; things like Boards of Trade, Heads of Governments, and Police Commissioners. This miracle was performed single-handed by one woman, Mrs. E.K. Marshall.'[41]

The cleaners suspended on Elizabeth Tower on the morning of 6 March 1930 looked down at the sight that greeted them. Below the dull sky, which would resolve itself into sunshine, the traffic had been stopped and around 500 women marched past the Houses of Commons to Victoria Tower Gardens. Their women's garments were enlivened by the colourful gowns worn by university graduates and mayors, surrounded by sprays of purple and white flowers. Commandant Mary Allen was once again dressed in her uniform, accompanied by her colleagues, on hand to police the crowds, those onlookers who did have the fortune of possessing one of the deep purple-coloured tickets to the event but wished to pay their respects. When the procession reached the Victoria Tower Gardens, more colour awaited them. Swathed in WSPU colours was Mrs Pankhurst's statue, designed by Royal Academy mosaicist, illustrator, painter and sculptor Arthur George Walker. Among his previous works were several war memorials, and famously, the statue of Florence Nightingale at Waterloo Place. His statuette of *Christ at the Whipping Post* (1925) exhibited Walker's skill using the medium of ivory and marble to portray sacrifice. Jesus's pale torso twists against his manacles as he looks up expectantly from the black bollard of the post, brows contracted in expectant pain, his mind focused on a higher purpose. Mrs Pankhurst's statue's Portland stone plinth was the brainchild of the renowned architect Sir Herbert Baker, who worked with Cecil Rhodes. Inside an iron casket hidden in a hollow in the plinth he had designed was Rosamund Massy's prison badge and hunger strike medal along with other articles of warfare such as a letter from Mrs Pankhurst on Prime Minister Asquith.

While guests waited, the Metropolitan Police Central Band entertained the audience. Their repertoire included the works of four women composers. Shortly before the day, Ethel had been told that only the bandmaster was entitled to conduct the police band. She had phoned Kitty in a panic and Kitty told her not to worry. Kitty pulled a few strings and Ethel soon started rehearsals, locked up in a basement with the 'cats' and their wind instruments. On the day itself at noon, the composer took to the stage and told the band: 'Well, gentlemen, you have "conducted" me a few times, now I am going to conduct you.' As 'The March of the Women' swung into progress, Dame Ethel cut an imposing, winged figure as she wielded the baton with ardour, wearing her doctoral robes and her prison badge, encouraging the officers into a musical tempest.

Written only a small handful of years after the event, Edwin T. Woodhall's memoir gives us a clue as to the thoughts of the officers who now performed under Ethel's directions:

Let it be said, here and now, of the Special Branch were, from the point of view of duty, the suffragists' avowed antagonists. Many of us openly declared our sympathy with their aims, but they were fighting against the Government, and if the State did not see its way clear to give women the vote, that ended the argument so far as we were concerned. ... I look back with great admiration, not unduly mixed with a certain amount of, shall I say, affection for those hectic days of 'Woman's Suffrage'. When all is said and done, one has to admit that they were splendid women, these suffragette pioneers. They fought with courage and desperation for their cause. To the determined and intrepid action of these Englishwomen – and there is no denying the fact – the women of to-day enjoy all they now so familiarly accept in the way of independence and freedom of action.[42]

To Ethel's displeasure, Sylvia was the only daughter of Mrs Pankhurst to attend her funeral, together with her son; Christabel sent word from Chicago and Adela was in Australia. Enid Goulden Bach, her mother and sisters were present, holding flowers, along with many key figures. Kitty Marion felt honoured to witness the event of old suffrage veterans cooperating with police officers. On the podium was Flora Drummond, who struck up a conversation with Stanley Baldwin. 'Half the women here are gaol-birds,' Flora Drummond said in an aside to the former prime minister, who had narrowly lost the General Election of 1929, the 'Flapper Election', under which newly qualified women could vote. Baldwin, who had admittedly once been against women's suffrage, then made his speech. He was a fitting choice, given that Mrs Pankhurst herself had given a speech to Baldwin in 1926 at the Royal Albert Hall:

Mrs. Pankhurst did not make, nor did she claim to make or to have been the creator of the Women's Movement. It was too big a thing for that, and many may have claimed to have played their part in it. ... But if Mrs. Pankhurst did not make the movement, it was she who set the heather on fire.

Trumpets sounded and then Baldwin pressed the electric button. The WSPU drapery fell away as Ethel conducted 'The Chorale' from her opera, *The Wreckers*. Kitty took a long breath out. Many wreaths were laid. The Pathé film clearly shows Mary Allen lowering hers to the foot of the statue. Ethel Smyth felt that by the end of the day Mrs Pankhurst was left to stand guard splendidly outside the Houses of Parliament like a regal sentinel. On the night of the unveiling, a dinner was held in Kitty's honour, with Kitty Marion seated to her right. Nurse Pine, who had snubbed the former arsonist in America, ate a proverbial slice of humble pie alongside her dessert course when Kitty Marion came up to say hello.

An impressed Stanley Baldwin wrote Kitty a letter on the day, thanking her for her hard work. He felt that Walker had achieved a good likeness of Mrs Pankhurst. Although Mrs Pankhurst was one of the most celebrated twentieth-century female figures, she was an intensely private person. Just as she did not wish her first name to be used, Mrs Pankhurst did not generally consent to photographs being taken of her, at least not in the later stages of her life. Baldwin told her that he liked the site of the statue – the setting was 'perfect'. This was no mere platitude. He and his wife had been sceptical and those in the know were aware of the effort Kitty had made, against the odds, to make everything fall into place. He knew how often Kitty had knocked on his door until he had finally agreed to endorse the project and give a speech for the day. Edith How-Martyn of the Suffragette Fellowship invited Christabel to present Kitty with a small replica of the statue, delaying Christabel's trip to America by a week. In 1956, Victoria Tower Gardens was re-landscaped and Mrs Pankhurst's statue was moved closer to the Houses of Parliament. The stone vase which Baker designed was omitted and replaced with an informative tablet. In 1959, a year after Christabel's death, Mrs Pankhurst's memorial was augmented by a semi-circular wall – a Classical 'exedra' which was in the original design proposals by Walker – with two coin-shaped bronze reliefs on columns either side of the main statue, featuring Christabel's image and the WSPU prison badge design. The unveiling was televised. Mrs Pankhurst would resist future attempts to move her again.

The National Portrait Gallery accepted Georgina Brackenbury's portrait, which had been commissioned in 1927, of Mrs Pankhurst in the summer of 1929. Kitty had a plan for the surplus £200 raised for the Memorial Fund. The Marshalls had become deeply involved in church matters in Ongar and in May 1931 Kitty sent a letter to the secretary of the church council about the new choir stalls she had in mind, inspired by those at Liverpool Cathedral, and which she had designed and constructed close to the Marshalls' Westminster home. However, enlarging the existing choir stalls had proved a sticking point. After much campaigning by the Marshalls, they were installed. They bear the carving of 'E.P. 1931', and those same 'E.P.' initials had featured on the rosettes worn by some of the women who attended the unveiling of Mrs Pankhurst's memorial.

As Mrs Pankhurst's statue was erected, Julian Phelps Allan (Eva Dorothy Allan) OBE was approached to create the Celtic headstone for Mrs Pankhurst's grave. 'That clever girl,' Kitty called her. The dedication service took place on the afternoon of 14 June 1930. The Bishop of Barking, who dedicated the headstone, praised Mrs Pankhurst but said that there was still plenty of work to do to tackle suffering in the world. The Temple choir sang, then the bishop unveiled the headstone, swathed in WSPU colours.

In 2018, which saw the centenary of the partial enfranchisement of women, Mrs Pankhurst's statue in Victoria Tower Gardens was lovingly decorated with a WSPU-themed sash. Her grave was also adorned with flowers in purple pots. Amongst the blooms was a laminated shape poem beautifully written by an 8-year-old girl. Her name was Kitty.

Dear Mrs Pankhurst
Every woman needs a choice
Every woman needs a vote
Do you know you gave us the opportunity
Suffragettes helped us get it to
Nothing could get in your way
Over and over you went to jail
To suffer very hard conditions
When you were released you carried on again
Over and over you got in the newspaper
Really spreading the word
Do you know how grateful we are
Suffragettes are womans heroes! [sic]
I love suffragettes

20.

The Final Hideout

In the early 1930s, Lieutenant Colonel Charles Thomas Samman decided to sell his house prior to his move to Ventnor on the Isle of Wight. The highly educated surgeon and lawyer had achieved the distinction of being elected Master of the Society of Apothecaries two years in a row in recognition of his services to the guild and he was known for his sartorial attention to detail as well as his forceful personality. Samman's dislike of black ties could prompt him to return guests to their dressing rooms to don white ones. His home, The Bridge House in Sible Hedingham, Essex, was equally imposing. It is easy to see why the Marshalls fell in love with it. The sweeping carriageway, picturesque duck pond, the river which runs through it (a tributary of the River Colne) and shaded gardens boasted an idyllic setting for the many charitable events which the Marshalls hosted. There were nooks in which to hide secret treasure, shading for stalls and abundant space for dancing with music by the Halstead Orchestra. Like her father, Kinton Jacques, Kitty was a devoted dog lover and in June 1936, Kitty, who was the chairman of the North-West Essex RSPCA, hosted a Dogs' Garden Party for eighty dogs including her own, Lily Dove and Jackette.

Kitchener became involved in the most famous case of his career. In 1932, pupils at St Bees School in the Lake District discovered a contraption hooked up to fireworks and filled with gunpowder. It was feared that the bomb might have been a murder attempt, having been installed right under the platform on which the speakers were standing and giving out prizes. An explosives expert created a replica at Woolwich and concluded that the school stage drapery would have caught fire. Kitchener, who was in charge of investigations, interviewed two brothers from Macclesfield. Their lawyer contended that the device was intended as a hoax and in the end, there was insufficient evidence and the summonses against them were dismissed.

Kitchener, who had served in the Met for over two decades and had risen to first-class detective inspector by 1932, wrote an essay entitled 'The Police as a Career: A Review of the Past, with Suggestions for the Future', which was published under the pseudonym 'Clifton Reynes', the name of a village near Olney. He observed that the increasingly diverse nature of required skills pushed police work towards the professions and included some recommendations for the further education of officers. Kitchener's ideas struck such a chord, resulting in him being placed first in the Police Gold Medal Essay Competition in 1933, and an award of 30 guineas in 1934. The prize was personally approved by the king and presented to him by the Home Secretary, Sir John Gilmour. The *Police Review and Parade Gossip* featured his photograph, along with a description of his career, a reference to his two decorations from King Albert of Belgium and his position as captain of the Metropolitan Police Rugby team. He received numerous letters of congratulations. Kitchener's likeness, taken as he was leaving his home, was widely reproduced. Did Arthur recognise the man smiling cordially in the photo as the one who gave evidence in court all those years ago?

A Suffragette Fellowship dinner was held on 13 October 1936, the anniversary of Christabel's and Annie Kenney's protest at the Free Trade Hall. By this point, some of the older officers who had had dealings with the suffragettes had passed away, including Sir Patrick Quinn, who had been knighted in 1919 and who had died only that summer. Inspector James Jarvis, the recipient of Mrs Pankhurst's slap decades ago, was in his seventies when he accepted an invitation from the Suffragette Fellowship group to attend the Fellowship dinner on, coincidentally, the same night as H.G. Wells was giving a birthday speech to the PEN Club. Founded in 1921, PEN was envisaged as a dinner club for poets, essayists and novelists but the society quickly grew into an international organisation promoting freedom of expression and human rights. Wells, whose writings would inspire the Universal Declaration of Human Rights, told his 200 listeners that he refused to put away his toys and go to bed, so to speak; he still had so much he wanted to achieve in his lifetime.[43] The Fellowship dinner would also be the anniversary of Jarvis's arrest of Flora Drummond, Christabel and Mrs Pankhurst following the 'rush' on parliament. Jarvis readily accepted, then felt shy and got cold feet before his wife persuaded him to join the ladies. Mrs Jarvis was the proud owner of a steel chain and padlock which her husband had removed from one of Mrs Pankhurst's staunchest followers. But one of the highlights of the evening was surely when Flora Drummond, the great general who had brandished a dog-whip at Churchill, raised her glass to the former police officer, noting how Jarvis had a pleasant manner of arresting the women.

In his lecture, H.G. Wells, the long-standing PEN member, warned about the rise of fascism. Some of Kitty's former WSPU colleagues, notably 'slasher' Mary Richardson and Commandant Mary Allen, were being drawn towards the extreme right-wing end of the political spectrum. Mary Allen met Hitler and Goering in the early 1930s and she shared with the latter an enthusiasm for uniforms for female police officers. The commandant became a member of Mosley's British Union of Fascists in 1939 which resulted in a restriction being placed on her movements during the Second World War. It is likely that Mary Allen was attracted to fascism by notions of loyalty to an authority figure in uniform as well as the propaganda which preached a sense of struggle between fascists and the 'Other' or enemy. Indeed, the WSPU recruitment drive had appealed to the public with images of valiant suffragettes fighting a blind and brutish patriarchy. But the thoughts of Bodyguard member Joyce Nettlefold, who was now Joyce Newton Thompson, provided a further insight into what could have attracted former fighters for emancipation to such an ideology. As Joyce later reflected, the pull of political movements was chiefly down to the cult of personality. She had seen this in action with Mrs Pankhurst who 'had a voice of silver which never failed to charm the heart' and often extracted astonishing sums of money from an enthralled crowd:

Enthusiasm is infectious. This piece of psychology has been made use of by many political parties, including the Nazis. Modern enthusiasm seems to be directed more to individuals than causes. This is possibly symptomatic of a generation that has experienced two world wars and the disillusion that has followed them.[44]

Rather cannily, the Marshalls used a garden party to promote their own views on who could manage the growing presence of the Far Right. On a glorious summer's day in 1937, Kitty hosted a resplendent pageant at The Bridge House in honour of the local Conservative Association. The theme was the Kings and Queens of England, with Britannia heading the procession of fifty-five characters in dress. A guest of honour was MP for Saffron Walden, Richard Austen (Rab) Butler. Now that Baldwin had just resigned, Butler called on visitors to Bridge House to support the new prime minister, Neville Chamberlain. A fluent German speaker, Butler became Under Secretary of State for Foreign Affairs in 1938 and, in the face of the growing expansion of Nazi Germany, persevered with a policy of appeasement. In 1944, he would guide the Education Act (called the Butler Act) through Parliament. Kitty and Butler shared a love of painting (Butler indeed painted with Churchill) as well as an interest in the area around St John's Smith Square; in 1938, Butler moved his town residence to 3 Smith Square. We do not know if the Marshalls learnt that their house on Gayfere Street, the home where they had sheltered Grace Roe and welcomed Mrs Pankhurst's mourners, was bombed in 1944. The legacy of the damage is that today half the houses in the street are shorter than those which were destroyed and rebuilt.

Kitty and Arthur had one more brush each with the police. On 3 June 1938, Arthur Marshall, the lawyer who had worked for suffragettes who appeared in the dock, found himself under scrutiny of the law. He was accused of driving dangerously over a bridge near Sible Hedingham to Braintree, but the charges were dismissed, while Kitty was fined for allowing a car to stand on the highway without lights. In the spring of 1939, Kitty had combined an interest in automobiles with her support for local nurses by successfully submitting an application for a timber and asbestos garage in Sible Hedingham for a district nurse's car. The vehicle was partly funded by the opening of the grounds and keep at Hedingham Castle. Kitty also continued her interest in art; she was an accomplished woodcarver and loom weaver, making silk and woollen textiles and she carved an overmantel which adorned her sitting room. She also gave demonstrations of spinning wheel weaving and her artwork, including oil and watercolour works, was displayed at her studio across the road from The Bridge House during the Marshalls' fundraising events. She exhibited her work in a number of places, including at the New English Art

Club (NEAC), which was founded in the 1880s as a reaction to what were perceived as the more rigid academic conventions and included Walter Sickert and Augustus John in its history.

Mrs Marshall amused the Women's Institute of Castle Hedingham with tales from Lancashire and her suffragette days, as part of an appeal to collect books for the troops, likely thinking of writing down her memoirs. By this point, an autobiography was suggesting itself to her. Rachel Barrett, who was also a member of the same local Women's Institute, was her typist and lived at Lamb Cottage, a very short walk from The Bridge House, around a third of a mile away. That the two women were politically at odds seems not have mattered at all. Standing under the oak beams of The Bridge House, Rachel, in her early seventies, shared memories of the suffragette days, watched by the weird, Tudoresque wood-carved faces of indeterminate origin which peered out from the corners of the walls. It is perhaps fitting that Mrs Pankhurst's bodyguard, who helped to hide her leader from the police, came to live in a house which itself boasted a priest's hideout, tucked away in a cupboard in the hallway. There may well have been the chatter of women's voices as Kitty reposed in bed where she was laid up for months with a kidney inflammation. Was there a twinge and a short gasp, followed by a silence and a solicitous change in Rachel's tone? Perhaps Arthur was called in. Kitty was in considerable pain by this stage, suffering from uraemia and infection as well as kidney stones, all of which would have made her feel sick and feverish. She had watched and painted the winter thaw from her bedroom and then made her will. Kitty left the bulk of her estate and her house contents to her husband with the remainder to her nieces, Mace Caroline and Cicely, the daughters of Kitty's sister Eleanor, who had offered her sanctuary after Kitty's first marriage fell apart. Her god-daughters received £10 each with the exception of Enid Goulden Bach, who remembered Kitty's prison playing cards and how she knitted strands of her own hair with hairpins to keep her busy in jail. However, her godmother may have privately given her a memento.

Suffragette Escapes and Adventures was evidently typed up with a great sense of urgency. A sentence or two trails off into a smudge and the occasional full stop has not made the cut in this breathlessly dictated document. The manuscript has the feel of a conversation with Kitty recollecting as Rachel listens, the speaker's words expressed in stops and starts, the story she communicates reflected in the random sizing of the memoir's paragraphs that range vastly in length and are then clipped short with three exclamation marks. *Did you catch that?* she might have asked. *You simply must tell readers that we arrived back in London after our jaunts in Littlestone just in time for the morning milk round.* And then Kitty might have chuckled softly. This former bodyguard, who had frequently flouted the law, was writing her memoir against the odds. It was her last act of defiance. She died on 28 November 1947.

Kitty's funeral took place on 2 December at St Peter's Parish Church, Sible Hedingham. Newcomers would have noticed the canopied arches of the memorial to Sir John Hawkwood who had fought in the Hundred Years War. Medieval graffiti could be spotted on the walls and pillars of the fourteenth-century church whose Roman bricks hinted at the village's origins as a Roman outpost. The rectors of Sible Hedingham and Castle Hedingham led the service. Kitty's courage and humour, qualities which radiate in her autobiography, were remarked upon as well as her sense of duty to the local community and the causes in which she had believed. But her crowning achievement, it was said, was the campaign for Mrs Pankhurst's memorial in Victoria Tower Gardens. Dame Christabel Pankhurst joined in singing the hymns, with the organ played by Ashley Ripper.

She had felt that Kitty was part of the Pankhurst 'Super-Family'. As the cortège filed out of the church, which was surrounded by fields, the Nunc Dimittis was chanted. Like her mother, who had been a popular local figure, Kitty was given a significant send off. Arthur was among the numerous chief mourners along with Kitty's youngest brother, Colonel George Philip Rigbye, as well as numerous nieces and nephews. And there were friends and various representatives from the charities she had helped, such as Mrs Goulden Bach and Dr Lorna Bach, who represented the Suffragette Fellowship. Also present was Kitty's executor, Arthur James Barnett, whose ill-fated visit to Grace Roe in prison had landed him in so much hot water. Did those who came to pay their respects to the artist notice the palimpsest on the pillar of the south-east of the nave which depicts a flowering plant and, overlaid, a childlike image of a horned devil, its teeth bared in a pronounced grimace?

In the late 1940s, Rachel gave some thought to a potential publisher for Kitty's memoir. Rachel and Ida Wylie had been friends with (Marguerite/John) Radclyffe Hall – the couple met the author in 1921 at an ill-fated dog show which caught fire and injured several dogs – and had supported her during the obscenity trials in America and Britain which ensued over Hall's groundbreaking and hotly debated lesbian novel, *The Well of Loneliness* (1928).[45] While an American court eventually overturned the verdict to Hall's benefit, in the UK, the book's publisher, Jonathan Cape, was prosecuted. Hall's solicitor was Harold Rubinstein, a former suffragist. He was also the brother-in-law of Victor Gollancz who had shown his support of Radclyffe Hall. Gollancz had published Wells's own prodigious two-part memoir, *Experiment in Autobiography: Discoveries and Conclusions of a Very Ordinary Brain (Since 1866)* in 1934. But, unfortunately for Rachel and Kitty, Rachel's contacts did not prove beneficial and her submission of *Suffragette Escapes and Adventures* to Victor Gollancz was unsuccessful.

After Kitty's death, Arthur moved to Devon and remarried. The situation bore some resemblance to that of Fred Pethick Lawrence, whose wife died in 1954. Knowing she did not have long to live, Emmeline had felt strongly that Fred should not feel lonely after her death and she encouraged him to think about marrying again. Only three years after his wife passed away, Fred married Helen McCombie, who, known as Helen Craggs, had been in love with Mrs Pankhurst's son Harry and had earned a name for herself in the attack on Harcourt's country home. The couple married at Caxton Hall. Lord Pethick Lawrence experienced the passing of the Life Peerages Act, 1958 before he died in 1961.

We do not know if Kitty gave her blessing in the same way as Emmeline had given hers to Fred but, as Kitty's will shows, Arthur's wife-to-be, Lily Berry, seems to have been regarded with some warmth, as Kitty left Lily (whom she described as a 'friend') a token sum of £10. Arthur and his new wife were, however, not together long before he too died in 1954. He left Arthur James Barnett the sizeable sum of £1,000 and left £100 to his nephew, the ambassador Sir Derwent Kermode, whose bromide print is kept at the National Gallery; it was taken in 1953, the year in which Rachel Barrett passed away at a nursing home in Sussex. As the papers reported, Ida Wylie was unable to make Rachel's funeral.

Both Rachel and Kitty had been described in local obituaries as 'friends' of Mrs Pankhurst. Lamb Cottage bears a blue plaque: 'Rachel Barrett B.Sc. Suffragette and political activist 1875–1953 Lived here.' Rachel's home was inherited by her niece, Gwyneth, who soon afterwards married teacher and leading modern poet of his time, John Redwood Anderson, to whom there is also a plaque at Lamb Cottage. There are blue plaques to Kitty and Arthur outside their Sible Hedingham home. All four commemorative markers were provided jointly by Essex Heritage Trust and by Sible Hedingham Parish Council. Arthur's reads: 'Solicitor Advocate for Women's Social and Political Union supporter of women's suffrage 1870–1954' and Kitty's says: 'Emily Katherine Marshall née Finch suffragist and artist 1870–1947 Lived here.' Kitty may well not have appreciated the Finch-related error. Yet, at St Peter's in Sible Hedingham we see another memorial to them in the form of a joint epitaph on the rounded stone with a Celtic symbol. The stone tilts forward and is initially difficult to spot. Because of the angle, much of the inscription is obscure but it reads: 'Either to either and each to God may the most holy name of Almighty God be praised.'

Epilogue

Enid's Wrecking Ball

The windows take a direct hit. Any remaining shards give themselves up and drop into the wasteland, shattering further. It is May 1977 and the suffragettes are at it again, but this time they have permission to demolish the cell windows of Holloway. Kitty's golf swing, executed by proxy by Enid Goulden Bach, is deadly. Enid, who is the chairman of the Suffragette Fellowship, makes sure that through her efforts, this suffragette hits home. The wrecking ball which she ceremoniously wields is decked in WSPU colours. She strikes out on behalf of all those who risked their lives behind its now diminished walls. When the Suffragette Fellowship members arrived, they had to pass through the wreckage of what was once the chapel where Kitty struggled to keep her hat in place, pass through cinders, walk on duckboards and observe the white-walled cell walls, now doorless, rendering escape easy. Enid is creating what Kitty would have described as 'a useful smash'. After the ceremony, life peer, Baroness Joan Vickers of Devonport, lays flowers on this disturbed earth of memories.

In 1968, on the fiftieth anniversary of the partial enfranchisement of British women, a tea party was held in the House of Commons on 14 July, attended by Fellowship members and Members of Parliament. Bouquets were placed at Mrs Pankhurst's statue, accompanied by uniformed female police officers, an image which invokes the original unveiling of the statue. As well as Enid Goulden Bach, Grace Roe (president of the Fellowship), Leonora Cohen (vice president), and Gwen O'Brien (committee member) were also there. Gertrude Harding sent her greetings from the United States to the Bodyguard and Enid: 'Remembering long skirts in defence of the leader.' Gwen Cook, who had nursed her husband for seventeen years before his death, felt that in the 1960s, when Kitchener was typing up his autobiography, she was a relic of a past era and yet, today, suffragettes' stories have never felt closer.

To Ida Wylie, it seemed that flouting the 'Cat and Mouse Act' had led to a series of escapes and adventures right out of a novel written by Edgar Wallace. Like Kitchener, Wallace was a self-made man, having worked in various jobs including in a mackintosh factory, on a Grimsby trailer and as a *Daily Mail* correspondent during the Boer War. By the 1920s, he had become a household name and was known as the 'King of Thrillers'. Indeed, Harold Brust, the Special Branch 'shadow', stepped into the limelight and became an advisor on a 1952 adaptation of Wallace's *The Ringer*, even giving cameo performances in various crime dramas. Suffragette history used the police officer as a backdrop to the story of the suffragettes but Kitchener's autobiography helps to illuminate the officers' backstories and explain their perspectives a little better.

What became of the Schützes and of Glebe House where this book began? Gladys, a journalist and author of over twenty novels, died in July in 1946 in Switzerland. Rumour had it that Peter, broken-hearted, followed her three weeks later by drowning himself. She had been the love of his life. After their deaths, the Schützes gave the lease of the house to the PEN Club. Later, Glebe House became the home of The de László Archive Trust. Not only does the balcony from which Mrs Pankhurst spoke survive but so do the contours of the Fig Tree Room which is now a dining room. And within is the fig tree, still rooted under the floor, which was saved from a workman's axe by the historian Reginald Blunt who was renting the house in the 1920s. It is heartening to see that those indomitable branches, so enjoyed by Gladys and the writers of the PEN club with whom she worked, still arc prettily across the skylight, enduring for future generations.

Acknowledgements
and Adventures

I would first of all like to thank the London Library for providing me access to the collection via the Carlyle Trust, while the Society of Authors' K Blundell Trust funded my various research trips. Furthermore, the Police History Society helped with the costs of obtaining the files relating to the Battle of Glasgow from the National Archives of Scotland.

Ray Wilson has been a vital link and he put me in touch with Janet Dennis and Elizabeth Lester, Kitchener's granddaughters. They shared with me photographs of Kitchener's medal from his prize-winning essay, their extensive family photograph collection, Kitchener's research into his family history and, importantly, the original memoirs. Their contributions to this book have made this story so engaging.

Thank you to Antony Smith, custodian of The Priest House, West Hoathly, Sussex for information behind the 'Votes for Women Holloway Prison March 1912' handkerchief which bears Kitty's signature. The handkerchief, which was rescued from a jumble sale bonfire in the early 1970s by custodian Dora Arnold, is displayed at the Priest House Museum. Member of the Men's League for Women's Suffrage John Godwin King CBE restored the Priest House which he opened to the public in 1908. His daughter Ursula was a member of the NUWSS. Sussex Archaeological Society kindly gave permission for the delightful image of the handkerchief to be reproduced. Thank you to David Brooks and Jeremy Harte of Bourne Hall Museum for access to Bunn's notebook. I am also grateful to Jonathan Ferguson, Keeper of Firearms and Artillery at the Royal Armouries, Leeds for his insight into the Scheintod used at the Battle of Glasgow.

A warm twelve-bell peal goes to Ann Jones for taking an interest in Kitty's story and for pointing me to some intriguing sources on Ancestry. As ever, a big hello to Tony Wolf – the *Bartitsu Compendium* boater still takes pride of place on my book shelf. Dr Renée Marie Shelby of the Sexualities Project at Northwestern University very kindly sent me a copy of the popular Edwardian game *Suffragetto!*, which she recreated for modern audiences to enjoy.

Peter Kennison and I shared research on the Rock sisters and he sent me a lovely photograph of the officers of A Division. Mary Walker wrote *A Mother's War*, based on the diary she kept as she awaited news when her son Graham was sent into the Iraq War in 2003. Her account was printed in *The Gravesend Messenger* in 2003. She shared with me her photograph of her ancestor PC Edwin Lapworth and the suffragettes and Lapworth's *Police Almanac*. Alastair Dinsmor, curator of the Glasgow Police Museum introduced me to the stories of the officers involved in Mrs Pankhurst's arrest in Glasgow. Many thanks to Richard Scantlebury for providing me with information on Chief Inspector Charles Scantlebury. Richard runs a website, One-Name Study, which traces the origins and variations of the name Scantlebury.

I would like to thank the following people and organisations: Reuben Library, British Film Institute; British Library; University of Cambridge Library; London Metropolitan Archives; Archives & Local History Manchester Central Library and the National Archives, Kew; Dr Clare Smith, Heritage Centre Manager of the Police Heritage Centre gave me some useful tips and Phill Barnes-Warden found an amusing police-suffragette painting which he shared with me; Dr Jane Pearson; Dr Mike Sherborne, H.G. Wells Society; Louisa Chapman; Tim Richardson; Dr Irene O'Brien, Archives Department, Mitchell Library, Glasgow; Andrew Potter, Royal Academy; Bridget Clifford, Keeper of Tower Armouries at the Royal Armouries at the Tower of London; Jim Davidson, Halstead District Local History Society; Ruby Ree-Sheridan of the Four Corners Gallery, Roman Road; Jim Monahan, architect; Owen Stanhope, BBC Written Archive Centre; Ian Moore, British Library Sound Archive; Dr Mari Takayanagi, Senior Archivist of the Parliamentary Archives; The

National Stalking Helpline, which also offers self-defence tips and legal advice for victims of street harassment; Katie from Greater Manchester Police Museum; Elissavet Ntoulia, The Wellcome Library; Melissa Scott-Miller of the New English Art Club; Bryony Dixon, Curator of Silent Film, British Film Institute National Archive; Lynn O'Mahony, Assistant Librarian, National Police Library; Emma Savage, Heinz Archive & Library, National Portrait Gallery; Kitty Ross, Curator and Nicola Pullen, Assistant Curator of Leeds and Social History, Leeds Museums and Galleries; Janet Few of the North Devon History Society; Professor June Purvis; Elizabeth Crawford; Dr Lise Schoeman; Amanda Thyme; Rohit Dhillon; Dr Mike Callan; and Calum MacKenzie of Brompton Cemetery. Showing interest and support in this project, Sarah Savitt and Clive Boutle have helped me make the challenging transition away from academic writing. Thank you too to Susan Scott, archivist at Savoy for reproducing the menus and seating plan for the suffragette banquet. Many thanks also to Overglam's Jan Long for dog-training tips.

John Walmsley of the Halstead Museum very kindly retrieved and scanned the obituary photograph of Kitty from the *Halstead Gazette* and sent me photographs of Kitty's and Arthur's gravestone. Frieda Midgley of Newnham College Library confirmed Agnes Smallpeice's name in the Newnham College Register. Another eye-opening moment was when Jill Geber found a series of photographs featuring Hugh Finch. Thank you to Peter Monteith, Archivist and Records Manager of Keble College Archives, for arranging the reproduction of two of these fabulous photographs which appear in the book. Helen and Emma at Guardian News and Media Archive sent me an anniversary piece and John Reeder, Club Manager of Theydon Bois Golf Club not only took an interest in the book but also gave me a copy of the anniversary publication.

My family had a great weekend in Lancashire in September 2018. It was lovely to meet churchwarden Martin Coane and Reverend David Ward, the Rector of Brindle, who gave us a church teddy and a lovely pot of local marmalade. Emma Foxall of St Andrew's Leyland very helpfully tracked down the William Baldwin memorial plaque, while Hugh Meteyard of St Mary's in Theydon Bois shared with me his photographs of the stained-glass window to Frances Buss, and her gravestone. Reginald May, churchwarden St Peter's Sible Hedingham, confirmed the inscription on Kitty's and Arthur's grave.

The Worshipful Company of Basketmakers and the Worshipful Society of Apothecaries shared their knowledge with me and I would like to thank Janet Payne in particular for the information she sent me about Lieutenant Colonel Charles Thomas Samman. It was a pleasure to meet Peter Clarke, Seif El Rashidi, Howard Benge and Rebecca Walker of the City of London Police Museum. Rebecca, who has been researching the lives of City of London officers, has been wonderfully supportive.

Thank you to Christopher Ripper, Judy Ford and their cousin Anne Shelim. Chris and Judy were given paintings featured in this book by Kitty from their late grandparents, Harry and Winifred Ripper of Sible Hedingham, who knew Kitty. Ashley Ripper, the organist at Kitty's funeral, was Chris and Judy's grandfather's first cousin. Barbara Harker Honorary Secretary Waltham Abbey Historical Society put me in contact with Honorary Curator Mary Salton, who dated Kitty's painting of Waltham Abbey. Colin and Margaret Walker of the Dymchurch & District Heritage Group very kindly put me in contact with John Henley who had in his collection a set of charming Edwardian postcards of the local area. The postcard of Gladstone's house features in this book. A key link is Adrian Corder-Birch who sent me my first photograph of Kitty, an obituary image from the *Halstead Gazette*. I was able to use this to identify Kitty from the Christina Broom photographs kept by the Museum of London and it was an exciting moment to go over the well-known images with Beverley. The Bridge House, where the Marshalls lived, boasts Essex Heritage Trust blue plaques to both Kitty and Arthur; Rachel is similarly commemorated down the road. Melanie and Afsheen Foroozan and their family invited Adrian and my family and we have lovely memories of that day. When Sandra de Laszlo welcomed us into her home one summer's evening, I just knew that the beginning, the middle and the end of this book would come together so nicely. The photographs speak for themselves.

I have been very lucky to meet the relatives of key people in this book. Jenny Cooper and Sybil shared their memories of Edith Garrud with me. The sections on Edith Garrud in this book are written in memory of Edith's grand-nephew, Martin Williams. Thanks to Martin, there are now two memorials to this former Islington resident: a People's Plaque at 60 Thornhill Square, Islington and a commemorative bench outside Finsbury Park tube station, erected following a public vote. Edith and her descendants were also featured on BBC's *The One Show* in a documentary presented by Honor Blackman in 2014.

Chris Jacques shared with me his family stories, from the anecdotes of how Kinton met Caroline Augusta. Lesley Griffiths very kindly gave me a copy of the Bodyguard Rules from the estate of Gladys N. O. Griffiths (née Dewar). When Gladys retired, aged 70, around the early 1970s, she wrote the story of her mother's involvement in the suffrage campaign and her own, but it was never published. Her Indian club and the Rules were passed on to Lesley. It was a very exciting day meeting Chris and Lesley and to see Beverley Cook from the Museum of London again. In fact, it is thanks to the museum's collections that this book has come into existence. I first encountered Kitty's memoirs at the Suffragette Fellowship Collection at the Museum of London whilst researching for my PhD on women's self-defence during what has been called the 'long nineteenth century', an era which begins with the end of the eighteenth century and ends in the years prior to the First World War. I knew instantly that this lady, who wrote with such energy, needed her own biography. This was what Rachel had in mind when she pitched her memoir to a publisher, albeit unsuccessfully.

In 2013, Kathy Wenborne from the Ongar Millennium Society shared with me the photographs of Kitty's divorce papers that she took at the National Archives, years before the files went online on Ancestry. I spent some time pondering over whether or not I should discuss the details surrounding Kitty's divorce. I felt the tension between honouring Kitty's memory and the expectations required of writing a biography. While she would have liked her story to have been told, Kitty no doubt would have wanted the Hugh Finch aspect of her life to be kept a secret. However, when Diane Atkinson hinted at the details of the divorce in her 2018 book *Rise Up Women! The Remarkable Lives of the Suffragettes* (which charmingly features a photograph of Bodyguard member Gwen Cook many years after the suffrage campaign), it became clear that this event, now in the open, demanded to be included in an account of Kitty's life.

I never had the privilege of meeting Ray Harrop who had taken such an interest in the Old House in Ongar and had undertaken significant research into its history. However, Simon Webb and his family welcomed us into Ray's home. I will treasure the items found in the house which they gave to me. It is thrilling to think that the Victorian baby's sock had lain under the floorboards when Mrs Pankhurst walked overhead, agonising over what to do about the situation with Sylvia. Thank you to Peter Dudeney and Jill Bowtle of St Martin's Chipping Ongar for permission to reproduce a photograph of the E.P. pews.

Learning a new martial art from scratch at a similar age to Kitty has given me an appreciation of what it may have been like for her to join Edith Garrud's classes. Many thanks to Sensei Ian Cuthbert of UKA Karate for guiding me and Peter from complete beginners to blue belt during lockdown and for all the insights this inspiring and daunting journey has given us as well as the Sunday morning qigong classes. 'Tuck under!' I would also like to give my warmest thanks to Jennifer Garside – it is her silhouette which features alongside Kitty's 'shadow' on this book's front cover. It has been fantastic to work with Amy Rigg and Rebecca Newton from The History Press. Amy's enthusiasm and critical eye for detail, as well as her marshalling of the jumble of picture files I sent her, have really shaped this book. I'm very grateful to Gaynor Haliday for her editing of this book and her attention to detail.

My husband Martin has come with me on so many trips and has taken the wonderful photos which accompany this book. Thanks to our Affenpinscher puppy, Tuppence, for her cuddles and her unfailing support in the shredding of old drafts. I often drive through the Marshalls' old haunts of Theydon Bois and Ongar and have commuted, as the Marshalls did, to London from there; my mother by chance moved to a street less than two minutes' walk from Kitty's and Arthur's Gayfere Street home. When I walk through this area, I see Kitty setting off with her contingents to Parliament, I imagine her on her traffic island in Broad Sanctuary tackling a policeman, see her tearful outside St John's Smith Square, I can sense her determination as she strides to the Office of Works with her plans for Mrs Pankhurst's memorial. And I often feel that as well as seeing family, I too am about to take tea with Kitty. Our son Peter grew up with this project and came with us on many of my research trips. Holding my hand in Victoria Tower Gardens, he once looked up at me and asked: 'Is Kitty your friend, Mummy?' I would like to think so.

Notes

1 Edwin T. Woodhall, *Guardians of the Great* (London: Blandford Press, 1934), p. 101.

2 Tony Wolf, 'An interview with "Year of the Bodyguard" director Noel Burch' <suffrajitsu.com/an-interview-with-year-of-the-bodyguard-director-noel-burch/> [Accessed 1 July 2022].

3 Adelaide Procter, *The Complete Works of Adelaide A. Procter* (London: George Bell and Sons, 1905), pp. 27–28.

4 'Fashionable Marriage at Brindle', *Preston Herald*, 8 April 1896, p. 5.

5 Kate Parry Frye, quoted in Elizabeth Crawford, *Campaigning for the Vote: Kate Parry Frye's Suffrage Diary* (London: Francis Boutle, 2013), pp. 178–179.

6 Camila Ruz and Justin Parkinson, '"Suffrajitsu": How the Suffragettes Fought Back Using Martial Arts', *BBC News Magazine* <www.bbc.co.uk/news/magazine-34425615> [Accessed 1 July 2022].

7 Mary S. Allen, *Lady in Blue* (London: Stanley Paul & Co, 1936), p. 191.

8 *Votes for Women*, 2 July 1909, p. 878.

9 Mary S. Allen, *Lady in Blue* (London: Stanley Paul & Co, 1936). p. 16.

10 Herbert Gladstone to Sir Charles Edward Troup, letter dated 9 September 1909, HO144/1043, National Records Office.

11 Edwin T. Woodhall, *Guardians of the Great* (London: Blandford Press, 1934), p. 101.

12 Garrud, Edith, Article for 'The World We Live In', *Votes for Women*, 4 March 1910, p. 355.

13 Cecil Bishop, *From Information Received: The Reminiscences of Cecil Bishop* (London: Hutchinson & Co., 1932), p. 176.

14 Colin Gifford, *The Asquiths* (London: John Murray, 2002), p. 146.

15 Edwin T. Woodhall, *Guardians of the Great* (London: Blandford Press, 1934), p. 92.

16 Elizabeth Robins, *Both Sides of the Curtain* (London: William Heinemann, 1940), pp. 164–168.

17 E. Katherine [Kitty] Willoughby Marshall, *Suffragette Escapes and Adventures*, p. 11.

18 Mrs [Emmeline] Pethick Lawrence, 'Inciting to Violence. Mr. Hobhouse Taunts Women with Being Less Militant than Men', *Votes for Women*, 23 February 1912, p. 9.

19 Kitty Marshall, *Suffragette Escapes and Adventures*, p. 13 (59).

20 *Votes for Women*, 8 March 1912, p. 360.

21 Mrs E[mily]. K[itty]. Marshall, 'Trade Union Tyranny', *Pall Mall Gazette*, 19 June 1912, p. 4.

22 W[alter]. H[enry] Thompson, *Guard from the Yard* (London: Jarrolds, 1938). pp. 25–26.

23 Emmeline Pankhurst, *My Own Story* (London: Eveleigh Nash, 1914), pp. 4–5.

24 Cecil Bishop, *From Information Received: The Reminiscences of Cecil Bishop* (London: Hutchinson & Co., 1932), p. 175.

25 Ibid..

26 *Suffragette*, 24 October 1913, p. 38.

27 'Why We Are Militant', speech by Mrs Pankhurst New York City, 21 October 1913, *Suffragette*, 14 November 1913, p. 99.

28 Women's Social and Political Union Eighth Annual Report Year Ending February 28th 1914, p. 19.

29 *Suffragette*, 27 February 1914, p. 446.

30 Ethel Smyth, *Female Pipings in Eden* (London: Peter Davies, 1933), p. 225.

31 Ibid.

32 Helen Crawfurd, Autobiographical Manuscript, dated 1940, HC/1/3, Marx Memorial Library & Workers' School, pp. 96–97.

33 'Hands, Feet and Tongue', *Morning Advertiser*, 22 July 1914, page unknown, Heinz Library and Archive, National Portrait Gallery.

34 I[da] A[lexa] R[oss] Wylie, 'Resurrection', *Suffragette*, 10 April 1914, p. 591.

35 'More About his Majesty's Police', *Suffragette*, 12 June 1914, p. 152.

36 'The Appointment of Policewomen. Opposition from Scotland Yard', *Police Review and Parade Gossip*, 22 May 1914, p. 246.

37 *Suffragette*, 5 June 1914, p. 133.

38 'The Revolutionaries', *Votes for Women*, 12 June 1914, p. 566.

39 Ethel Smyth, *Female Pipings in Eden* (London: Peter Davies, 1933), p. 263.

40 'The War', transcript of a speech by Christabel Pankhurst, dated 8 September 1914, Museum of London, First World War, David Mitchell Collection, Suffragette Fellowship Collection, pp. 5–6.

41 Ethel Smyth, *Female Pipings in Eden* (London: Peter Davies, 1933), p. 272.

42 Edwin T. Woodhall, *Guardians of the Great* (London: Blandford Press, 1934), p. 93.

43 'Leftism and Rightism', *Daily News*, 1936, p. 11. 'Our Friend – The Enemy', *Daily Mirror*, 14 October 1936, p. 1. See also *Daily Herald* for coverage of both Wells' party and the suffragette reunion with Inspector Jarvis. '500 Writers Honour Mr. Wells' and 'Women Boast of Bombs, Fire – & Jail. Man Who Arrested Them Just Laughs', *Daily Herald*, 14 October 1936, p. 13.

44 Joyce Newton Thompson, 'The Suffrage Movement', *NCW News*, June 1958, p. 7.

45 Sally Cline, *Radclyffe Hall: A Woman Called John* (London: John Murray, 1997), p. 172.

Bibliography

Collections and Archives Consulted

Bourne Hall Museum.
Emily Wilding Davison Personal Papers, the Women's Library, London School
    of Economics.
Epsom Crime Museum.
Heinz Archive & Library.
Houses of Parliamen.t
Jacques Family Archive.
Jill Craigie Collection, the Women's Library, London School of Economics.
Kitchener Family Archive.
National Portrait Gallery.
National Records of Scotland Parliamentary Archives.
New Scotland Yard.
Suffragette Fellowship Collection.

Cases

Boardman v. Boardman, 1866.
Brown v. Brown, 1865.
Campbell v. Campbell, 1886.
Chorlton v. Lings, 1868, Court of Common Pleas.
Finch v. Finch, 1901.
Kelly v. Kelly, 1869.
R. v. Jackson (The Clitheroe Abduction Case), 1891.
Wells v. Wells, 1894.

Radio, Television, Film

The Blaze of Day: The Suffragette Movement (Pearl/Pavilion Recordings, E. Sussex).

Boase, Tessa, *Mrs Pankhurst's Purple Feather: Fashion, Fury and Feminism – Women's Fight for Change* (London: Aurum Press, 2018), Audible Audio Book, read by Tessa Boase.

Clare Balding's Secrets of a Suffragette, Channel 4, first broadcast 26 May 2013.

Close, A.J., *A Petrol Scented Spring* (2016) Lamplight Audio, narrated by Jilly Bond.

Enola Holmes (2020), directed by Harry Bradbeer.

The Lost World of the Suffragettes, BBC Radio 4, 2 October 2016.

Suffragette (2015), directed by Sarah Gavron.

Suffragettes Meet Again, 1955, British Pathé <www.britishpathe.com/video/suffragettes-meet-again> [Accessed 1 July 2022].

Suffragettes with Lucy Worsley, first broadcast BBC, 23 June 2018.

Suffragettes: Women Recall Their Struggle to Win the Vote <www.bbc.co.uk/archive/suffragettes> [Accessed 1 July 2022]: 'In Town Tonight: The Suffragette Movement', Home Service, first broadcast 29 January 1955; 'Lilian Lenton', first broadcast 1 January 1960; 'Aileen Graham-Allen', The Light Programme, 28 September 1962; 'Eleanor Higginson and Grace Roe', Radio 2, 6 February 1968; 'Grace Roe', Radio 2, 6 February 1968; 'Up and About: Elizabeth Dean', Regional Programme, 30 June 1978; 'Profile: Victoria Lidiard', Radio 4, 3 May 1983.

The Year of the Bodyguard: Conflicting Thoughts on the Politics of Violence, directed by Noel Burch, 1982.

Interviews from British Library
Sound and Vision Archive

Cicely Hamilton, Marguerite Bowie and Rosemary Menzies-Wilson, *Women and the Vote*, 2 May 1943, T929712.

Enid Goulden Bach, BBC Light Programme, 14 July 1958, B590/3.

Gladys Griffiths, 9 September 1977, 1LPO197454.

Sir Brian Harrison taped interviews
The Women's Library, LSE

Grace Roe, 4 October 1974, 8 SUF/B/017.

Leonora Cohen, 26 October 1974, 8SUF/B/018.

Cicely Hale, 6 November 1974, 8 SUF/B/021.
Maude Kate Smith, 14 January 1975, 8SUF/B/030.
Olive Bartels, 27 March 1976, 8SUF/B/078.

Directories

Vincent, Sir Howard, the Late Colonel Sir, *The Police Code and General Manual of the Criminal Law* (London: Butterworth & Co., 1912). And other years.
The Suffrage Annual and Women's Who's Who, ed. by A.J.R. (London: Stanley Paul & Co, 1913), p. 355.

Exhibitions

'Voice and Vote: Women's Place in Parliament Exhibition', Houses of Parliament, 2018.
'Votes for Women', Museum of London, 2018–2019.

Journals and Newspapers

Britannia.
Daily Herald.
Glasgow Herald.
Halstead Gazette.
Illustrated London News.
Illustrated Police News.
Illustrated Sporting and Dramatic News.
Kinematograph and Lantern Weekly.
Leeds Mercury.
Listener.
Lloyd's Weekly Paper.
Manchester Guardian.
Morning Advertiser.
Nottingham Evening Post.
Pall Mall Gazette.
Police Review and Parade Gossip.
Scotsman.
Suffragette.
Times and *Sunday Times.*

Votes for Women.
West London Observer.
Woman's Leader and Common Cause.
The Women's Hall Dreadnought, Issue 1, Tuesday, 29 May 2018.
Yorkshire Post.

Websites

Charles Booth's London: Poverty Maps and Police Notebooks
    <booth.lse.ac.uk/map/14/-0.1174/51.5064/100/0> [Accessed 1 July 2022].
Britishnewspaperarchive.co.uk
Life's Work for Women Crowned 1930, British Pathé <www.britishpathe.com/
    video/lifes-work-for-women-crowned/query/pankhurst> [Accessed 1 July
    2022].
Copped Hall Trust www.coppedhalltrust.org.uk [Accessed 1 July 2022].
First 100 Years <first100years.org.uk/digital-museum/timeline/>
    [Accessed 1 July 2022].
Free BMD <www.freebmd.org.uk> [Accessed 1 July 2022].
Hansard <api.parliament.uk/historic-hansard/index.html> [Accessed 1 July 2022].
Hawley Harvey Crippen and Ethel Le Neve. Photograph by Arthur Barrett,
    1910, Wellcome Collection <wellcomecollection.org/works/a34e8y85>
    [Accessed 1 July 2022].
In global pursuit of Scantleburys & Skentelberys for a one-name study
    [Accessed 1 July 2022].
Olney and District Historical Society, Family History Searches[Accessed 1 July 2022].
Plodd in the Square Mile [Accessed
    1 July 2022].
Suffragettes victims of image doctoring <www.dailymail.co.uk/news/article-
    5723239/Rare-pictures-reveal-suffragettes-victims-image-doctoring-100-
    years-ago.html> [Accessed 1 July 2022].
The Proceedings of the Old Bailey, 1674–1913 <www.oldbaileyonline.org>
    [Accessed 1 July 2022].

Unpublished Works/Exhibition Pamphlets

Crawfurd, Helen, Autobiographical Manuscript, dated 1940, HC/1/3, Marx
    Memorial Library & Workers' School.
Gliddon, Katie, 'A Day in My Life', typescript account, The Women's Library,
    LSE, 7KGG/1/7.

Gliddon, Katie, Prison Diary 1 (1912), 7KGG/1/1 Gliddon, Katie, Prison Diary typescript transcript, ed. by Elaine Silver (2007), 7KGG/1/1, The Women's Library.

'Personal Recollections of Ada Cecile Wright – typed', 50.82/1135, Group C, pp. 63–68 (64–65), Suffragette Fellowship Collection, Museum of London.

Kitchener, Ralph Frederick, *The Kitcheners of Olney: A Family Saga (c. 1956–1974)*, Personal Collection of Janet Dennis.

Kitchener, Ralph Frederick, *From Olney Cottage to Scotland Yard*, Personal Collection of Janet Dennis.

Kitchener, Ralph, *The Memoirs of an Old Detective*, ed. by Ian Adams (2010).

Kitchener, Ralph, *Memoirs of an Old Detective* (1969).

Marion, Kitty, Autobiography, Museum of London, Suffragette Fellowship Collection, pp. 50.82/1124, Museum of London.

Marshall, E[mily]. Katherine Willoughby, *Suffragette Escapes and Adventures*, 50.82/1132, Group B, pp. 1–43.

Rhondda, Viscountess, Women & the House of Lords: Achieving Equality for Women in the House of Lords, Vote 100 pamphlet, Houses of Parliament.

Setchfield, Gertrude, diary, Women's Library, LSE, 7/GLS/01.

Smith, Kevin Charles, 'The Militant Suffragettes as a Police Problem: London, 1906–1914', unpublished PhD thesis, The Ohio State University, 1974.

Terrero, Jane, Prison Experiences, Group A, 60.15/13, pp. 119–137, Suffragette Fellowship Collection, Museum of London.

Trueman, Emma, 'Leonora Cohen: The Making of a Freelance Militant', History Dissertation, Keele University (Copy at the Tower of London), 2011.

Anonymous or Unsigned

'An Appalling Danger', *Suffragette*, 14 May 1914, p. 67.

'Another Picture Slashed with a Hatchet: Sensational Scene at the Academy', *Suffragette*, 15 May 1914, p. 107.

'Answers to Correspondents', 30 July 1908, *Votes for Women*, p. 342.

'The Appointment of Policewomen. Opposition from Scotland Yard', *Police Review and Parade Gossip*, 22 May 1914, p. 246.

'The Arrest of Mrs. Pankhurst', *Police Review and Parade Gossip*, 20 March 1914, p. 133.

'Back to Jail', *Daily Herald*, 22 July 1913, p. 5.

'Bishop of Barking Unveils Headstone', *Nottingham Evening Post*, 16 June 1930, p. 3.

'The Bishop of London and Forcible Feeding: Second Visit to Holloway: Conversations with Two Suffragists', *The Times*, 10 February 1914, p. 5.

'Bishop of London's Visit to Holloway: Treatment of Suffragists: Allegations of Cruelty Refuted', *The Times*, 31 January 1914, p. 5.

'The Case of William Ball', *The Times*, 9 May 1912, p. 13.

'The Cat-and-Mouse Act', *Suffragette*, 18 July 1913, pp. 578–579.

'Cat and Mouse or Votes for Women?: Miss Barrett's Statement', *Suffragette*, 27 June 1913, pp. 618–619.

'Cecilia Russell, 88, and Still An Angry Suffragette', *Glasgow Herald*, 9 December 1982, p. 8. HH5_336_2, National Records of Scotland.

'Charge, Girls!', *Leeds Mercury*, 24 February 1914, p. 7.

'Chicago Women Greet Militant English Suffragette Leader', *Chicago Daily Tribune*, 26 November 1909, p. 3.

'City Earnest in Observing Bastille Day', *Rochester Democrat and Chronicle*, 15 July 1918, p. 15.

'The Close of the Women's Exhibition': 28 May 1909, *Votes for Women*, pp. 722–723.

'Crime and Criminals: Dynamite and Dynamiters', *Strand*, 7 (1894), pp. 118–132.

'The Death of Metro. Chief Inspector', *Police Review and Parade Gossip*, 7 August 1914, p. 379.

'Dedication of Mrs. Pankhurst's Headstone', *Vote*, 20 June 1930, p. 3.

'Deputation of Welsh Women Received by Mr. Lloyd George', 30 September 1910, *Votes for Women*, p. 848.

'Deputation to Mr. Asquith', *Common Cause*, 15 August 1913, pp. 319–321.

'Descriptive Accounts in the London Press', *Votes for Women*, 25 June 1908, pp. 260–263.

'Do the Government Intend to Murder Mrs. Pankhurst?', *Suffragette*, 20 February 1914, p. 420.

'The Double of Mrs. Pankhurst', *The Times*, 21 July 1913, p. 10.

'Dr. Ingram's Holloway Report: Suffragist Demonstration', *The Times*, 2 February 1914, HO 144 1305, National Archives.

'Drugging Women Hunger-Strikers', *Leeds Mercury*, 15 June 1914, p. 7.

'The End and the Beginning', *Common Cause*, 25 July 1913, pp. 267–268.

'The Exhibition Day by Day', *Votes for Women*, 21 May 1909, p. 691.

'Fashionable Marriage at Brindle', *Preston Herald*, 11 April 1896, p. 12.

'First Woman to Fly the Atlantic', *Daily Herald*, 19 June 1928, p. 1.

'Food for the Police on Duty: The Unnecessary Cruelty of Long Fasts', *Police Review and Parade Gossip*, 20 January 1911, p. 34.

'Forcible Feeding: Position of the Bishop of London: No Sympathy with Militants', *The Times*, 6 July 1914, p. 5.

'Forcibly Fed 232 Times: Miss Kitty Marion Released', *Suffragette*, 24 April 1914, p. 33.

'Fought Like Men', *The Evening Telegraph and Post*, 18 June 1906, p. 2.

'Four Years for Spying', *Illustrated Police News*, 24 June 1915, p. 4.

'Free Speech for Women – The Fight in Hyde Park: Militant Women Defy the Government', *Suffragette*, 10 April 1914, pp. 592–593.

'From the World's Scrapbook: New Items of Topical Interest', *Illustrated London News*, 23 June 1928, p. 1178.

'Glasgow Militant at the High Court', *Suffragette*, 3 July 1914, p. 199.

'Government Spies and Bullies: The Political Police at Work', *Suffragette*, 13 February 1914, p. 399.

'Government's Persecution of Women: Terrible Scenes in Court: Tortured Woman's Magnificent Courage', *Suffragette*, 5 June 1914, pp. 132–133.

'The Grimsby Spy Trial', *Leeds Mercury*, 18 June 1915, p. 4.

'Hands, Feet and Tongue', *Morning Advertiser*, 22 July 1914, page unknown.

Heinz Library and Archive, National Portrait Gallery.

'He Will Dine with His Suffragette Prisoners', *Daily Herald*, 29 September 1936, p. 11.

'H.G. Wells At Seventy', *Leeds Mercury*, 14 October 1936, p. 5.

'I Defy Them To Make Me Submit', Verbatim Report of Mrs. Pankhurst's Speech at Glebe Place, Chelsea, Saturday, Feb, 21', *Suffragette*, 27 January 1914, pp. 443 and 446.

'I Have Kept My Promise in Spite Of His Majesty's Government's: Unprecedented Enthusiasm in Glasgow', *Suffragette*, 13 March 1914, p. 493.

'In the Park', *Votes for Women*, 18 June 1908, p. 250.

'Inspiring Women: In Search of Women's History on Campus', *LSE Connect*, Autumn 2018, pp. 10–13.

'Jujitsu: Some Means of Attack and Defence', *Pall Mall Gazette*, 23 October 1900, p. 10.

'"Kill Me, Or Give Me My Freedom!": A Speech Delivered by Mrs. Pankhurst at the London Pavilion, July 14', *Suffragette*, 18 July 1913, p. 677.

Khomami, Nadia, 'Anger Over Plan to Move Pankhurst Statue Away from Parliament', *Guardian*, 17 August 2018, <www.theguardian.com/culture/2018/aug/17/anger-over-plan-to-move-pankhurst-statue-away-from-parliament> [Accessed 28 September 2018].

'A Message from Mrs Pankhurst', *Suffragette*, 18 June 1915, p. 160.

'Metro. Pay Increased: The New Figures', *Police Review and Parade Gossip*, 1 September 1911, p. 412.

'The Metropolitan Police: A Station', *The Times*, 28 December, 1908, p. 6.

'The Metropolitan Police: The King's Highway', *The Times*, 15 January 1909, p. 4.

'Militancy', *The Woman's Leader and the Common Cause*, 22 June 1928, p. 159.

'Militancy in Scotland', *Suffragette*, 17 July 1914, p. 244.

'Militant Brawling and Arson: Prison Drug-Smuggling', *The Times*, 8 June 1914, p. 48.

'Militants in Prison: Solicitor's Clerk Fined', *The Times*, 15 June 1914, p. 4.

'Militant Outrages: Headquarters Seized by Police', *The Times*, 25 May 1914, p. 34.

'The Militants: Their Leader's Defiance': "The Real Enemy"', *The Sunday Times*, 22 February 1914, p. 8.

'Mr. Francis Powell, Ex-Detective-Inspector Metro', *Police Review and Parade Gossip*, July 1912, p. 330.

'Mr. Lloyd George's Attack on the Conciliation Bill', *Votes for Women*, 19 August 1910, p. 768.

'Mrs. Pankhurst Again Triumphs', *Suffragette*, 20 March 1914, p. 511.

'Mrs Pankhurst's Arrest', *Police Review and Parade Gossip*, 3 April 1914, p. 157.

Mrs. Pankhurst Memorial, *The Times*, 16 June 1930, p. 11.

'Mrs. Pankhurst's Release – Prison News', *Suffragette*, 18 April 1913, p. 445.

'Mrs. Pankhurst's Tour Ends: Will the Government Arrest Mrs. Pankhurst: A Bodyguard in Readiness', *Suffragette*, 28 November 1913, p. 146.

'No Peace Anywhere in the Kingdom: Suffragettes at Lossiemouth', *Suffragette*, 5 September 1913, p. 816.

'Obituary: Christopher Newton Thompson', *Telegraph*, 25 March 2002. <www.telegraph.co.uk/news/obituaries/1388740/Christopher-Newton-Thompson.html> [Accessed 24 March 2018].

'Obituary: Sir Patrick Quinn', *The Times*, 10 June 1936, p. 9.

'Obituary: Richard Pankhurst', *The Times*, 24 March 2017, p. 55.

'Official Secrets. Charge Against a Swede', *Midland Daily Telegraph*, 18 May 1915, p. 2.

'Our Perfect Police!: Law and Order Acquits Itself of the Charge of Brutality: Rebels Always Wrong', *Votes for Women*, 13 February 1914, p. 3.

'The Outlook', *Votes for Women*, 18 November 1910, p. 97.

'Pankhurst Statue Unveiling: Suffragists' Homage to Leader', *Manchester Guardian*, 7 March 1930, p. 8.

'The Pentonville Atrocity', *Votes for Women*, 16 February 1912, p. 303.

'Policewomen?', *Police Review and Parade Gossip*, 3 June 1913, p. 272.

'The Political Police: Liberal Government's Agents of Repression', *Suffragette*, 6 February 1914, p. 371.

'Public Opinion: Representative Men and Women Condemn the "Cat and Mouse" Bill', *Suffragette*, 27 June 1913, p. 617.

'Put Me Near a Suffragette – Memories of the Battle', *Listener*, 8 February 1968, pp. 175–181.

'To Hyde Park on Saturday!', *Suffragette*, 3 April 1914, p. 559.

'Re-Arrest of Miss Kenney', *Manchester Courier*, 15 July 1913, p. 3.

'A Remarkable Woman', *Halstead Gazette*, 5 December 1947.

'Retribution!: Mary Richardson's Reply', *Suffragette*, 13 March 1914, p. 491.

'Review: Book of the Week: A Liberator of Women', *Votes for Women*, 8 July 1910, p. 666.

'The St. Bees Bomb: Two Young Men Charged', *The Times*, 26 July 1932, p. 9.

'The Scandal of King's Thursday', *Suffragette*, 5 June 1914, p 137.

'Sequel to Pavilion Meeting', *Suffragette*, 1 August 1913, p. 725.

'Solicitor's Clerk Fined', *Daily Herald*, 15 June 1914, p. 1.

'Strange Outrage: A Bomb at St. John's Church', *West London Press Chelsea News*, 6 March 1914, p. 963.

'The Stricken Brave', *Yorkshire Post*, 16 June 1915, p. 6.

'The Suffragette Athlete', *Daily Mail*, 27 June 1910, p. 9.

'The Suffragette Athlete. Jiu-Jitsu Test. The Little Woman and a Big Policeman', *Daily Mail*, 27 June 1910, p. 9.

'Suffragette Leader's Funeral', *Sheffield Daily Telegraph*, 19 June 1928, p. 9.

'Suffragettes Dine with the Man Who Arrested Them', *Leeds Mercury*, 14 October 1936, p .5.

'Suffragist Deputation to the King', *The Times*, 21 May 1914, p. 5.

'Suffragist Riot at Glasgow', *Police Review and Parade Gossip*, 20 March 1914, p. 142.

'Suffragists and the King', *The Times*, 15 December 1913, p. 5.

'Swede Spying for Germany', *Dundee Evening Telegraph and Post*, 18 June 1915, p. 4.

'Three Pears', 'P.C. Hodge's Lesson in Ju-Jitsu', *Police Review and Parade Gossip*, 2 June 1911.

'To-Day in the Courts: Suffragettes Armed with Clubs: Woman Tries Policemen's Belts in Court: Princess Knocked Down', *Globe*, 11 February 1914, p. 7.

'To Hyde Park!: Portraits and Biographies of the Twenty Chairmen for Sunday June 21', *Votes for Women*, 7 May 1908, pp. 141–145.

'To Kill Mrs. Pankhurst: Suffragist's Extraordinary Allegations', *Manchester Evening News*, 19 February 1914, p. 4.

'The Unnamed Suffragettes', *West London Observer*, 20 February 1914, p. 10.

'The unveiling of Mrs. Pankhurst's Statue', *Vote*, 14 March 1930, pp. 81–82.

'Victory is Assured.: A Verbatim Report of Mrs. Pankhurst's Speech at Campden Hill Square, Feb. 10, 1914', *Suffragette*, 13 February 1914, p. 397.

'Visit of A Famous American Detective', *Police Review and Parade Gossip*, 23 June 1911, p. 294.

'Votes for Women. Memorial Statue of Mrs. Pankhurst', *The Times*, 7 March 1930, p. 13.

'Whitewashing the Police: Mrs. Pankhurst's Arrest in St. Andrew's Hall', *Suffragette*, 10 April 1914, p. 598.

'"Why We Are Militant", speech by Mrs Pankhurst New York City, 21 October 1913', *Suffragette*, 14 November 1913, p. 99.

'Women Carried Into Court: Government Again Charged with Drugging Prisoners', *Daily Herald*, 10 June 1914, p. 2.

'The Women's Party.: Victory, National Security and Progress', *Britannia*, 2 November 1917, pp. 171–172.

'A Woman Suffrage Bill This Session: Proposals of the Woman Suffrage Parliamentary Conciliation Committee', *Votes for Women*, 27 May 1910, p. 561.

Selected Primary and Secondary Sources

Adie, Kate, *Fighting on the Home Front: The Legacy of Women in World War One* (London: Hodder & Stoughton, 2013).

Allen, Mary S., *Lady in Blue* (London: Stanley Paul & Co, 1936).

Anand, Anita, *Sophia: Princess, Suffragette, Revolutionary* (London: Bloomsbury, 2015).

Arnold, Matthew, *Culture and Anarchy* (Oxford: Oxford World's Classics, 2006).

Asquith, Herbert, *Moments of Memory: Recollections and Impressions* (London: Hutchinson & Co, 1937).

Atkinson, Diane, *Rise up, Women! The Remarkable Lives of the Suffragettes* (London: Bloomsbury, 2018).

Atkinson, Diane, *The Suffragettes in Pictures* (Museum of London, 2010).

Austin, L.F., 'Our Notebook', *Illustrated London News*, 6 January 1900, p. 2.

Baird, Julia, *Victoria The Queen: An Intimate Biography of the Woman who Ruled an Empire* (London: Blackfriars, 2016).

Baldwin, William Charles, *African Hunting and Adventure: From Natal to the Zambesi* (London: Richard Bentley and Son, 1891).

Bartley, Paula, *Emmeline Pankhurst* (London: Routledge, 2002).

Barton-Wright, Edward William, 'The New Art of Self Defence' (Part 1), *Pearson's Magazine*, 7 (1899), pp. 268–75; (Part 2), *Pearson's Magazine*, 7 (1899), pp. 402–410.

Barton-Wright, Edward William, 'Self-Defence with a Walking-Stick: The Different Methods of Defending Oneself with a Walking-Stick or Umbrella when Attacked under Unequal Conditions' (Part 1), *Pearson's Magazine*, 11 (1901), pp. 11–20; (Part 2), *Pearson's Magazine,* 11 (1901), pp. 130–139.

Billington-Greig, Teresa, 'The Woman with the Whip' (1907), in *Towards Woman's Liberty* (London: Women's Freedom League, 1913).

Bishop, Cecil, *From Information Received: The Reminiscences of Cecil Bishop* (London: Hutchinson & Co., 1932).

Bonham Carter, Mark and Mark Pottle (eds), *Lantern Slides: The Diaries and Letters of Violet Bonham Carter 1904–1914* (London: Weidenfeld & Nicholson, 1996).

Bonham Carter, Violet, 'The Suffragettes: Some "Militant" Memories', *Manchester Guardian*, 2 February, 1957, p. 6.

Brust, Harold, *'I Guarded Kings': The Memoirs of a Political Police Officer* (London: Stanley Paul & Co, 1935).

Buckley, Angela, *The Real Sherlock Holmes: The Hidden Story of Jerome Caminada* (Barnsley: Pen & Sword, 2014).

Caird, Mona, 'Ideal Marriage', *Westminster Review*, 130 (1888), pp. 617–636.

Caird, Mona, 'Marriage', *Westminster Review*, 130 (1888), pp. 186–201.

Churton Braby, Maud, 'G. B. S. and a Suffragist: "I Am Not a Woman – I Have Got the Suffrage", An Intimate Interview', *Tribune*, 12 March 1906, newspaper cutting, no page given, Box File 20, 7JCC/B/Survey/20, The Jill Craigie Collection, The Women's Library, London School of Economics.

Cherrill, Fred, *Cherrill of the Yard: The Autobiography of Fred Cherrill* (London: George, G. Harrap, 1954).

Churchill, Randolph S., *Winston S. Churchill, 1874–1956, Volume II, Young Statesman, 1901–1914* (London: Heinemann, 1967).

Clifford, Bridget, 'Curator@ War: A continuing story of museum – ffoulkes – The Tower Armouries' – February 1913 <https://royalarmouries.org/stories/the-armouries-at-war> [Accessed 20 March 2018].

'Clifton Reynes' [Ralph Kitchener], 'The Police as a Career: A Review of the Past, with Suggestions for the Future', *Police Journal*, 7 (1934), pp. 292–320.

Cline, Sally, *Radclyffe Hall: A Woman Called John* (London: John Murray, 1997).

Collette, Carolyn, P., *In the Thick of the Fight: The Writing of Emily Wilding Davison, Militant Suffragette* (Michigan: University of Michigan Press, 2013).

Crawford, Elizabeth, *Art and Suffrage: A Biographical Dictionary of Suffrage Artists* (London: Francis Boutle, 2018), pp. 47–48.

Crawford, Elizabeth, *Campaigning for the Vote: Kate Parry Frye's Suffrage Diary* (London: Francis Boutle, 2013).

Crawford, Elizabeth, 'Police, Prisons and Prisoners: The View from the Home Office', *Women's History Review*, 14 (2005), pp. 487–505.

Crawford, Elizabeth, *The Women's Suffrage Movement: A Reference Guide 1866–1928* (London: Routledge, 1999).

Dangerfield, George, *The Strange Death of Liberal England* (London: Constable, 1936).

Davison, Emily Wilding, 'Josephine Butler: Pioneer of Social Purity', *Votes for Women*, 25 August 1911, p. 756.

Dickens, Charles, 'Detective Police', *Charles Dickens: Selected Journalism: 1850–1870*, ed. by David Pascoe (London: Penguin, 1997).

Drabble, Margaret, 'Freedom Fighters: Keep the Torch Burning', *Radio Times*, 30 March–5 April 1974, pp. 62–67.

Drummond, Flora, 'My Campaigning Days', *People's Journal*, 24 June 1939, p. 20.

Drummond, Flora, 'Votes for Women', *The Listener*, 25 August 1937, p. 405.

E.H.H., 'Holloway Prison Comes Down', *Calling All Women*, 12 May 1977.

Ekstein, Eve and June Firkins, *Hat Pins* (Buckinghamshire: Shire Books, 2006).

Emsley, Clive, *The Great British Bobby: A History of British Policing from the 18th Century to the Present* (London: Quercus, 2009).

Eustance, Claire, 'Suffragettes in Trousers: The Men who Supported Women's Suffrage in Parliament, 1860–1930', <www.parliament.uk/about/living-heritage/transformingsociety/electionsvoting/womenvote/case-studies-women-parliament/suffragettes-in-trousers/suffragettes-in-trousers> [Accessed 21 August 2018].

Ferguson, Rachel, *Victorian Bouquet: Lady X Looks On* (London: Ernest Benn, 1931).

ffoulkes, Charles, John, *Arms and the Tower* (London: John Murray, 1939).

Fitch, Herbert T., *Traitors Within: The Adventures of Detective Inspector Herbert T. Fitch* (London: Hurst & Blackett, 1933).

Flanders, Judith, *The Invention of Murder: How the Victorians Revelled in Death and Detection and Created Modern Crime* (London: Harper Collins, 1911).

Gardiner, A.G., *Prophets, Priests, and Kings* (London: Alston Rivers, Ltd., 1908).

Garrett Fawcett, Millicent, *What I Remember* (London: T. Fisher Unwin, 1924).

Garrett Fawcett, Millicent, 'Letter to the Editor: The Imprisoned Suffragists', *The Times*, 27 October 1906, p. 8.

Garrett Fawcett, Millicent, *The Women's Victory – And After: Personal Reminiscences, 1911–1918* (London: Sidgwick & Jackson, 1920), p. 94.

Garrud, Edith, Article for 'The World We Live In', *Votes for Women*, 4 March 1910, p. 355.

Geddes, Jennian, F., 'Deeds and Words in the Suffrage Military Hospital in Endell Street', *Medical History*, 51 (2007), pp. 79–98.

Gifford, Colin, *The Asquiths* (London: John Murray, 2002).

Gifford, Denis, *The British Film Catalogue, Volume One: Fiction Film 1895–1994* (London: Fitzroy Dearborn, 2001).

Gilmour, Ian, 'Butler, Richard Austen [Rab], Baron Butler of Saffron Walden', *Oxford Dictionary of National Biography* (2004).

Gissing, George, *The Odd Women* (London: Penguin, 1983).

Greg, W.R., *Why Are Women Redundant?* (London: N. Trübner & Co, 1869).

Godfrey, Emelyne, 'Aim High: The Lives of the Women Who Fought for the Vote', *Times Literary Supplement*, 9 February 2018, pp. 14–15.

Godfrey, Emelyne, *Feminity, Crime and Self-Defence in Victorian Literature and Society: From Dagger-Fans to Suffragettes*, (Basingstoke: Palgrave Macmillan, 2012), pp. 79–82.

Godfrey, Emelyne, 'Jujutsuffragettes', *Martial Arts of the World: An Encyclopedia of History and Innovation*, II, ed. by Thomas A. Green and Joseph R. Svinth ABC-CLIO (Santa Barbara, California: 2010), pp. 632–637.

Godfrey, Emelyne, 'Wright, Edward William Barton (1860–1951), martial arts instructor', 2012, *Oxford Dictionary of National Biography*.

Graef, Roger, *Talking Blues: The Police in their Own Words* (London: Collins Harvill, 1989).

Greville, Lady Violet, *Vignettes of Memory* (London: Hutchinson & Co, 1927).

Hale, Cicely, *A Good Long Time: The Autobiography of an Octogenarian* (London: Regency Press, 1973).

Harrison, Brian, *Separate Spheres: The Opposition to Women's Suffrage in Britain* (London: Croom Helm, 1978).

Herbert, A. P., *Holy Deadlock* (Methuen & Co, London: 1934).

Hickman, Tom, *Churchill's Bodyguard* (London: Headline, 2006).

Humphreys, Christmas, 'Bodkin, Sir Archibald Henry (1862–1957), lawyer' (revised by Mark Pottle), *Oxford Dictionary of National Biography* (2004).

Jackson, Sarah and Rosemary Taylor, *East London Suffragettes* (Gloucestershire: The History Press, 2016).

Jacques, Kinton, *Memoirs of the late Rev. Canon Jacques, Rector of Brindle and Hon. Canon of Manchester* (Chorley: S. Fowler & Sons, 1915).

Jewell, J. St A., 'The Gymnasiums of London: Pierre Vigny's', *Health and Strength*, 8 (1904), pp. 173–177.

Jeyes, S.H., *The Life of Sir Howard Vincent* (London: George Allen and Company, 1912).

John, V., Angela, *Elizabeth Robins: Staging a Life* (Gloucestershire: The History Press, 2013).

Jones, Ian, *London Bombed, Blitzed and Blown Up: The British Capital Under Attack Since 1867* (Barnsley: Frontline Books, 2016).

Kenney, Annie, *Memories of a Militant* (London: Edward Arnold & Co., 1924).

Kenney, Jessie, '"Jostling" the Premier at Lympne', *Votes for Women*, 10 September 1909, pp. 1157–1158.

Laski, Harold, 'The Militant Temper in Politics', Z6061, Group B, p. 103–122, Suffragette Fellowship Collection, Museum of London.

Leslie, Henrietta [Gladys Schütze], *More Ha'pence than Kicks: Being Some Things Remembered* (London: MacDonald & Co, 1943).

Leslie, Henrietta, *A Mouse with Wings* (London: Collins' Clear-Type Press, 1920).

Leslie, Henrietta, *Mrs. Fischer's War* (London: Jarrold's, 1930).

Lewis, Lionel S., 'Food for the Police on Duty', *The Times*, 6 January 1911, p. 10.

Liddington, Jill, with Elizabeth Crawford, *Vanishing for the Vote: Suffrage, Citizenship and the Battle for the Census* (Manchester: Manchester University Press, 2014).

Linton, Eliza Lynn, 'Modern Mannish Maidens', *Blackwood's Edinburgh Magazine*, 147 (1890), pp. 252–264.

Lock, Joan, *Scotland Yard Casebook: The Making of the CID 1865–1935* (Endeavour Press, 2014).

Logan, Mrs John A., *The Part Taken by Women in American History* (Delaware: The Perry-Nalle Publishing Company, 1912).

Lytton, Lady Constance and Jane Warton, *Prisons and Prisoners: Some Personal Experiences* (New York: George H. Doran Company, 1914).

M[arshall], E[mily]. K[atherine], 'More About His Majesty's Police': 'The Treatment of Women on King's Thursday, The Scene on Constitution Hill', *Suffragette*, 12 June 1914, p. 152.

Marshall, Mrs E[mily]. K[atherine]., 'Trade Union Tyranny', *Pall Mall Gazette*, 19 June 1912, p. 4.

Martindale, Louisa, *Under the Surface* (Brighton: The Southern Publishing Company, 1909).

Masefield, John, 'The White Slave Trade', *Votes for Women*, 29 April 1910, p. 495.

May, James with Phil Dolling, *James May's Magnificent Machines: How Men in Sheds Have Changed Our Lives* (Hodder & Stoughton, London, 2008).

McKenna, Stephen, *Reginald McKenna: 1863–1943* (London: Eyre & Spottiswoode, 1948).

Mitchell, David, 'Life in Mrs Pankhurst's Second Family', [interview with Mary Hodgson], *The Times*, 25 July 1975, p. 10.

Morris, William, *News from Nowhere and Other Writings* (ed. By Clive Wilmer) (London: Penguin, 2004).

Morse, Elizabeth, J., Schütze [née Raphael; other married name Mendl], (Gladys), Henrietta [pseud. Henrietta Leslie] (1884–1946), writer and pacifist, *Oxford Dictionary of National Biography*, 2004.

Moss, Alan and Keith Skinner, *Scotland Yard's History of Crime in 100 Objects*, (Gloucestershire: The History Press, 2015), p. 205.

Moss, Alan, and Keith Skinner, *The Victorian Detective* (Oxford: Shire Library, 2013).

Murray, [Dr] Flora, *Women as Army Surgeons: Being the History of the Women's Hospital Corps in Paris, Wimereux and Endell Street, September 1914–October 1914* (London: Hodder & Stoughton, 1920).

Murray, Jessie, Dr., and Henry Brailsford (eds) *Treatment of the Women's Deputations of November 18th, 22nd, & 23rd, 1910 by the Police* (Woman's Press, London, 1913), pp. 4–6.

The National Association of Decorative and Fine Arts Societies: Record of Church Furnishings (Brindle St James Archives).

Nevinson, Henry Woodd, *More Changes, More Chances* (London: Nisbet & Co., 1925).

Nevinson, Henry, 'An Impression' in 'The Great Protest of Women: Demonstration in Parliament Square. Many Windows Broken. 223 Arrests', *Votes for Women*, 24 November 1911, p. 123.

Newton Thompson, Joyce, 'The Suffrage Movement', *NCW News*, June 1958, pp. 6–8.

Nott-Bower, William (Sir), *Fifty-Two Years a Policeman* (London: Edward Arnold, 1926).

O'Brien (Cook), Gwen, 'Profile', *Calling All Women*, February 1969, pp. 6–8.

Pankhurst, Christabel, 'To Cure White Slavery: A Medical Question', *Suffragette*, 25 April 1913, p. 475.

Pankhurst, Christabel, 'In Fear of Women', *Suffragette*, 19 December 1913, p. 225.

Pankhurst, Christabel, 'Militant Tactics to Date', *Votes for Women*, 17 September 1909, pp. 1180–1181

Pankhurst, Christabel, 'Plain Facts about a Great Evil', *Suffragette*, 29 August 1913, p. 797.

Pankhurst, Christabel, 'Political Notes: "What Women Want"', *Votes for Women*, 2 July 1908, p. 281.

Pankhurst, Christabel, 'The War: A Speech', delivered to the London Opera House, 8 September 1914, pp. 5–6. Museum of London, First World War Folder, 1914–1918, David Mitchell Papers, Suffragette Collections (accession ref: 73.83 & 80.116), Museum of London.

Pankhurst, Christabel, 'The Truth about the Piccadilly Flat', *Suffragette*, 25 July 1913, p. 693.

Pankhurst, Christabel, *Unshackled: The Story of How We Won the Vote* (London: Hutchinson, 1959).

Pankhurst, Emmeline, *My Own Story* (London: Eveleigh Nash, 1914).

Pankhurst, Mrs [Emmeline], 'The Argument of the Broken Pane', *Votes for Women*, 23 February 1912, p. 319.

Pankhurst, E. Sylvia, *The Life of Emmeline Pankhurst: The Suffragette Struggle for Women's Citizenship* (London: T. Werner Laurie, and Kraus reprint, 1969).

Pankhurst, E. Sylvia, *The Suffragette: The History of the Women's Militant Suffrage Movement, 1905–1910* (London: Gay & Hancock, 1911).

Pethick Lawrence, Emmeline, 'Across the Atlantic', *Votes for Women*, 11 October 1912, p. 25.

Pethick-Lawrence, Emmeline, 'Book of the Week: Josephine E. Butler', *Votes for Women*, 28 May 1909, pp. 720–721.

E[mmeline.P[ethick]. L[awrence]., 'Books of the Month: The Heart of Women', *Votes for Women*, November 1907, p. 19.

Pethick Lawrence, Mrs [Emmeline], 'Inciting to Violence. Mr. Hobhouse Taunts Women with Being Less Militant than Men', *Votes for Women*, 23 February 1912, p. 9.

Pethick Lawrence, Emmeline, 'In Quest of Freedom', *Votes for Women*, 29 April 1910, p. 499.

Pethick-Lawrence, Emmeline, *My Part in a Changing World* (London: Gollancz, 1938).

Pethick Lawrence, Emmeline, 'Review of Mary Wollstonecraft: A Study in Economics and Romance by G.R.S. Taylor', *Votes for Women*, 24 February 1911, p. 338.

P[ethick]. L[awrence]., E[mmeline]. 'The Story of Old Japan', *Votes for Women*, 2 September 1910, p. 789.

Pethick Lawrence, Emmeline, 'What the Vote Means to the Woman as Wife; 1. Women's Status in the 19th Century', *Votes for Women*, November 1907, p. 17.

Pethick Lawrence, Emmeline, 'What Women Are Worth', *Votes for Women*, 9 July 1908, p. 296.

Porter, Bernard, *Plots and Paranoia: A History of Political Espionage in Britain, 1790–1988* (London: Unwin Hyman, 1989), p. 131.

Porter, Bernard, *The Origins of the Vigilant State: The London Metropolitan Police Special Branch Before the First World War* (London: Weidenfeld and Nicolson, 1987).

Procter, Adelaide, A., *The Complete Works of Adelaide A. Procter* (London: George Bell and Sons, 1905).

Pullein-Thompson, Josephine, 'International P.E.N. in Chelsea', *The Chelsea Society Annual Report*, 1978, pp. 25–28.

Purvis, June, *Christabel Pankhurst: A Biography* (Routledge, London and New York, 2018).

Purvis, June, *Emmeline Pankhurst: A Biography* (London: Routledge, 2002).

Purvis, June, 'We Owe Them the Vote', *The Guardian*, 10 July 2008. <www.theguardian.com/commentisfree/2008/jul/10/women> [Accessed 2 October 2018].

Quilter, Harry, (ed.), *Is Marriage a Failure?* (London: Swann Sonnenschein, 1888).

Raeburn, Antonia, *The Militant Suffragettes* (London: Michael Joseph, 1973).

Reed, Michelle, 'Chirpy Chipping Ongar', *Essex Life & Countryside*, December 2004, pp. 54–57.

'Reynes, Clifton', 'The Police as a Career: A Review of the Past, with Suggestions for the Future', *Police Journal*, 7 (1934), pp. 292–320.

Reynolds, K.D., Campbell [neé Blood], 'Gertrude Elizabeth [Lady Colin Campbell] (1857–1911), art critic and journalist', *Oxford Dictionary of National Biography* (2004).

Rhondda, Viscountess, Margaret Haig (Thomas Mackworth) *This Was My World* (London: Macmillan and Co., 1933).

Richardson, Mary, *Laugh A Defiance* (London: Weidenfeld and Nicholson, 1953).

Riddell, Fern, *Death in Ten Minutes: Kitty Marion Activist, Arsonist, Suffragette* (London: Hodder and Stoughton, 2018).

Robins, Elizabeth, *Both Sides of the Curtain* (London: Heinemann, 1940).

Robins, Elizabeth, *The Convert* (1907), ed. by Emelyne Godfrey (Victorian Secrets, 2013).

Robins, Elizabeth, *'Where Are You Going To …?'* (London: William Heinemann, 1913).

Robinson, Jane, *Hearts and Minds: The Untold Story of the Great Pilgrimage and How Women Won the Vote* (London: Doubleday, 2018).

Rounds, C.R. (ed.), *Ruskin's Sesame and Lilies* (American Book Company, 1916).

Rouse, Wendy, *Her Own Hero: The Origins of the Women's Self-Defense Movement* (New York: New York University Press, 2017).

Ruz, Camila and Justin Parkinson, '"Suffrajitsu": How the Suffragettes Fought Back Using Martial Arts', *BBC News Magazine* <www.bbc.co.uk/news/magazine-34425615> [Accessed 1 July 2022].

St. John, Christopher, *Christine Murrell, M.D. Her Life and Her Work* (London: Williams & Norgate, 1935).

Savage, Gail, '"The Wilful Communication of a Loathsome Disease": Marital Conflict and Venereal Disease in Victorian England', *Victorian Studies* (34) 1990, pp. 35–54 and 47.

Sebba, Anne, 'A Rebel in the Family', *The Times*, 2007, 26 July p. 10.

Sebba, Anne, 'A Suffragette in the Family', *The London Library Magazine*, Spring (2018), pp. 14–17.

Sharp, Evelyn, Hertha Ayrton, *1854–1923* (London: Edward Arnold & Co., 1926).

Sharp, Evelyn, 'The Fighting Woman', *Votes for Women*, 3 September 1908, p. 418.

Shaw, George Bernard, '"We Are Members of One Another", Verbatim transcript of a speech delivered at Kingsway Hall', 18 March 1913, *Suffragette*, 28 March, p. 380.

Shaw, George Bernard and Violet R. Markham, 'Letters to the editor. "Woman Suffrage"', *The Times*, 31 October 1906, p. 8.

Sherborne, Michael, *H.G. Wells: Another Kind of Life* (London: Peter Owen, 2010).

Shpayer-Makov, Haia, *The Ascent of the Detective: Police Sleuths in Victorian and Edwardian England* (Oxford: Oxford University Press, 2011).

Smith, Sir (William) Henry, K.C.B., *From Constable to Commissioner: The Story of Sixty Years, Most of them Misspent* (London: Chatto & Windus, 1910).

Smyth, Ethel, *Female Pipings in Eden* (London: Peter Davies, 1933).

Snow, Keith, and David Thompson, 'Emmeline Pankhurst at St. Martin's Church, Chipping Ongar', *Ongar Millennium History Society Newsletter*, May 2012 <omhs.org.uk/newsletters>.

Soames, Mary (ed.), *Speaking for Themselves: The Personal Letters of Winston and Clemmie Churchill* (London: Doubleday, 1998).

Sparham, Anna, *Soldiers & Suffragettes: The Photography of Christina Broom* (London: I.B. Tauris & Co., 2015).

Stapleton, Suzannah, *The Adventures of Maud West, Lady Detective* (London: Picador, 2019).

Stevenson, Kim, '"An English Gentleman": Joseph Davidson Sowerby Chief Constable of Plymouth 1892–1917', *The Journal of the Police History Society*, 30 (2016), pp. 61–69.

Strachey, Ray, *The Cause: A Short History of the Women's Movement in Great Britain* (London: G. Bell and Sons, Ltd, 1928).

'Suffrage Fallacies. Sir Almroth Wright on Militant Hysteria', *The Times*, 28 March 1912, p. 7.

Swanwick, Helena, Maria, *I Have Been Young* (London: Victor Gollancz, 1935).

Theydon Golf Club: The First 100 Years, Celebratory Publication (Theydon Bois Golf Club, 1997).

Thomson, Sir Basil, *My Experiences at Scotland Yard* (New York: A.L. Burt Company/Doubleday, 1923).

Thomson, Sir Basil, *The Scene Changes* (London: Collins Publishers, 1939).

Thompson, W[alter]. H[enry]., *I Was Churchill's Shadow* (London: Christopher Johnson, 1951).

Thompson, W[alter]. H[enry]., *Guard from the Yard* (London: Jarrolds, 1938).

Tidcombe, Marianne, *The Doves Press* (London: British Library/Oak Knoll, 2002).

Turnour Winterton, Rt. Hon. Earl Edward, *Orders of the Day* (London: Cassell, 1953).

Wheeldon, G.H., *Self-Defence: A Treatise upon the Art of Defence against attack, Specially Designed for Police Instruction* (London: John Kempster, Police Review Office, 1904).

Vincent, Howard, C.E., *A Police Code and Manual of Criminal Law* (London: Cassell, 1881).

Vincent, Colonel Sir Howard, *The Police Code and General Manual of Criminal Law* (London: Francis Edwards, 1907).

deVries, Jacqueline R., 'Sounds Taken for Wonders: Revivalism and Religious Hybridity in the British Women's Suffrage Movement' in *Material Religion in Modern Britain: The Spirit of Things*, ed. by Timothy Willem Jones and Lucinda Matthews-Jones (Basingstoke, Palgrave Macmillan, 2015), pp. 101–123.

Wainright, Robert, *Miss Muriel Matters: The Fearless Suffragist who Fought for Equality* (London: Allen & Unwin, 2017).

Ward, Margaret (ed.), *Hanna Sheehy Skeffington, Suffragette and Sinn Féiner: Her Memoirs and Political Writings* (Dublin: University College Dublin Press, 2017).

Watts, Emily, *The Fine Art of Jujutsu* (London: William Heinemann, 1906).

Webb, Simon, *Suffragette Bombers: Britain's Forgotten Terrorists* (Barnsley: Pen & Sword, 2015).

Wells, H.G., *Ann Veronica: A Modern Love Story* (London: T. Fisher Unwin, 1909).

Wells, H.G., *The First Men in the Moon* (London: Penguin, 2005).

Wells, H.G, *Experiment in Autobiography: Discoveries and Conclusions of a Very Ordinary Brain (Since 1866)*, 2 vols (London: Victor Gollancz & The Cresset Press, 1934).

Wenborne, Kathy, 'Kitty Marshall and Ongar', Millennium History Society Newsletter, February 2013. <omhs.org.uk/newsletters> [Accessed 23 August 2018].

Wheeldon, Sergeant G.H., *Self-Defence: A Treatise upon the Art of Defence against attack, Specially Designed for Police Instruction* (London: John Kempster, Police Review Office, 1904).

Wilding Davison, Emily, 'The Corruption of the Metropolitan Police', Emily Wilding Davison Personal Papers, 7EWD/A/5/1, The Women's Library 5.5, Reel 1, pp. 1–5.

Wilding Davison, Emily, 'The Price of Liberty', *Suffragette*, 15 June 1914, p. 129.

W[ilding]. D[avison]., E[mily]., 'The World We Live In', 'The Japan-British Exhibition', *Votes for Women*, 27 May 1910. p. 563.

Willmott Dobbie, B. M., *A Nest of Suffragettes in Somerset* (Batheaston, 1979).

Wilson, Gretchen, *With All Her Might: The Life of Gertrude Harding Militant Suffragette* (Goose Lane, New Brunswick, 1996), pp. 95–96.

Wilson, Ray and Ian Adams, *Special Branch. A History: 1883–2006* (Biteback Books, 2015, Kindle Edition).

Winn, Godfrey, 'Dear Mrs. Garrud – I Wish I'd Known You Then … ', *Woman*, 19 June 1965,pp. 22–25.

Wood, Adam, 'War in the Shadows: Detecting the Dynamitards', *Journal of the Police History Society* (2020), pp. 53–61.

Wood, Christopher, *Victorian Painting* (London: Weidenfeld & Nicolson, 1999).

Woodhall, Edwin T., *Guardians of the Great* (London: Blandford Press, 1934).

Wolf, Tony, 'An interview with "Year of the Bodyguard" director Noel Burch', <suffrajitsu.com/an-interview-with-year-of-the-bodyguard-director-noel-burch/> [Accessed 1 July 2022].

Wolf, Tony (ed.), *The Bartitsu Compendium: Volume III: What Bartitsu Was and What it Can Be* (Kindle Direct Publishing, 2022).

Wolf, Tony, 'The Mystery of Miss Sanderson's First Name' <www.bartitsu. org/index.php/2015/11/solved-the-mystery-of-miss-sandersons-first-name> [Accessed 1 July 2022].

Wollstonecraft, Mary, *A Vindication of the Rights of Woman with Strictures on Political and Moral Subjects* <digital.library.lse.ac.uk/objects/lse:dur688faq> [Accessed 15 January 2019].

Wright, Sir A[lmroth] E[dward], 'Letter to the Editor: "Suffrage Fallacies"', *The Times*, 28 March, 1912, p. 7.

Wylie, I[da]. A[lexa]. R[oss]., *My Life with George: An Unconventional Autobiography* (New York, Random House, 1940).

Wylie, I[da]. A[lexa]. R[oss]., 'Resurrection', *Suffragette*, 10 April 1914, p. 591.

Index

Ainsworth, Laura 56–8, 75
Allan, Janie 169, 177
Allan, Julian Phelps (Eva Dorothy) 212
Allen, Commandant Mary 49, 55, 76,
    140, 192, 202, 204, 209, 211, 215
Anderson, Dr Elizabeth Garrett 69,
    97
Anderson, Dr Louisa Garrett 69, 193,
Anderson, John Redwood 219
Asquith,
    Herbert Henry, 1st Earl of Oxford
    47, 51, 52, 56, 59, 60, 63, 68, 69,
    70, 72, 81, 84, 85, 91, 100, 119,
    146, 201, 209, 228
    Herbert Dixon 47, 60
    Violet (Baroness Asquith of
    Yarnbury) 63–4, 123–4,

Baldwin,
    William Charles 21–2, 24, 53, 68,
    147, 176, 199, 225
    Caroline see Caroline Jacques
Ball, William, the case of 88
Barrett, Arthur 44, 67, 142
Barton-Wright, Edward William 48
Bartitsu 48–9, 59, 224
Billinghurst, Rosa May 87, 111, 115,
    147

Billington-Greig, Teresa, 76
Bishop, Cecil 39, 71, 145–9, 163
Boyle, Nina 193
Black Friday 71, 74, 81, 91, 119, 177,
    201
Bodkin, Sir Archibald Henry 114–15,
    123, 12–7, 181–3
Bombs
    Aerial 152, 192
    St Bees Bomb 213–14,
    Suffragette 114, 117–18, 130, 216
    Fenian 103, 152
Bonham Carter,
    Helena (CBE), 63
Botchkareva, Maria, 196
Brackenbury,
    Georgina, frontispiece, 115, 122,
    130, 142, 205, 207, 211
    Marie, 68, 122, 130, 142
Brown Women March 145–6
Brust, Harold 84, 106, 148–9, 222
Bunn, Frank 40, 129, 223
Burkitt, Hilda 181
Butler, Josephine 115 135
Butler, Rab 216

Capper, Mabel 53, 56
Cass Case 136

Churchill,
    Winston, Sir 48, 65, 70, 71, 73–8,
        80, 97, 106, 111, 195, 215, 216
    Clemmie 111
Cohen, Leonora 86, 134–5, 221
Cook, Gwen(doline) ('Ethel Cox')
    128, 132, 150, 173, 178, 197,
    222, 227
Crawfurd, Helen 135, 168–9, 171, 196
Criminal Investigation Department
    (CID) 76, 103–5, 139, 154, 167
Crippen, Dr Hawley Harvey 67–8,
    73, 104, 139

Dacre Fox, Norah 139, 146–7, 154, 180,
    227
Damer Dawson, Margaret Mary
    (OBE), 193
Dewar, Ellen 130, 138, 177, 227
Dog-whips 73, 75–6
Dove-Willcox, Lillian Mary 53, 135,
    146, 168, 172
Doyle, Sir Arthur Conan 47, 49, 63,
    117, 123
    see also Sherlock Holmes
Drummond, Flora 43, 73, 84, 107,
    124, 126–7, 146–7, 151, 168,
    171, 197, 205, 210, 215

East London Federation of the
    Suffragettes 123

Fawcett, Dame Millicent Garrett 25,
    145–6, 200
Finch, Hugh 26–34, 220
Franklin, Hugh 74–6, 120–1
Fonblanque, Florence de 110, 145
Fussell, Maud 53, 72, 74, 86

Garrud, Edith 11, 15, 17, 19, 46–9,
    66, 82, 85, 129, 131–2, 134, 137,
    138, 197, 226
General Strike 202

Gladstone,
    William Ewart 35
    Herbert, 1st Viscount 44, 57–9,
        61–5, 122, 226
Goulden Bach,
    Ada 203, 205, 210, 218
    Enid 205, 210, 217, 221
Griffiths, Gladys 130, 138, 192, 227

Hale, Cicely 124
Hall, Nellie 180–3, 204
Hamilton, Cicely 11, 194
Hasler Helby, Dr Ernest 57–8
Haverfield, Hon. Evelina 54, 69, 86,
    125
Henry, Sir Edward 51, 54, 65, 105,
    140
Hockin, Olive 115
How-Martyn, Edith 211
Howey, Elsie 59, 66, 63, 121, 125

Jacques,
    Caroline 22–5, 29, 53, 28, 155,
        196, 227
    Emily Katharine (Kitty) *see*
        Marshall
    Lieutenant Francis Augustus 22,
        195
    James Kinton 22, 26
    Reverend Kinton 22, 24–8, 54,
        123, 196

Kano, Jigoro 38
Kenney,
    Annie 41, 55, 93, 94, 115, 123–4,
        126–7, 130, 131, 142, 146, 192,
        197, 214
    Jessie 59, 63, 92, 126, 185, 196
Kitchener,
    Helen (Nellie) 190
    Detective Inspector Ralph 9, 11,
        35–9, 40, 60, 63, 67, 75, 74,
        79–81, 86, 90, 101–8, 118–19,

121–2, 126, 127, 137, 139, 146, 149, 181, 188–91, 201–2, 214, 122, 123

Lake, Agnes 124
Leigh, Mary 56–8, 68
Lenton, Lilian 118, 131, 133, 139, 160, 200
Livingstone, Dr David 21–2, 53, 199
Lytton, Lady Constance 58, 66, 68

MacDougall, Eilidh 105
Marion, Kitty 29, 43, 53, 72, 74, 86, 123, 128–9, 140–1, 153, 181, 189, 191, 201, 210, 211
Marshall,
    Arthur Edward Willoughby 20, 34, 46, 52–4, 57–8, 66, 73–8, 82–4, 86–7, 96, 99, 108–11, 114–5, 118–20, 122, 124, 125–7, 129–30, 134, 140, 143, 146, 147, 156, 163, 181, 182, 184, 188, 199, 200–4, 214, 214–20, 225, 226
    Emily Katharine (Kitty) 9–11, 15–35, 39, 41–3, 46, 49–54, 57, 60–3, 65–78, 81–100, 109–10, 121, 122–8, 131, 133, 135, 138, 143, 144–5, 147, 150, 155–6, 159–62, 168, 173, 175, 177, 179, 184–5, 191, 193–6, 199, 200–5, 207–13, 125, 216–17, 220–1
Massy, Rosamund 114, 205, 207, 209
McKenna, Reginald 97, 105, 118, 120–1, 125, 129, 146, 148, 154, 156, 165, 178
Men's Political Union for Women's Enfranchisement 74–5, 88, 95, 126
Men's League for Women's Suffrage 126, 223
Murray, Dr Flora 59, 130, 154, 181, 193

Neligan, Dorinda 51, 69
Newnham College, Cambridge 24–5
Nettlefold, Joyce 133, 194, 215

Ogston, Helen 75

Pankhurst,
    Adela 48, 59, 63, 188–9, 210,
    Dr Alula 203
    Christabel 33, 41–5, 49, 51, 66, 86, 92–4, 107–10, 121, 124, 129, 151, 158–60, 174–5, 178, 185, 188–9, 200–5, 208, 210, 211, 214–5, 218
    Mrs Emmeline 9, 13, 16–20, 32–43, 46–7, 51–4, 61–3, 69, 71–3, 89–98, 102, 109–10, 114–19, 120–4, 129, 131–5, 139, 142–4, 149–51, 154–65, 167–89, 192–3, 196, 199–219, 221–2, 224, 227–9
    Harry 46, 71, 219
    Dr Helen 203
    Dr Richard 32
    Richard Keir Pethick (OBE) 203
    Sylvia 45, 110, 147, 148, 150, 178–9, 188–9, 193, 196, 203, 205, 210, 227
Parry Frye, Kate 33
PEN Club 214, 222
Pethick Lawrence 107–9, 202, 204
    Emmeline 13, 29, 42, 51, 61, 73, 86, 91, 94, 108, 219
    Fred 219

Quinn, Sir Patrick 65, 76, 85, 93, 101–4, 107, 113–5, 118–20, 122, 146, 151–2, 189, 190, 214

Radclyffe Hall 218–19
Rhondda, Lady (Mrs Humphrey Mackworth) 200–1, 204, 207
Richardson, Mary 141, 172–4, 215
Right to Serve March 192

Robins, Elizabeth 86, 139, 196
Roe, Grace 50–1, 53, 87, 98, 126, 129, 131, 179, 180–1, 183, 218, 221
Rolfe, Chief Inspector Francis Henry 86, 178–9
Royden, Maude 203
Rush Trial 44, 49, 51

Scantlebury, Chief Inspector Charles 42, 51, 70, 224
Scott, Arabella 184
Schütze 17, 20, 30, 160, 103, 164, 184, 222
    Gladys (nom de plume Henrietta Leslie) 160, 176, 177, 187, 222
    Peter 160, 171, 187, 222
Sennett, Maud Arncliffe 76
Six Point Group 200–1
Sherlock Holmes 36, 47, 63
Singh, Princess Sophia Duleep 69, 71, 110, 155, 161
Smyth, Dame Ethel 85, 88, 96, 147, 160, 178, 182, 202, 208, 211
Solomon, Georgiana 51, 69, 96
Stead, W.T. 99, 125
Suffragette Fellowship Collection 153, 194, 215

Taylor, Jane 199
Terrero, Jane 76, 94, 97, 150
Thomson, Sir Basil 111, 142, 167–8, 188, 201

Troup, Sir Charles Edward 64–5
Tuke, Mabel 89, 90, 92–3, 97, 151

Uyenishi, Sadakazu 48

Vassall, Archer 27
Vickers, Joan, Baroness of Davenport 221
Vincent, Sir Howard 39, 103
Vigny, Pierre 48

Walker, Arthur George 209, 211
Wallace-Dunlop, Marion 51–2, 55, 61, 77, 205
Watts, Emily Diana 48, 144
Wells, H.G. 30, 31, 60, 61, 159, 214, 215, 219
Wentworth, Vera 59, 63
Wheeldon, Inspector George Henry Edwin 39
Wilding Davison, Emily 40, 53, 58, 62, 100, 128, 153, 204
Williamson, Adolphus ('Dolly') 102–3
Winsonosaurus 55, 77
Women's Freedom League 47, 65, 76, 81, 82, 110, 145
Women's Party 197
Wyles, Chief Inspector Lilian 105
Wylie, Ida 147, 218

Also from The History Press ...

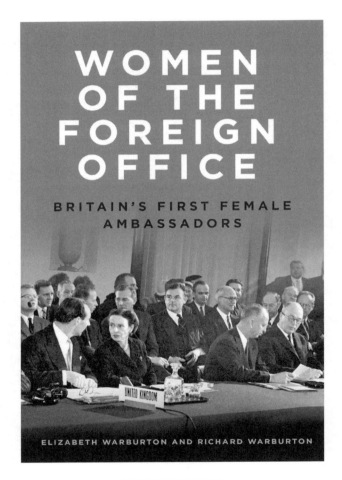

978 0 7509 9300 5